THE SPLENDID
CHINESE GARDEN

THE SPLENDID CHINESE GARDEN

Origins, Aesthetics and Architecture

HU JIE

中國古典園林

Better Link Press

Note

The names of the Chinese gardens and scenic spots usually have only a few characters which contain a wealth of meaning. To give the readers a deeper understanding of them, this book uses three different methods when referencing the names of gardens and scenic spots:

1. **Pinyin**. Pinyin is the official system that transcribes Chinese characters into Latin script in China, Singapore, and Malaysia. It is often used to spell out Chinese names in foreign language publications. For example: the pinyin for 仙人承露 (Platform of Immortal Receiving Heavenly Dew) is Xian Ren Cheng Lu. If you want to find a specific location, you may encounter some difficulties with inquiries using the English names, because the translation of many names is not uniform; but with the use of pinyin there would be no problem. The short-comings and advantages of pinyin are obvious: simple and helps with character pronunciation, but it cannot express the meaning of them.

2. **English**. Compared to pinyin, English names can express more information and cultural meaning. The same example would literally be: Platform of Immortal Receiving Heavenly Dew. However, the names of many Chinese gardens and attractions have only a few Chinese characters, yet are infused with a rich philosophical meaning, but the translation into English would be too long and not conducive to a smooth reading.

3. **A combination of pinyin and English**. This method combines the characteristics of the above two expressions, which is relatively simple, yet still allows the reader to understand the type of architecture. The same example would be known as Xianren Chenglu Platform.

The book will use the above three forms of expression:

1. The third method will be used in the body of the text—a combination of pinyin and English. At the first occurrence, the second method, which is the literal English translation, will be added in brackets for reference (e.g. "Xianren Chenglu Platform [Platform of Immortal Receiving Heavenly Dew]").

2. In the ichnographies of chapter four, the first and second methods will be used together with some spaces in between (e.g. "17. Xian Ren Cheng Lu Platform of Immortal Receiving Heavenly Dew").

3. When translating the architectural types, most of the English names correspond with the Chinese name. There are only two exceptions: the *ge* and *lou* are both translated into "tower" and *dian*, *tang*, *ting* are translated into "hall" (see Glossary of Chinese Garden for more details). To keep the reader aware of its original Chinese name, the pinyin will be added in the first occurrence (e.g. "Yuanxiang Hall [Yuan Xiang Tang, Hall of Remote Fragrance]").

Copyright © 2013 Shanghai Press and Publishing Development Company

This book is edited and designed by the Editorial Committee of *Cultural China* series

Managing Directors: Wang Youbu, Xu Naiqing
Editorial Director: Wu Ying
Editors: Zhang Yicong, Yang Xiaohe, Susan Luu Xiang
Editing Assistant: Wu Yuezhou

Text by Hu Jie
Translation by Li Yan
Photographs by Hu Jie, China Architecture and Building Press, Quanjing
Ichnographies by Wang Peng
With a Foreword by Peter Walker

Cover Design: Diane Davies
Interior Design: Li Jing, Zhang Yan (Yuan Yinchang Design Studio)

ISBN: 978-1-60220-010-4

Address any comments about *The Splendid Chinese Garden: Origins, Aesthetics and Architecture* to:

Better Link Press
99 Park Ave
New York, NY 10016
USA

or

Shanghai Press and Publishing Development Company
F 7 Donghu Road, Shanghai, China (200031)
Email: comments_betterlinkpress@hotmail.com

Printed in China by Shenzhen Donnelley Printing Co., Ltd.

1 3 5 7 9 10 8 6 4 2

Contents

Contents

On page 1
FIG. 1 Xianren Chenglu Platform (Platform of Immortal Receiving Heavenly Dew) on Qionghua Island, Beihai Park, Beijing
Beihai Park, located to the north of Zhongnanhai, Beijing, has 38.87 hectares of water surface and 32 hectares of land, and is currently the most representative imperial garden in China. All the architectures that were preserved up to now were built when Emperor Qianlong was in power.
　　Xianren Chenglu platform was located at the west side of the north slope of Mt. White Pagoda on Qionghua Island. A white marble column was situated in the center of 12 white marble balustrades (with "auspicious clouds" relief pattern) standing on this square platform. On the top of the column stands a bronze statue of a celestial being holding a bronze plate above his head. The celestial being wears a high hat and a costume typical of the Han Dynasty. His floppy sleeves droop and fold onto his shoulders. His lower hem is so long that it touches the ground. The bronze plate in his hands, decorated with clouds and hornless dragon patterns, is nearly 70 cm in diameter and 16 cm in depth. Standing there day and night, loyal to his mission, he raises the plate high and waits for celestial dew. The bronze statue is a symbol of the emperors' expectation for immortal life.

On pages 2 – 3
FIG. 2 Kunming Lake and Seventeen Arches Bridge in the Summer Palace, Beijing
Located in the western suburb of Beijing, the Summer Palace is the largest and best preserved imperial garden in China. Kunming Lake, the major lake in the Summer Palace, occupies three quarters of its entire floor space, approximately 220 hectares. Located at the south section, the vast front lake with blue waves and misty ripples is facing the rolling mountain ranges to its west and architectural complexes to its north. Seventeen Arches Bridge is the largest-scaled stone bridge in the garden. More than 500 stone lion statues of various postures and sizes are sitting on the top of railing on both sides.

Contents

Foreword

It is common knowledge that China is a great culture that has developed over many centuries. And yet it is only in the last several decades that greatly increased numbers of visitors from the outside have been exposed to the modern dynamism that is China today. These travelers from around the world have visited the great Chinese cities for business and pleasure and as a result they have experienced the beautiful imperial gardens of Beijing as well as the gardens of Shanghai and Suzhou and the gardens and parks of contemporary landscape designers throughout the country. Much of China's contemporary landscape design aspires to be Western in approach. Yet there remains a rich heritage that is solely and importantly Chinese, and this heritage can be seen in some contemporary Chinese gardens today; in many ways, it may constitute their greatest strength. In some cases the Chinese landscape designers of today are, perhaps unknowingly, including historic Chinese ideas that have been cycling through Western garden design ever since the European Enlightenment, for so long in fact that they have ceased to be recognized as Chinese.

It's not surprising that in recent years this heightened world interest in Chinese gardens has resulted in many new books, studies that have ranged from art history and Chinese cultural perspectives to picture books for visiting tourists. Now comes a new book authored by a distinguished, contemporary Chinese landscape architect and educator who, over many years, has produced a work that will serve garden lovers—both professionals and amateurs, from tourists to the Chinese themselves. Professor Hu Jie, educated both in China and the United States, is the designer of the much acclaimed Olympic Park in Beijing. He is an associate professor at Tsinghua University in Beijing, where he serves as Chief Designer of Landscape Architecture at Tsinghua Urban Planning and Design Institute.

Few Western landscape architects understand the purposes and artistic heights achieved by the creators of Chinese gardens over many centuries; even many Asian designers are not fully aware of the extraordinary varieties of compositions represented in gardens still in existence both north and south of the Yangtze River. And many designers are unaware of the influence Chinese gardens played in landscape design not only in Korea and Japan, but in Europe and the United States from the seventeenth through the nineteenth centuries. Professor Hu Jie explores these influences and makes a strong and interesting case for their impact on Western garden thought.

He begins with a useful examination of Chinese garden layout and composing elements, followed by a careful and detailed examination of twenty of the most important gardens and their designers. These are beautifully illustrated with a profusion of handsome photographs, detailed plans (often in color), and related examples of Chinese sculpture and painting. The clarity and detail of these descriptions makes them of great use to all landscape architects and designers, and the sensitive explanations will deepen the understanding and appreciation of all the new travelers to China from all over the world.

Principal of PWP Landscape Architecture

FIG. 3 Qionghua Island (Jade Sparkle Island) in Beihai Park, Beijing
Qionghua Island is gracious, dignified, and well proportioned, ornamented with architectures painted into strongly contradistinctive colors—red, yellow, and all other colors—appearing or disappearing within the greenery. A snow-white pagoda concludes the entire design on the hilltop, on which you can overlook the Forbidden City in the heart of Beijing.

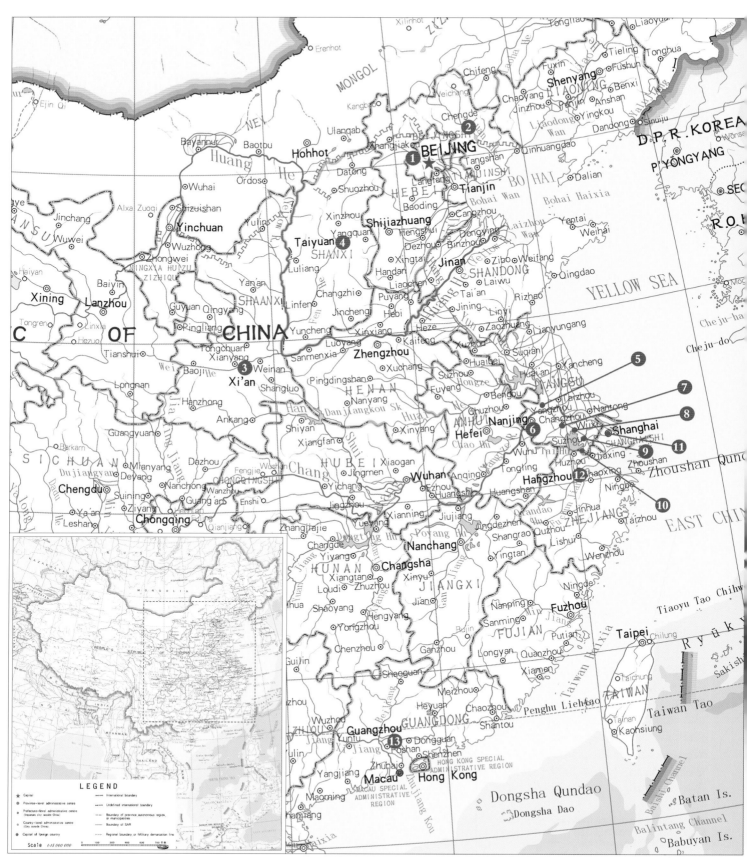

Map of China

Chinese Gardens Accessible to Visitors

❶ Beijing

Beihai Park	Bei Hai Gong Yuan	北海公园
Circular Wall	Tuan Cheng	团城
Imperial Garden in Forbidden City	Yu Hua Yuan	故宫御花园
Old Summer Palace	Yuan Ming Yuan	圆明园
Prince Gong's Mansion	Gong Wang Fu	恭王府
Summer Palace	Yi He Yuan	颐和园
Tanzhe Temple	Tan Zhe Si	潭柘寺
Xiangshan Park	Xiang Shan Gong Yuan	香山公园

❷ Chengde, Hebei province

Mountain Resort	Bi Shu Shan Zhuang	避暑山庄

❸ Xi'an, Shaanxi province

Huaqing Pool	Hua Qing Chi	华清池

❹ Taiyuan, Shanxi province

Jin Ancestral Temple	Jin Ci	晋祠

❺ Yangzhou, Jiangsu province

He Garden (Resort for Ease of Singing)	He Yuan (Ji Xiao Shan Zhuang)	何园(寄啸山庄)
Individual Garden	Ge Yuan	个园
Xiaopangu Garden	Xiao Pan Gu	小盘谷

❻ Nanjing, Jiangsu province

Outlook Garden	Zhan Yuan	瞻园
Warm Garden	Xu Yuan	煦园

❼ Changzhou, Jiangsu province

Nearby Garden	Jin Yuan	近园

❽ Wuxi, Jiangsu province

Garden for Lodging One's Expansive Feelings (Jichang Garden)	Ji Chang Yuan	寄畅园

❾ Suzhou, Jiangsu province

Couple's Retreat Garden	Ou Yuan	耦园
Five Peaks Garden	Wu Feng Yuan	五峰园
Garden of Cultivation	Yi Pu	艺圃
Garden of Pleasure	Yi Yuan	怡园
Garden of Zeng's and Zhao's Families	Zeng Zhao Yuan	曾赵园
Great Wave Pavilion	Cang Lang Ting	沧浪亭
Humble Administrator's Garden	Zhuo Zheng Yuan	拙政园
Lingering Garden	Liu Yuan	留园
Lion Grove Garden	Shi Zi Lin	狮子林
Master of the Nets Garden	Wang Shi Yuan	网师园
Mountain Villa with Embracing Beauty	Huan Xiu Shan Zhuang	环秀山庄
Zigzag Garden	Qu Yuan	曲园

❿ Wujiang, Jiangsu province

Retreat and Reflection Garden	Tui Si Yuan	退思园

⓫ Shanghai

Garden of Autumn Vapors	Qiu Xia Pu	秋霞圃
Guyi Garden	Gu Yi Yuan	古漪园
Winding Water Garden	Qu Shui Yuan	曲水园
Yu Garden	Yu Yuan	豫园

⓬ Hangzhou, Zhejiang province

Guo's Villa	Guo Zhuang	郭庄

⓭ Guangzhou, Guangdong province

Garden of Abundant Shade	Yu Yin Shan Fang	余荫山房

Note: The first column indicates the citys and garden names in English accessible to visitors, and the second and third ones are the garden names in pinyin and Chinese characters.

FIG. 4 Yuanxiang Hall in the Humble Administrator's Garden, Suzhou
The Humble Administrator's Garden, the largest ancient garden in the Yangtze River Delta, was
located at the northeast corner in Suzhou. The Yuanxiang Hall (Yuan Xiang Tang, Hall of Remote
Fragrance) is a four-sided hall structure sitting right in the center of the central area of the garden.

Introduction
Chinese Gardens from a Western Perspective

The centuries-old history, original style and glorious artistic achievement of Chinese garden construction have earned it a title of the "Mother of World Gardens." It has profoundly influenced Western gardening arts and enjoys an esteemed reputation in the history of world architecture. It is not only one of the most important tourism resources of China, but is also one of the most valuable, tangible and cultural heritages of the Chinese people.

In line with the essential philosophies of Chinese Taoism, such as the "harmony of heaven and men" and "letting things take their natural courses," Chinese gardens are the imitations of natural landscapes, taking "to capture the spirit of nature" as its essential and distinctive feature. It combines the beauties of natural creation and human creation, and unifies the realm of art and those of real life, to create a poetic and picturesque space where people can have a rest, take a walk or view a scene that is "completely free of artificial elements." It is like a hymn praising the beauty of nature or a landscape painting of visitors who indulge so deeply in its beauty that they would linger on and on with no thought of leaving.

When looking back on the history of world garden construction, G. A. Jellicoe, Hon. President of The International Federation of Landscape Architecture, wrote in an article entitled *The Search for A Paradise Garden*: "The three indeed the landscape of almost the whole world are based are the Chinese, the Western Asian, and the ancient Geek.

"The first of these, the Chinese, sprang from its own land, spread to Japan, and began to influence Europe seriously from the middle of the eighteenth century. It was an art based upon a philosophy that man was a part of organic nature and just like nature did not change after having reached a 'climax.' It was undoubtedly extremely restful and contented. The only real excitements were the grotesque in nature, such as storms, twisted trees, waterfalls, for these disturbed the quiet flow of Japan were brought to a state of sensitivity unknown to the western world. It is said, for instance, that trees were planted in order that the sound of the breezes through the leaves would to be the ear like music.

"My universal garden would remind us also that we are always a part of nature and would turn us to that delicate response to nature which has almost passed from our experience."

Chinese Garden Arts: Trip To West

Europeans had knowledge of Chinese gardens in as early as Marco Polo's time (1254 – 1324). After seeing the gardens of the Southern Song Dynasty in Hangzhou City in 1279, Marco Polo wrote in his *Travels* that the gardens he saw there were the most beautiful and entertaining gardens in the world. By the end of the 15th century, after the great Portugal navigator Vasco da Gama (1460 – 1524) successfully opened the shipping line connecting Europe and India through the Cape of Good Hope in South Africa, trade between the Eastern and Western worlds soon escalated to a whole new level. Chinese silk, china, lacquer ware and tea soon became favorable luxuries in 17th century European high society. From the late 17th century to the end of the 18th century, Europe witnessed an unprecedented China Rush that lasted for over 100 years.

Between the 16th century and the 18th century, the connection between China and the Western world became increasingly inseparable as domestic economies and major foreign trade countries thrived after the new shipping line was opened. Through the work of Western missionaries, there appeared a large-scale equal exchange of architectural cultures between China and the West. During this period, the Western world was experiencing a profound social transformation and capitalism began to take the leading role in the historical stage. After the Renaissance, advocators of the Enlightenment in the 17th

and 18th centuries needed new ideological weapons to fight against the power of Feudalism and the Church. Some Enlightenment thinkers quickly look to Chinese culture, which was totally different from Western culture, as a source for new ideas. Chinese culture became in fashion and swept through Western societies. Chinese silk, ceramics, tea and other goods changed the lifestyle of Western people to a certain extent. The dissemination of Chinese gardening arts overturned the rigid traditional Western garden construction theories. Free style or asymmetrical arrangement, a feature that is typical in Chinese gardens and entirely different from traditional Western designs which centers on geometrical patterns, began to appear in Western garden designs and, later on, gave rise to a revolution in the Western garden construction world. The ideals of Enlightenment, such as "respecting nature and human rights" happened to coincide with the essential Chinese gardening theories like "learning from nature" and "free style arrangements," which added to the ideological preparation for the upcoming revolution of Western gardening arts.

First Emergence of Landscape Gardening in U.K.

In Europe, the charm of Chinese gardening was first felt in the United Kingdom. The British Isles had a unique natural landscape characterized by grass, woods and hills, but a large proportion of the land was converted to pasture

because of the development of the wool textile industry. What's more, nature is a strong element in the British cultural tradition and the people's deep love of it made it particularly easy for them to understand and accept the basic ideas of Chinese gardening. Sir Francis Bacon, the great English philosopher, and an acknowledged proponent of "natural style gardens," was the first British individual who saw the value of wildness in nature. In his book *On Gardens* (published in 1625), he insisted that an ideal garden must have in itself a large wild land where grass and plants can flourish freely. In his volume of essays *Sermons*, he condemned "symmetrically trimmed plants and stagnant pond" and advocated "complete charm of wildness and indigenous trees and bushes."

Sir William Temple (1628 – 1699) was the first British individual who introduced Chinese gardens into the British Isles. In 1685, his writings in *Upon the Gardens of Epicurus*, he spoke highly of Chinese gardening arts, saying "Chinese created beautiful and dazzling images with their extraordinary imagination."

In 1712, when expressing his dissatisfaction with the works of British garden designers and his admiration for Chinese gardens in a feature article in his magazine the *Spectator*, Joseph Addison (1672 – 1719, a great English realistic essay writer) said "Chinese people would laugh at Europeans for how we rely on ropes and rulers to plant trees, because anybody knows how to plant trees and keep them in the same line and the same spacing distance. They'd rather bring out the creativity of nature. So, they

FIG. 5 The Chinese pagoda in Kew Garden, UK
The picture is taken from *Art of Garden Construction Abroad* composed by Chen Zhihua, designed by Sir William Chambers, the founder of Picturesque Garden in the second half of the 18th century, modeling from the Porcelain Pagoda in Bao'ensi (Temple of Gratitude) in Nanjing.

always try to hide the techniques they used behind the landscape. In contrast, our British gardens always try to separate themselves from nature, as farthest as they can, instead of adapting themselves to nature." In fact, Mr. Addison practiced his theory on his own land. Aside from him, Alexander Pope (1688 – 1744, a great British poet) was more radical than anyone else. He leveled his geometric garden in Twinkenheim and spent five years, from 1718 – 1723, to

rebuild a free-style garden. It was a rectangular garden occupying an area of about 5 acres with three roads running along three sides and one side opening to the Thames River. Although there was a central axis, nothing was forced into symmetric patterns. Two randomly winding paths formed the left and right boundaries. Inside the garden, a single trimmed tree could never be found, but instead a few caves created with man-made rockeries were present. These are the typical features of Chinese gardens. The Twinkenheim Garden was the first of the kind in the Great Britain.

The true representatives of British Landscape Garden designers, however, were William Kent (1685 – 1748) and Lancelot

"Capability" Brown (1715 – 1783). In their hands, a garden was just like a pasture, or simply a field, and their arrangements blended in with the background as if it was a part of rural nature. In order to eliminate obvious boundaries that visually separate a garden from its surroundings, British designers creatively replaced enclosing a wall or fence with a waterway. People would hardly notice the existence of such waterways. When suddenly realizing that they are stopped at such a partition, people usually could not help but utter their surprise with an exclamation of "Ha-ha." As a result, such waterways were named "Ha-ha." This new garden type emerged during the 17th century to the first half of the 18th century. This period was later officially called the "Landscape Garden."

Beginning in the second half of 18th century when Romanticism was developing in the British Isles, the British Landscape Garden evolved into the British Picturesque Garden. During this time, it was Sir William Chambers (1723 – 1796) who tinted British gardens with romantic dyes. He had been to China several times from 1742 to 1744 as a transportation supervisor and was able to recognize the charm of Chinese gardens. In 1757, he published his *Design of Chinese Buildings, Furniture, Dresses, and Utensils*. In 1772, he published his masterpiece, *Dissertation on Oriental Gardening*, the first formal introduction of Chinese gardens to British people. In this book, he suggested his British peers borrow from Chinese garden styles and theories in their gardening works and pointed out that British gardening over-emphasized on the roughness of nature and looked empty, uncouth and tasteless because of the fanciless language it confined itself to. From 1785 to 1759, as the architect of Kew Garden, he created quite a number of garden buildings in Chinese style. Among his buildings that still exist, the Pagoda is the most famous one (Fig. 5).

Development of British-Chinese Gardens in France

In the 18th century, as British colonialism expanded in the world, France, too, began to feel the influence of Chinese garden style. The French called this newly emerged gardening art as British-Chinese Gardens or simply, Chinese Gardens. The French Enlightenment Movement also played a very important role in the popularity of Landscape Gardens in France. Both Montesquieu (1689 – 1755) and Francois-Marie Arouet De Voltaire (1694 – 1778), two representatives of the Enlightenment, had been to the British Kingdom and were admirers of Chinese culture. In addition, the famous remark of Jean Jacques Rousseau (1712 – 1778), i.e. "Back to Nature," helped landscape gardening to further submerge into the hearts of the French people. In 1743, Jean-Denis Attiret (1702 – 1768, a French Jesuit painter, a Painter in Emperor Qianlong's court) wrote a letter to one of his friends, H. d'Assaut Toises, in France. In this letter, *A Special Feature of Chinese Emperor Garden*, he described the beautiful scenery of Old Summer Palace in detail

FIG. 6 Chinese cottage in Petit Trianon of Versailles (taken from *Art of Garden Construction Abroad* composed by Chen Zhihua)
Such "cottage" of Chinese style, a fashionable construction, occupied an independent section in a garden, constituted of a mill, a chicken house, a cattle shed, a barn, farmer residence, and like architectures.

and called it "heaven on earth" and "the garden of all gardens." In addition, by virtue of his artistic sensitivity and a vivid analytical comparison between Chinese aesthetic theories and Western theories, he captured the most important aesthetic principle of Chinese gardening: learn from nature, and value the charm of nature, thus adding less manual work. He said, "What people try to express is a simple and natural village instead of a palace arranged in accordance with the strictest symmetric rules. Chinese gardens are gardens made by nature." This

famous letter was first published in *Lettres Edifiantes et Curieuses Ecrites des Missions Etrangères* in 1749 and then translated into different languages and adopted by many important books and magazines in the Western countries. In addition to that, he participated in the production of the series of paintings *Forty Scenes of Old Summer Palace* and sent a copy of this back to Paris. The images of Chinese gardens immediately created a sensation in the West. Victor-Marie Hugo, a master in modern literature, enthusiastically gave his highest remark, "In a corner of the world there existed a man-made miracle, the Summer Palace … If only you could imagine an ineffable architectural structure, like a palace in the moon, a fairyland, that is the Summer Palace."

In 1767, P. Michel Benoit (1715 – 1774), the designer and construction supervisor of Dashuifa Waterworks (Great Fountain) in Changchun Garden, said in his letter to M. Papillon d'Auteroche, "In terms of garden decoration, Chinese artists are very successful in completing nature with art. A Chinese garden designer would never be highly recognized before he could imitate nature without releasing the traces of his techniques … Your eyes will never get bored or tired in a Chinese garden because your sight will always be confined in a space that perfectly matches your vision."

In 1770, a French duke, Duc De Choiseul, made it his recreational activity to build Chinese gardens in his vegetable fields. He even employed an architect, Le Ca-nius, to build a 7-floor Chinese pagoda from 1775 to 1778. The pagoda was 39 meters high with a golden ball embedded at the pinnacle. During the time from 1780 to 1787, Steinfort Park, located near Münster, Westphila, had been the most exquisite British-Chinese Garden in France. Some of its designs were based on the paintings drawn by John Nieuhof who visited China as a member of a Holland delegate. In the garden, you could find a three-cornered pavilion and other Chinese buildings. From 1775 to 1784, Queen Marie Antoinette built a British Chinese garden in Petit Trianon. Inside the garden, you will see a big greenhouse full of exotic plants, a Chinese

pavilion, a large attic, a pagoda, a cow shed, a sheep shed, a Chinese bird cage, a big rock overhang, a headstream of a small river and rock pieces where sediment in the river would be blocked (Fig. 6). Queen Marie probably was inspired by Jean-Denis Attiret's description of Yuanming Yuan and asked her gardener, Antoine Richard, to design this garden. The popularity of Chinese gardens in France, which began in the second half of the 17th century, lasted for over 100 years until the end of the 18th century.

Landscape Gardens Thriving in Germany

Seeing the rise of Chinese gardens in the U.K. and France, other European countries began to follow their examples. In Germany, Gessner, a German writer who advocated for landscape gardens, made it very clear that "in contrast to green wall labyrinth and yew obelisks lined up by strictly equal spacing, idyllic pastures and wild forest are more exciting."

In 1773, in his *Uber Die Chinesischen Garden*, Ludwig A. Unzer insisted that Chinese gardens be the example of all gardening. The Garden Kingdom of Dessau-Worlitz was the most splendid gardening endeavor in early German landscape gardens. It was a summer residence built by Duke Francis, the Lord of Dessau, from 1769 to 1773, and is still kept in good condition. The foundation itself being a large swamp, the Garden Kingdom of Dessau-Worlitz creatively took advantages of the geographic features by

excavating lakes and ponds, digging bays and ditches, and piling up islands, which brought about boundless variation to the scenery. The dykes around this garden were hidden in the forms of hills and low cliffs.

Built in 1781, the Wilhelmshohe Garden near Kassel is one of the largest Chinese gardens in Germany. In Weissenstein, a place south to Wilhelmshohe Garden, a Chinese village was built in 1781 at the foot of a hill, facing water. All village houses were in Chinese style. Standing in the center of the village, there is a small round temple with double eaves. In addition, there is a small river spanned by a Chinese wooden bridge. Johann Wolfgang Von Goethe (1749 – 1832, the great German scholar and poet) was also enthusiastic about Chinese gardens and architecture. In 1778, after his visit to the Garden Kingdom of Dessau-Worlitz, he personally took part in the design and construction of his landscape garden in Weimar. Goethe built a Chinese style hermit house in his garden and surrounded it with Chinese rockeries. In Stockholm, Sweden, Piper, a garden design expert, designed two Chinese gardens for the King of Sweden; Drottningholm Garden and Haga Garden. Drottningholm Garden is characterized by waterways and waterscapes, while Haga Garden is famous for its paths rolling up and down rhythmically in accordance with the local geographic features, bridges leading to the island in the center of a river, as well as a variety of fruit trees. Among the plants, there are various tiny buildings, including a Chinese pagoda.

Appearance of Landscape Gardens in the United States of America

Since it was British colony, it was only natural that the style of landscape gardens was brought to America. In 1850, when Chinese gardening was in full bloom in the British Isles, Andrew Jackson Downing (1815 – 1852) visited the country where he deeply felt the charm of landscape gardening. When he returned to America, he was committed to showing his fellow Americans the beauty of the natural sceneries in the continent. After his death, his successor Frederick Law Olmsled continued spreading the essential ideas of landscape gardening.

Essential Elements of Chinese Gardens

During the Chinese Gardening Rush that lasted from the 17th century to the 18th century, many techniques and elements of Chinese gardening, such as buildings, rockeries, water, roads and path and plants were accepted and borrowed as essential parts of a Chinese garden. The first of them was small buildings. In Europe, small buildings were considered as a typical feature and an important gardening element of a Chinese garden. Among all small buildings, palaces, temples, pagodas, decorated archways and bridges are the favorites of Europeans, and palaces and pagodas are particularly heatedly recommended, It was in the

Trianon de Porcelaine of Chateau de Versailles that the first Chinese palace in Europe was built. Trianon de Porcelaine was a French classical building covered with glazed tiles. Its steep roofs were covered with glazed tiles, too. The reason for such extensive use of glazed tiles was that Europeans at that time thought the use of porcelain materials was a key feature of Chinese architecture. Since Chinese palaces were too complicated to copy, the Western designers turned to Chinese pagodas. Sir William Chambers was the first European to design a Chinese pagoda; a beautiful brick one that was built in his Kew Garden. He said, "With such a tower standing in a garden, the owner can proudly invite his guests to climb it and enjoy a bird's eye view of his garden." In the second half of the 18th century, imitations of small Chinese buildings like pavilions, belvederes, waterside pavilions and bridges were widely seen in Western landscape gardens.

Rockery was another key element in Chinese gardens for the creation of sceneries. For a long time, Europeans have known of the existence of Chinese rockeries. A lot of missionaries and envoys had already given detailed description about rockeries, seeing them as the most important and unique feature of Chinese gardens. As a result, rockery became a popular choice for many landscape gardens in Europe, such as Stowe Garden, Peimshill Garden and Fontainbleau (Fig. 7).

The third element was water. In classical Western gardens, water was always confined to geometrical pools or ditches. Water surface only accounted for a small proportion of

FIG. 7 The Palace of Fontainbleau in France has rockeries of this kind.

a garden. The relationship between men and water was not close at all. Thanks to Marco Polo's description, Europeans for the first time in history had a glance of the water surface in Chinese royal gardens and the scenes of Chinese emperor and his wives enjoying themselves in boats. It was Sir William Chambers who for the first time in history elaborated and spoke highly of the beauty of Chinese water scenery. In fact, he was the first European who realized the roles water could play in adjusting the microclimate in a garden and in affecting the emotions of viewers. Because of their introduction, the use of water surface in Western gardens was completely changed, and in general, was largely expanded. Water banks were shaped in curves. The width of a waterway started to vary randomly. Rocks were scatter freely along the banks. Plants began flourishing on bank slopes. More importantly, water was getting much closer to human and buildings.

The fourth was the arrangement of plants. Plants in a Chinese garden were arranged differently than a European garden. Trees were not in lines, nor trimmed in geometric shapes. Spacing between trees was rarely equal. Plants were grouped together in line with the circle of seasons. All these arrangements brought great changes into the Western gardens. During the 18th century, symmetric arrangement of plants was completely abandoned by European landscape garden architects. Plants were given room to grow freely. Botanic diversification and the selection of complementary plants became a widely accepted practice. In addition to that, a lot of Chinese garden plants were introduced to the West, making great contribution to the development of ornamental horticulture.

The last element was roads and paths. European garden-makers completely fell in love with Chinese winding roads and paths that create surprising scenic contrasts. According to Sir William Champers, "no other people in the world are more skillful than Chinese people in awaking a feeling of surprise in you by creating changes in scenery. Sometimes, they'd lead you through a cave or a dark path and suddenly you'd find yourself in front of a dulcet scene composed of every beautiful thing that the nature could offer. Sometimes, it would be a narrow and barely visible trail that leads you to a cluster of bramble, grass or rocks. You'd think you've come to the end of the trail, but suddenly, there is a delightful open space stretching before you. You'd be overwhelmed by an extra pleasant moment because you'd never foreseen its coming. "

All in all, during the cultural exchange between the West and China in the 17th and 18th centuries, Chinese gardening arts brought a great impact to the Western world. The "China Rush" found its way into many European countries and moved on prosperously until the 19th century. Even when the China Rush faded, the Western gardening art didn't fall back into the old track of pure classicalism. Today, landscape gardening still serves as a keynote in world garden designs.

In May 1980, the Astor Court (Ming Xuan, 明轩), a classic Chinese garden court designed by a Chinese garden architect according to the patterns and spirit of Dian Chun Yi of Master of the Nets Garden in Suzhou, was exhibited in the Metropolitan Museum of Art, New York, U.S.A. This was the first step that Chinese gardening art made towards the world. In 1983, a Chinese garden named Fanghua Garden (Fanghua Yuan, 芳华园) received the Gold Award in the 16th International Horticultural Exposition. In 1984, another Chinese garden, Yanxiu Garden (Yanxiu Yuan, 燕秀园), swept the Gold Award, the Best Pavilion Award and the Best Artistic Design Award (permanent retention) in the Liverpool International Garden Festival in the U.K. The glorious Chinese gardening tradition shined in front of the world once again.

In his book, *Gardens of China*, the famous landscape garden architect said, "Being a typical landscape garden, Chinese gardens have more attributes of an artwork than any other parks or gardens (in the West). Or, to put it in another way, Chinese gardens are closer than any other gardens to the criteria of a work of art. They are not the result of direct imitation of the nature, nor the result of abstraction and transformation of the nature. Chinese gardens are an expression of artistic conception inspired by people's feeling for the nature. Although Chinese gardens often contain complicated facilities and seem lacking in unified planning, their extraordinary charm and the picturesque sceneries they create are enough for it to present an unparalleled style. The most exciting thing is that it has a rhythm that only appears in artistic masterpieces or the work of the nature. "

FIG. 8 Jinghuiyi Pond in Jichang Garden, Wuxi

Chapter One
The History and Genres of Chinese Gardens

The Chinese landscape gardens have a long history and diverse genres. Their superb techniques and exquisite classical examples are widely recognized throughout the world. Chinese classical gardens are reproductions of natural landscapes. The waterscapes are reflections of streams, waterfalls, and ponds. The land sceneries are artistic abstraction of natural terrains. The plant arrangements are picturesque representations of botanic nature. The garden buildings are exemplary constructions downsized to fit into their landscape surroundings. The integration of ancient architectural construction techniques with garden engineering created physical and artistic environments used for habitation, relaxation, entertainment, and literary and artistic activities. Therefore, they are a critical part of Chinese traditional culture and natural heritage.

Great quantities of significant classical gardens have been officially recognized as national, provincial, city, or county Historical and Cultural Sites under government protection. Some of the gardens that embody the greatest historical, artistic, and scientific value have been registered in the World Heritage List compiled by the World Heritage Committee of UNESCO. The Mountain Resort at Chengde, Summer Palace in Beijing, Humble Administrator's Garden, Lingering Garden, Mountain Villa with Embracing Beauty, Master of the Nets Garden, Couple's Retreat Garden in Suzhou city, and Retreat and Reflection Garden in Wujiang city are all within this category. They are now part of a global cultural legacy endowed to the human race.

As a valuable historical legacy for mankind, Chinese classical gardening has its own system and unique style that have earned it a high position in world history. Its influence was not only felt in neighboring regions like the Korean Peninsula and Japanese Islands, but also in European countries. In the 18th century, it played an active role in contributing to the rise of the Romanticism movement of European gardens. It is acknowledged as one of the origins of world gardening arts.

FIG. 9 *Play Bamboo Flute and Attract Phoenix*, **by Qiu Ying, Ming Dynasty**
This is a colored painting on a piece of silk 41.1 cm long and 33.8 cm wide, mounted like an album and collected by the Palace Museum in Beijing, China. The story it portrays is that of Nong Yu, the daughter of Duke Mu of Qin, who was playing a vertical bamboo flute. The music was so appealing that it lured a phoenix to the platform. Qiu Ying was one of the representative painters in the Ming Dynasty, and one of "Greatest Four Painters of Ming" (the other three were Shen Zhou, Wen Zhengming, and Tang Yin). This piece is carefully and neatly structured without showing any sign of rigidity. It is flamboyantly and delightfully colored but not bending to vulgar taste. The blue mountains and green waters on the picture are splendid and elegant. And even the fine folds on the cloth appear nice and fluent.

1. A Brief History

Chinese gardening history can be traced back to over 3,000 years. It has evolved into a unique landscape gardening system perfected by great techniques. Its development can be divided into six stages, i.e. budding stage, growing stage, transformation stage, bloom stage, mature stage, and prime stage.

Budding Stage—Slave Society (1100 – 300 BC)

In the later slave society period, about 3,000 years ago, human productivity increased to such a level of efficiency that slave owners themselves no longer had to be a part of the physical production. Thus, a privileged social class emerged. The slave owners accumulated a great multitude of wealth and compelled countless farmers and artisans to start the early garden construction activities. The natural mountains, rivers, forests, springs, and animal habitats were adopted as their places for living, production, and entertainment. Gradually, they started designing and building gardens instead of simply enclosing the natural landscape as they did before. *You* (囿, hunting garden) was the earliest garden in China.

In his hunting garden, a slave owner would usually raise birds and other animals, plant flowers, grass, trees, and vegetables. Waterways and ponds were excavated to create beautiful landscape for relaxation and hunting. *Tai* (台, platform) was the most important architecture in a hunting garden. Piled with soil, a platform was originally used for observing celestial phenomena and worshipping divinities, but sometimes it also served as a place to enjoy landscape and scenery (Fig. 9). It is said that Emperor Zhou, the last emperor of the Shang Dynasty (1105 – 1046 BC), once built for himself a Shaqiu Garden, and Emperor Wen, the founder of the Zhou Dynasty (1152 – 1056 BC), constructed three parts in his garden: Ling Tai (灵台, Nimbus Platform), Ling You (灵囿, Nimbus Hunting Garden), and Ling Zhao (灵沼, Nimbus Pond); Ling Tai was a series of high platforms, while Ling You was a bird and animal zoo, and Ling Zhao was a fish pool. Together, they organized a comprehensive garden with appointed officials and professional working staff.

In the Spring and Autumn and Warring States Periods, China transformed from a slave society to a feudal society. Powerful principalities competed with their rivals in building large luxurious palaces and gardens. The possession of lofty platforms and splendid palaces and halls became a trend among the rulers of principalities who wanted to boast their wealth. Two outstanding examples were Zhanghua Platform (章华台, Platform of Brilliant Poetry) in Chu Principality and Gusu Platform (姑苏台, Gusu is the old name of Suzhou city) in Wu Principality. Zhanghua Platform was a 30-meter high, 3-floor platform with a 50-meter wide foundation. Located at the bank of Taihu Lake, Gusu Platform was an incredibly grandiose palace made up of a group of interconnected lofty platforms stretching along the slope of a hill.

In the budding stage of Chinese classical gardens, the key functions of gardens were still limited to hunting, production, worshipping divinities, and praying for immortality. Landscape-related enjoyment was only a minor or secondary function. At this stage, not all specific genres of Chinese gardens had been developed. The gardens built by slave owners and the aristocracies were the predecessors of later imperial gardens. The garden during the budding stage featured too many elements jumbled together, rough overall planning, and vague gardening concepts.

Growing Stage—Qin and Han Dynasties (300 BC – 300)

In the third century BC, the founder of the Qin Dynasty, Emperor Qin Shihuang (259 – 210 BC), set up a giant centralized feudal empire after he united the several principalities into one kingdom. The system of fiefdom was replaced by the dictatorship of one individual emperor, making it possible to mobilize more labor force undertake various construction works. In 206 BC, Liu Bang led an insurrection that ended the reign of the Qin Dynasty before founding the Han Dynasty. He later became Emperor Gaozu (256 – 195 BC) and borrowed from the Qin's administrative systems. Thus, the unified government formed during Emperor Qin Shihuang's period proceeded. The royal gardens built in the Han Dynasty were more spacious than ever, encompassing lands as wide as several hundred *li* (an ancient

Chinese unit of length measurement, one *li* equals 0.5 km or 0.31 mile). What's more, gardening art and techniques depicted obvious advancements, and Chinese gardens flourished during the Qin and Han dynasties.

As the symbol of a united empire and a centralized dynasty, gardens in this period were spacious due to following the ideas of "embodying the heaven and earth" and "weaving yin and yang together" as guidelines for space arrangement. The Three Celestial Islands in One Pond arrangement was also perfected during this period.

At that time, due to the lack of resources and technology, the

FIG. 10 *Penglai Celestial World,* by Yuan Yao, Qing Dynasty
This is a colored painting on a 266.2 cm long and 163 cm wide silk scroll. Based on his masculine vision and extraordinary imagination, Yuan Yao portrayed a magnificent world of mountains and waters in which the sun and moon rotate. The zigzagging composition has lasting appeal, giving a heart-quickened image of the dynamic movement of a surging river. Mountains and slopes, either far away or close by, stand upright in the mist of dense fog and clouds, exactly like a celestial world. Legend says that there are three celestial islands in the East Sea: Penglai, Fangzhang, and Yingzhou. And on each island, there are celestial mountains, grandiose architectures, rare animals and exotic birds, precious flowers and trees, and most importantly, celestial medicines that could keep one living forever. Therefore, they are places deserving the most respect.

monuments of nature were mysterious and undiscoverable. Thus, people created myths for the existence of vast oceans and inaccessible mountains. Among them, Kunlun Mountain is the symbol of veneration to magnificent mountains and Penglai Island is the symbol of veneration to massive oceans. These were the sources from which Chinese imperial or paradise gardens originated (Fig. 10).

The earliest history about paradise gardens was Long Pond in Lanchi Palace (兰池宫, Orchid Pond Palace) of Qin Dynasty. Historical records notes: "Emperor Qin Shihuang constructed the Long Pond and heaped Penglai Island on its center. Water from Wei River was put into the pond, filling up an artificial waterway as long as 200 *li* (100 km, 62.14 miles) from east to west and as wide as 20 *li* (10 km, 6.21 miles) from south to north." In another garden Shanglin Palace Garden (上林苑, Palace Garden of Forest), numerous palaces, ponds, platforms, and waterside pavilions spread over 300 *li* (150 km, 93.20 miles). Later, E'pang Palace (阿房宫, E'pang Gong), a front hall 500 paces in length from its eastern end to its western end, and 50 *zhang* (an ancient Chinese unit of length, one *zhang* equals roughly 3.33 m) in width from its southern end to its northern end, witnessed its own completion in the year of 212 BC in the Shanglin Palace Garden. The trees of Shushan Mountain were felled and numerous artisans took great pains to accomplish this grandiose royal garden, yet such efforts were in vain. Xiang Yu (232 – 202 BC), a talented militarist in ancient China, ignited an extensive fire shortly after the construction activity was completed.

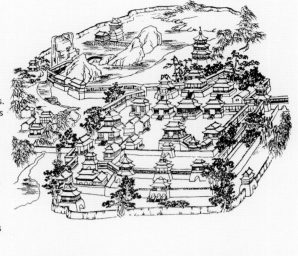

FIG. 11 A bird view of Jianzhang Palace
The Jianzhang Palace was built in 104 BC as one of the twelve main palaces in Shanglin Palace Garden, the imperial garden of the Western Han Dynasty. The south area of the garden was dominated by palace halls. While, the north part, Taiye Pond, was a well-organized landscape area. Just like Emperor Qin Shihuang, Emperor Wu of Han had a blind faith in the celestial world and immortal life. So, just like what Emperor Qin Shihuang had done, he built three islands in his Taiye Pond to symbolize the celestial islands—Penglai, Yingzhou, and Fangzhang—and even named them after the islands. Jianzhang Palace was the first imperial garden in Chinese history that followed exactly the celestial patterned royal garden with all these three islands. This illustration is selected from *History of Chinese Ancient Garden* by Wang Juyuan.

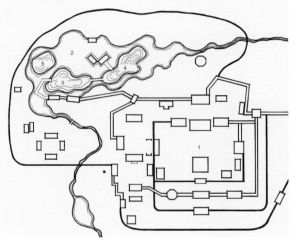

FIG. 12 Ichnography of Jianzhang Palace
The dominant elements in its north part were gardens and those in its south part were palace halls, which created a permanent model for the planning of all imperial gardens after it. As a result, its "Three Celestial Islands in One Pond" arrangement had been the essential pattern for all imperial gardens in China up to the Qing Dynasty. This illustration is selected from *History of Chinese Ancient Garden* by Wang Juyuan.
1. Palace Halls 2. Taiye Pond
3. Penglai Island 4. Yingzhou Island
5. Fangzhang Island

The imperial gardens created during the Han Dynasty were far grander than those in the Qin Dynasty. Emperor Wu of Han (156 – 87 BC) made Taiye Pond in Jianzhang Palace (建章宫, Palace of Establishing Institutions) and constructed three celestial islands, i.e. Penglai Island, Fangzhang Island, and Yingzhou Island, to create a "worldly paradise on earth." (Figs. 11, 12) Quite a few classical gardens in existence so far were laid out likewise—Three Celestial Islands in One Pond, such as Beihai (北海, North Sea), Zhonghai (中海, Middle Sea)and Nanhai (南海, South Sea) Gardens, Summer Palace and Old Summer Palace in Beijing (Fig. 13).

When Emperor Wu of Han was in power, the Shanglin Palace Garden built in Qin Dynasty was further enriched and expanded, making it a garden complex with "12 gateways, 36 interior gardens, 12 palaces, and 35 amusement palaces." In addition, he ordered an excavation of a number of waterscapes, including Kunming Pond and Taiye Pond. As far as vegetation was concerned, the garden had an impressive collection of plants, with over 3,000 kinds of "famous fruits and exotic trees" brought in by his courtiers and officials in addition to a wide variety of local plants. Inside the

FIG. 13 Pengdao Yao Tai (Immortal Platform on Penglai Island) of Old Summer Palace
This portrays three small islands in Fuhai. Since the Qin and Han dynasties when imperial gardens first came into being, palaces and gardens had already been closely combined together and "Jade Celestial Platform on Penglai Island" had already become the theme of landscape designs in imperial garden construction, expressing worship to nature.

This romantic image of "Jade Celestial Platform on Penglai Island" originated from two ancient Chinese myth systems: Kunlun Mountain System and Penglai Island System. Kunlun myth is a reflection of reverence to lofty mountains, while Penglai myth revered the vast ocean. Both systems had strong theocratic consequences. This such worship to nature gave birth to the Chinese imperial celestial palaces and gardens.

garden, hundreds of different animals and birds were raised for hunting.

In addition to Shanglin Palace Garden, Emperor Wu of Han constructed a monumental project, Ganquan Palace Garden (甘泉苑, Sweet Spring Palace Garden), which covered land as wide as 540 *li* (270 km, 167.77 miles). More than 100 palace structures were built within its boundaries. Other famous imperial gardens built in the Han Dynasty include Leyou Palace Garden (乐游苑, Palace Garden of Enjoying Tour), Sixian Palace Garden (思贤苑, Palace Garden of Expecting Sages), Bowang Palace Garden (博望苑, Palace Garden of Boundless Vision), Yusu Palace Garden (御宿苑, Palace Garden of Accommodation), Xijiao Palace Garden (西郊苑, West Suburban Palace Garden), Xi Palace Garden (西苑, Western Palace Garden of Eastern Han Dynasty), Xianyang Palace Garden (显阳苑, Unveiled Sunshine Palace Garden), and Yichun Palace Garden (宜春苑, Palace Garden of Tender Spring). Both the feudal empires of the Qin and Han were alike in that garden construction was largely a source of pride to the emperors. And the scale of imperial gardens was astonishing. It is during this time that the imperial garden established itself as an individual genre of Chinese classical gardens, although the aesthetic reach was still at a beginning phase. These imperial gardens were built in the hopes of communicating with celestial beings, and thus, tinted with an ethereal sense of paradise. The garden construction was still limited to sheer objective reflection of natural scenery and still had a few more steps to take before it could be abstracted and lifted to a level beyond nature. During the later Han Dynasty, private gardens began to emerge, such as the private garden built by a wealthy person named Yuan Guanghan in Maoling. But judging by the elements and patterns they had applied, these private gardens were only imitations of imperial gardens, and also much smaller.

Transformation Stage— The Era of Wei, Jin, and the Northern and Southern Dynasties (220 – 589)

The era of Wei, Jin, and the Southern and Northern Dynasties was a time of great turmoil in Chinese history that lasted for over 300 years. During this era, the Three Kingdoms, two Jin dynasties (Western Jin and Eastern Jin), and the 16 kingdoms built by the northern minorities, which the Southern and Northern Dynasties took turns to dominate part of China. Even under the threat of war, both emperors and their courtiers were desperately eager to amass more wealth and to be indulged in the most dissolute and luxurious enjoyments. Strangely enough, along with this turbulent period of time, came one of the most exuberant and energetic times in the history of Chinese ideological and philosophical development. Just as lively as the competition of divergent thoughts in the ideological field, the frontier of artistic field was pushed forward to a great extent. While experiencing the impact brought about by these changes, Chinese garden construction at that time continued advancing.

During this era, imperial garden construction activities were mainly implemented in three cities: Yecheng and Luoyang in northern China, and Jiankang (modern day Nanjing) in southern China. Yecheng was well structured with its imperial center seated right in the core of the city. Wenchang Palace (文昌殿, Palace of Prosperity), where the emperor dealt with his court business, was located exactly on the central north-to-south axis of the city. Adjacent to its western palace city wall was an imperial garden, Tongque Garden (铜雀园, Garden of Copper Sparrow). And Xuanwu Palace Garden (玄武苑, Palace Garden of the Black Turtle and Snake), a temporary palace outside the capital, was located to the north of Yecheng. Years later, Yecheng was chosen as the capital city of Five Dynasties, i.e. Zhao, Ran Wei, Former Yan, Eastern Wei, and Nothern Qi. During the time of these Five Dynasties, Emperor Wu of Later Zhao (Shi Hu) built a Hualin Garden (华林园, Splendid Woods Garden) and a Sangzi Palace Garden (桑梓苑, Palace Garden of Hometown) in the north suburb of the city. Then, Murong Xi (385 – 407, emperor of the later Yan Dynasty—one of the 16 kingdoms

set up by the northern minorities) made a Longteng Palace Garden (龙腾苑, Palace Garden of Flying Dragon) as his imperial garden. After him, the last emperor of the Northern Qi Dynasty expanded the Hualin Garden extensively and made it as fabulous as a celestial residence in paradise. Because of that, the garden was later named Xiandu Palace Garden (仙都苑, Palace Garden in Celestial Capital).

Luoyang was the capital of the Eastern Han Dynasty, Wei Dynasty, Western Jin Dynasty, and the Five Dynasties during the Northern Dynasties period. Emperor Ming of Wei (204 – 239) expanded Fanglin Garden (芳林园, Garden of Fragrant Woods), which was later renamed Hualin Palace Garden (华林苑, Splendid Woods Palace Garden). It was located to the north of his imperial city. Its design had already presented an image of man-made landscape garden where real landscapes were downsized into a smaller space— for instance, the Jingyang Hill in the northwest corner of the garden, a soil-and-rock rockery piled up with colorful aragonite rock pieces, which was extensively covered with bamboos and pine trees. Another example was the Tianyuan Pond (Pond of Heaven and Abyss) in the southeast corner of the garden. The stream of Gu River was led into an excavated pond, which extended to the front of the major palaces to organize a holistic water system. Various waterscapes were constructed along its bank for a boat tour and sight-seeing. In the center of the Tianyuan Pond, the Jiuhua Platform (九华台, Platform of Nine Flowers) rose up, upon which a Qingliang Hall (Qing Liang Dian, Hall of Cool Breeze)

was built. Animals and birds were also purposely moved. What's more, a square spacious enough to accommodate nearly 1,000 people was built in front of this main palace hall for performance or other activities. In addition to the Hualin Yuan, there were a large number of small-scaled gardens in Luoyang, e.g. Chunwang Garden (春王园, Garden of Earliest Spring), Hongde Palace Garden (洪德苑, Palace Garden of Enormous Merit), Lingkun Palace Garden (灵昆苑, Palace Garden in Nimbus Kunlun), Pingle Palace Garden (平乐苑, Palace Garden of Peaceful Happiness), Buddhist Sarir Pond, Tianquan Pond (Pond of Heavenly Spring), and Donggong Pond (Eastern Royal Pond).

Jiankang (modern day Nanjing) had been the capital of six dynasties during this period; Wu (during the Three Kingdoms period), Eastern Jin, Liu Song, Southern Qi, Liang, and Chen dynasties. Here, the most prosperous days for imperial garden came when Emperor Wu of Liang (464 – 549, the father of the Liang Dynasty) was in power. These dynasties were set up by the royal Han families, who were content with the temporary peace in a small piece of land in the southern downstream area of the Yangtze River, and paid less attention to the scale of their imperial gardens but more to their exquisiteness and luxury. Hualin Garden located in the northern part of the imperial city in Jiankang was one such tiny garden. The construction work of Hualin Garden started during the Wu Dynasty, and all the dynasties that came after Wu (i.e. Eastern Jin, Liu Song, Southern Qi, Liang, and Chen dynasties) had added something new to it, and made it a work of paradise. Another important garden interior to the imperial city was Fangle Palace Garden (芳乐苑, Palace Garden of Fragrant Pleasure). Aside from it, there were more than 20 temporary palaces and gardens built around Xuanwu Lake in the suburb of Jiankang. Among them, the most famous ones were Leyou Palace Garden, Shanglin Palace Garden, Qingxi Palace (清溪宫, Palace beside Green Brook), Bowang Palace Garden, and Jianxin Palace Garden (建新苑, Palace Garden of Constructing New World).

Quite a number of private gardens of this period had been recorded in historical documents. The most prestigious among these private gardens was Jingu Garden (金谷园, Golden Millet Garden), which was built by Shi Chong (249 – 300), a wealthy person who lived in Luoyang during the Emperor Hui's reign. The reason Shi Chong built Jingu Garden was to create a beautiful environment for himself to enjoy the natural views, entertain, and purse intellectual endeavors after retirement. To serve his purpose, not only garden buildings like pavilions, terraces, and belvederes were luxuriously constructed and decorated, but also the overall planning of landscape was handed over to some of the most prominent garden designers of the time. The garden rested on a piece of rolling land alongside a river and introduced the water from Jingu Creek to create a complete water system. People could either take a boat tour in its waterways or enjoy fishing at any bank. In fact, the exceptionally charming waterscapes and botanic scenery made it one of the best places of its time for

FIG. 14 *Jingu Garden*, by Qiu Ying, Ming Dynasty
This painting captures a moment in the Jingu Garden built by Shi Chong, ex-governor of Jingzhou region in the Western Jin Dynasty as he listens to the music from a vertical bamboo flute played by his concubine Lü Zhu. In this picture, human figures were expressed with neat and fine lines. The landscape was painted in both meticulous (*gongbi*) and freehand (*xieyi*) styles. The painting demonstrates the extraordinary mature artistic skills of the painter, perfectly melting human emotions with the natural views. This illustration is selected from *Painting Collection of Qiu Ying*.

entertainment and dining (Fig. 14). Literati and scholar-bureaucrats —Xie Lingyun (385 – 433, the pioneer of Chinese landscape poems) and Tao Yuanming (365 – 427, poet, litterateur, and ode and essay writer in Chinese history), to name a few—also admired garden construction. Chinese literati usually paid little attention to or even distain the ostentatious and extravagant gardens, which appealed to the more powerful bureaucrats and noble families. Consequently, their gardens placed more emphasis on the natural beauty or the freshness of the natural world to express their detached attitudes toward earthly power and their love for peaceful and solitary life.

The ravages of frequent wars

in this era led to a prosperity of religions, especially Buddhism and Taoism, all over China. In the wake of such prosperity, Buddhist temples and Taoist temples were erected in great quantity. In Emperor Wu of Liang's time, Jiankang alone had over 500 Buddhist temples and over 100,000 Buddhist monks and nuns. Subsequently, the temple gardens emerged along with more and more Buddhist and Taoist temples as an independent genre of Chinese gardens. The Buddhist temples were first constructed during the Eastern Han Dynasty as special sites to worship Buddha. Later, gardens were built and attached to temples beside or behind them in answer to the needs of saramana and benefactors for residence and relaxation. When society was avidly donating palaces and private mansions to Buddha as temples, a great number of gardens, ones belonging to royal families or attached to private mansions, were reconstructed into Buddhist temples. Understandably, these temple gardens achieved quite a high artistic influence. A case in point is Songyue Temple (嵩岳寺, Temple on Songshan Mountain) in Dengfeng county, Henan province. It was a temporary imperial palace outside the capital before it was dedicated to Buddha, and previously called Xianju Temple (闲居寺, Leisure Life Temple) in the Northern Wei Dynasty. From the perspective of overall planning, a private garden was usually composed of two sections; places for accommodation and an attached garden. Likewise, a temple garden was usually composed of a main hall for worshiping Buddha and an attached garden. Yet, as a tranquil space often used for deep meditation and self-cultivation, a temple garden had a high requirement for natural landscape for its surroundings. That's why a temple garden usually locates itself inside woods or beside water. Qixia Temple (栖霞寺, Temple of Perching Rosy Glow) is a typical example of this for its peaceful and charming environments; the Mirror Lake and laurel trees bathed in moonlight, the belvederes and houses hidden in clouds, the cliffs and valleys overshadowing all worldly annoyance, and the views from high places in the mist of a rosy glow. With all these fascinating wonders, Qixia Temple is still a renowned scenic spot in Nanjing. In the Southern and Northern Dynasties, there were countless Buddhist temple gardens

among which we could find many masterpieces of high artistic scope. One of the largest Buddhist temples of that time was Tongtai Temple (同泰寺, Temple of Common Peace), i.e. Jiming Temple (鸡鸣寺, Rooster Crowing Temple) today in Nanjing, Jiangsu province. Buddhist Halls of diverse scales were constructed and an elegant garden was located beside Xuanji Hall (Xuan Ji Dian, Hall of Armillary Sphere), where rockeries and a fountain were arranged. Other famous temple buildings constructed around the same time include Lingyin Temple (灵隐寺, Temple of the Soul's Retreat) in Hangzhou, Yunyan Temple (云岩寺, Temple on a Hill in Clouds) in Huqiu Hill, Suzhou, and the Beisi Pagoda (North Temple Pagoda), also in Suzhou.

Thanks to the influences from the literati and temples, "excavating waterways and ponds" and "piling up hills" were given special attention, and as a result, became the mainstream of Chinese garden constructions. An aesthetic system in respect to garden landscape appreciation was also established. Landscape gardens featuring creative use of waters and hills gradually replaced the previous imperial gardens dominated by various palace halls and filled with animals and birds. In this era, three genres of garden construction—imperial, private, and temple gardens—developed simultaneously, which then pushed Chinese garden construction art to a turning point.

Bloom Stage—Sui and Tang Dynasties (581 – 907)

When the Southern and Northern

Dynasties were conquered by the Sui Dynasty, the previous political separation that had lasted for over 300 years came to an end, and China once again became a giant united empire. Short-lived as the Sui Dynasty was, it handed down a great quantity of precious heritage to later generations, such as the Grand Canal and Daxing city (renamed as Chang'an in the Tang Dynasty). Its subsequent great empire, the Tang Dynasty, had been a formidable expansive empire lasting for more than three centuries. In addition to that, Tang surpassed its predecessors both in military and cultural accomplishments. It is recognized as another golden time during which culture and arts blossomed after the first flourishing phase in Chinese history—the Qin and Han dynasties.

Emperor Yang of Sui (569 – 618, the second emperor of the Sui Dynasty) squandered recklessly, building a great number of new buildings and royal gardens to meet his insatiable hunger for pleasure. Since 605, he recruited roughly one million laborers and launched the construction of Xi Palace Garden, a super-sized, man-made landscape imperial garden only second in scale to the Shanglin Palace Garden built in the Western Han Dynasty. Its water planning, hill piling, plant arrangements, and building construction works consumed tremendous amount of human labor and material resources. Its overall layout divided the garden into three sections: front, middle, and back. The front section was composed of five lakes and 16 minor gardens. The five lakes symbolized the territory under the ruling of the empire, while the 16 grandiose minor gardens were constructed in

FIG. 15 Jiulong Hot Spring (Hot Spring of Nine Dragons) in Huaqing Pool
Being one of the famous gardens built in the Tang Dynasty, Huaqing Palace is still in good condition today. Its characteristic feature lies in its artistic style as the earlier natural landscape garden in China. That is to say, constructions were in line with every change of the terrain, be it high or low, winding or straight. It is a good example of "adapting garden design to local condition." Jiulong Hot Spring, located near the West Gate of Huaqing Palace, was open only to the imperial families, so it had the most luxurious facilities of all the hot springs in the palace. Emperor Xuanzong of Tang and his royal concubine Yang Yuhuan bathed together here.

between, independent to each other and surrounded by the waterways. The central view of the middle section was a wide and open water surface—the North Sea, extending as wide as 40 *li* (20 km, 12.43 miles). Within the North Sea, Penglai, Yingzhou and Fangzhang islands were piled up to meet with the arrangement of Three Celestial Islands in One Pond, which was passed down through history from the Han Dynasty. On those islands, platforms, waterside pavilions, and winding corridors were built. The pavilions and temples, operated with machinery, might well appear or disappear all of a sudden. Rising up and then vanishing into thin air, they seemed to be celestial architectures in paradise. The back section featured the wilderness. To fill this wilderness with life, the emperor commanded that all species of rare animals and unusual plants be shipped to the capital by post. Thereafter, the garden presented a charming view with lush trees and dense grass, where herds of animals and flocks of birds leisurely settled.

Being the successor of the Sui Dynasty, the Tang rulers redecorated some of the Sui's imperial gardens and constructed a number of new gardens. Huaqing

Palace in Mt. Li and Jiucheng Palace (九成宫, Palace of Nine Perfections) in Linyou, which are still in good condition today, were two representatives. Huaqing Palace, the contemporary Huaqing Pool in Lintong county, was located at the foot of Mount Li (to the north of Lintong county, about 30 kilometers away to the east of Xi'an). It was a perfect example of "adapting garden design to local conditions," offering a clear demonstration of the concepts in early Chinese landscape gardens. Various architectures like pavilions, platforms, galleries, gazebos, towers, and belvederes were proportioned along with the rise and fall of the mountain slopes, only to achieve a sense of diverse unity with the changeable geographical features. The rows of buildings linked with each other and ornamented by exotic flowers and trees in between. The entire landscape presented an impressive and beautiful picture (Fig. 15).

The Tang Dynasty was a glorious time of cultural development. It was during this time that the landscape poem became a magnificent genre of Chinese poetry. At the same time, landscape painting made a great breakthrough, freed from the

limitation of being a background in murals, and became an independent art form for aesthetic appreciation. Also, during this time, Chinese landscape poems and landscape paintings began influencing and melting into each other. Wangchuan Villa, designed by Wang Wei, a renowned poet and painter, was a typical example of natural garden villa based on his own paintings. The villa contained 20 scenic spots, presenting both wild flavor and poetic and picturesque sceneries (Fig. 16). This villa gave prominence to natural beauty, located on a mountainous area with rolling hills, waterfalls, springs, creeks, lakes, and thick vegetation. Bai Juyi (772 – 846, known as the "Magician of Poetry" or "King of Poetry," a great realistic poet and litterateur in the Tang Dynasty) admired gardens, too. He personally led the construction of four gardens, i.e. private gardens attached to his mansions in Lüdao Lane in Luoyang and Xinchang Lane in Chang'an, Mount Lu Cottage Garden, and his Villa Garden at the bank of Weishui River. He believed that a rural villa must go with the natural surrounding, in agreement with the conditions and laws of nature. While a garden attached

to a private mansion in an urban setting must achieve the effect of "enjoying the peace in a bustling environment." This concept was realized in Bailian Hamlet (白莲庄, White Lotus Hamlet) in the Lüdao Lane in Luoyang, which was built when he served as the governor of Hangzhou and Suzhou, and ideally reflected the taste of a fresh, elegant, and tranquil landscape in an urban setting.

Another prominent poet garden designer of that time was Du Fu (712 – 770, the "Sage of Poets," one of the greatest realistic poets in the golden time of Tang Dynasty, having profound influence over poets after him, leaving about 1,500 poems behind). He built a Huanhuaxi Cottage (浣花溪草堂, Cottage beside Washing Flower Brook) at the bank of Huanhua Brook (Washing Flower Brook) west of Chengdu. And Li Deyu (787 – 849, a famous statesman and poet in the middle period of the Tang Dynasty) built Pingquan Hamlet (平泉庄, Leveled Spring Hamlet) 30 *li* (15 km, 9.32 miles) away south of Luoyang.

The Sui and Tang dynasties were another critical period for the development of imperial gardens after the Qin and Han dynasties.

During this era, imperial gardens shrugged off the roughness, spaciousness, and the simple imitation of nature that featured the imperial gardens of Qin and Han, and began presenting a genuine royal aesthetic. Both overall planning and details in such gardens had gone through painstakingly careful handling. It was also during this time that the three major branches of imperial gardens came into being, i.e. the imperial gardens interior to the imperial city, those within temporary dwelling palaces, and those inside detached palaces away from the capital city. At the same time, private gardens gradually developed to a mature stage. Chinese landscape painting, landscape poetry, and landscape garden had already begun to influence and blend into each other. People in the Tang Dynasty had already attempted to reproduce what had been a poetic and painting composition to create a scenic spot or a garden. In addition to the garden genres mentioned above, a host of temple gardens began appearing in scenic sites in mountainous areas in the heyday of Buddhism and Taoism in Chinese history.

Mature Stage—Song, Liao, Jin, and Yuan Dynasties (960 – 1368)

Despite the fact that the Song brought the separatist era (the Five Dynasties and Ten Kingdoms) to an end, it had never been able to reunite the entire country. The Northern Song's territory only covered the major proportion of the Yellow River Basin, the Yangtze River Basin, and the Pearl River Basin. The Northern Song had to guard against three rival regimes: Liao, Western Xia, and Jin. Although the garden scale of the time was no match for that of the Sui and Tang, the planning and design were much more exquisite than their ancestors.

As far as gardening technique was concerned in the Song Dynasty, hill and rockery piling welcomed the climax of its development, and the scale of rockeries had grown much larger. For instance, the Taihu Lake rock displayed in front of Renshou Hall (Ren Shou Dian, Hall of Benevolence and Longevity) in Hou Palace Garden (后苑, Rear Palace Garden) of the Northern Song Dynasty was as high as 9 meters. Another Taihu Lake rock displayed in Gen Yue Garden (艮岳, Gen Yue) built by Emperor Huizong of Song (1082 – 1135, the eighth emperor of Northern Song Dynasty) was as high as 15 meters. Both were rare creations in the history of Chinese garden construction.

After the royal court of the Song Dynasty was compelled to move its capital from Bianjing (now Kaifeng, Henan province) to Lin'an (now Hangzhou, Zhejiang province), all previous royal gardens were pitifully damaged, and the deserters started to build new imperial gardens in the new capital. If taking private gardens built by royal families, powerful bureaucrats, and wealthy persons all into consideration, during the Southern Song's reign, more than a hundred gardens stood alongside West Lake or scattered in the suburb of the capital.

Meanwhile, Jin, the conqueror, moved its capital to Zhongdu (today's Beijing) and began to build Xi Palace Garden to the west of its imperial city. The original water system of the site for Xi Palace Garden was expanded into a wide Taiye Pond in which Qionghua Island was piled up. As an imperial garden, it had a lot of halls, towers,

belvederes, a large patch of bamboo groves and apricot trees, and flocks of birds. Later, after sweeping Jin's regime, Yuan Dynasty chose Dadu (today's Beijing) as its capital and began to build its imperial city around the Taiye Pond, further uniting palaces and gardens into a holistic art work.

Imperial garden construction in the Northern Song Dynasty began with the "Four Gardens" in Dongjing city (the capital of Song, also named Bianjing, today's Kaifeng), i.e. Qionglin Palace Garden (琼林苑, Palace Garden in Jade Forest), Yichun Palace Garden, Yujin Garden (玉津园, Garden beside Jade Harbor), and Jinming Pond (Golden Brightness Pond). A painting named *Boating Contest in Jinming Pond*, painted by Zhang Zeduan (1085 – 1145, one of the greatest painters in the Northern Song Dynasty), gives us a vivid description of a humorous aquatic sport (Fig. 17).

However, large-scale garden

construction in the Northern Song's did not start until the time of Emperor Huizong of Song (1082 – 1135), an emperor who was weak in politics, but talented in painting and calligraphy. He was also passionate about garden rockeries. While appreciating those art rocks, he even took them down in paintings and composed inscription or poems to finish the paintings. A piece named *Rock of Auspicious Dragon*, now preserved in the Palace Museum in Beijing, is one of his art works (Fig. 18). He even gave an edict to a man named Zhu Mian (1075 – 1126) to help him collect unusual rocks and flowers for his imperial gardens. Subsequently, a department named "*ying feng ju*" was established to organize the searching and shipping works. In order to deliver the flowers, timbers, and rocks collected, i.e. "Flower and Rock Shipment," local governments often had to draft over 1,000 men as boat trackers. With enormous

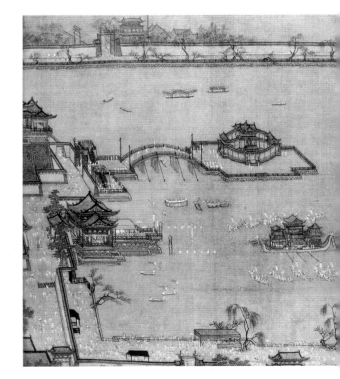

FIG. 17 *Boating Contest in Jinming Pond*, by Zhang Zeduan, Northern Song Dynasty
This silk scroll, collected by Tianjin Museum, is 28.5 cm long and 28.6 cm wide. This painting recorded an old custom of the emperors of the Northern Song Dynasty watching a dragon boat contest in Jinming Pond from a Linshui Palace. On the pond, there are barges with luxurious decorations, music boats, small boats, brightly painted pleasure boats, small dragon boats, and tiger-head boats serving either as ornaments on the water surface or carrier of music bands. In addition to those small boats, there is a giant dragon boat 40 *zhang* (133 m, 0.08 miles) in length. Except for the big dragon boats, other dragon boats are lined up and ready for a contest to entertain their audiences.

FIG. 18 *Rock of Auspicious Dragon*, by Emperor Huizong of Song, Northern Song Dynasty
This is a colored silk scroll, 53.8 cm long and 127.5 cm wide, preserved in the Palace Museum in Beijing. The rock in the painting is a Taihu Lake rock, which is famous for intricate hollows, twisting but lively shape, up-and-down surface, and especially, a "full of variety" sense. There is a precious flower planted in a small bed in a hollow on the top of the rock. In addition, a few elegant bamboos are standing beside it to show its master's temperament and interest. The painter first used thin but powerful lines to bring out the profile and texture of the rock and then applied an ink dyeing technique to vividly reproduce the hardness of the rock. It is obvious that the painter is very careful with every touch, leaving no room for anything unnecessary. The use of colors and composition are attractive to the eye but don't intentionally appeal to it, showing a true noble aesthetic.

in the garden, sitting on the peak of Wansui Mountain like a lord. A brook winding to the northwest of the garden was introduced into the garden to entertain the imperial families. And in the east section, a kingdom of rare flowers and trees set off the various architectures which were arranged in line with natural landforms.

In 1127, Jin troops ferociously invaded Song, conquering Bianjing (the capital of Song) and making Emperor Huizong of Song and Emperor Qinzong of Song (1100 – 1161) their prisoners. Zhao Gou (1127 – 1162, the first emperor of the Southern Song Dynasty) escaped to Southern China. In 1129 he promoted Hangzhou as Lin'an prefecture, and officially announced Lin'an (present day Hangzhou) as the capital of the Southern Song

Dynasty in 1138. From then on, this city served this role in the following 152 years. Although the Southern Song was a small regime, its achievements in governance, economy, and culture were still the most brilliant in the world at the time, which consequently made its capital, Lin'an, the largest metropolis among its peers in the globe. According to Marco Polo, Lin'an was the most beautiful and luxurious fairy city in the world (Fig. 19).

Emperors of the Southern Song Dynasty built a multitude of imperial gardens in and around Lin'an. Marco Polo described them in his travel notes that "the palaces deserve to be ranked as the largest scaled construction in the whole universe … the enclosed garden could house extreme splendor and

investment of human, financial, and material resources, and as much as 7 years of hard work, an unprecedented elegant garden in history, Gen Yue Garden, was created.

As a man-made landscape garden, Gen Yue Garden placed a huge rockery hill, the Wansui Mountain (Mt. Longevity), in the center of the overall blueprint, and set up Wansong Ridge (Ridge with Ten Thousand Pines) and Yanchi Pond (Wild Goose Pond) as its wings. The various buildings in Wansui Mountain were the starting points of scenery design. Although the Wansui Mountain was piled up by human, it had every essential features of a natural mountain. When walking in it, one would definitely mistake it for a real mountain. Jie Pavilion (Pavilion of Connection) was the highest point

Fig. 19 The locative relationship among Lin'an in West Lake and neighboring mountains
1. Imperial Garden
2. Deshou Palace 3. Jujing Garden 4. Zhaoqing Temple
5. Yuhu Garden 6. Jifang Garden 7. Yanxiang Garden
8. Pingshan Garden 9. Jingci Temple 10. Qingle Garden
11. Yujin Garden 12. Fujing Garden 13. Wuliu Garden
14. West Lake 15. Su Causeway 16. Bai Causeway
17. Qiantang Gate
18. District of Government Offices 19. Fenghuang Mountain 20. Wansong Ridge
21. Long Bridge
22. Qiantang River
23. White Pagoda
24. Liuhe Pagoda
25. Nanping Mountain
26. Southern Peak 27. Mt. Geling 28. Mt. Gushan
29. Imperial Road 30. Yuhang Gate 31. Yongjin Gate
32. Qingbo Gate 33. Genshan Gate 34. Dongqing Gate
35. Chongxin Gate 36. Xin Gate 37. Bao'an Gate
38. Houchao Gate 39. Jiahui Gate 40. Hening Gate
41. Palace Walls

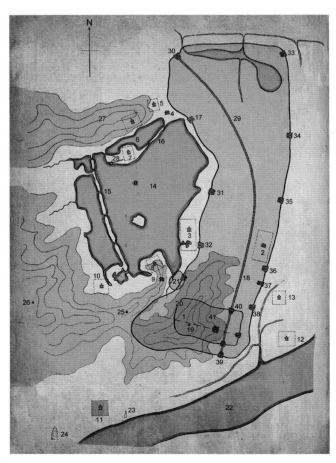

entertainment."

In Deshou Palace (德寿宫, Palace of Virtue and Longevity), a construction situated to the east of Wangxian Bridge (Bridge of Expecting Celestials), gardening elements played the dominating role. Here, chrysanthemum, lotus, bamboo, and plum trees were planted, water was introduced to fill in a large pond, and a rocky hill was piled up in imitation of the famous Flying Peak.

Besides, there were other constructions like Jujing Garden (聚景园, Garden of Accumulating Sceneries) outside Qingbo Gate (Gate of Crystal Ripples), Yujin Garden outside Jiahui Gate (Gate of Wonderful Meeting), Pingshan Garden (屏山园, Garden of Mountain Screen) outside Qianhu Gate, Yuhu Garden (玉壶园, Jade Pot Garden) outside Qiantang Gate, Fujing Garden (富景园, Garden of Wealthy Scenes) outside Xin Gate, Jifang Garden (集芳园, Garden of Housing Fragrance) on Mt. Geling, Yanxiang Garden (延祥园, Garden of Prolonged Auspicious Omen) on Mt. Gushan, as well as Qionghua Garden (琼华园, Garden of Jade Sparkle), and Xiaoyin Garden (小隐园, Minor Solitude Garden). All of them were proper matches for their neighboring natural landscapes of lakes and mountains.

What's more, the capital sceneries were further enriched by uncountable private gardens which were possessed by noble families and wealthy merchants and the Buddhist and Taoist temple gardens, which rested at random at the bank of West Lake, at the foot of mountains, or inside the city. All of the top ten scenic sites around West Lake during the

Southern Song Dynasty came into being and were well recognized by later generations, namely the Yuan, Ming, and Qing dynasties. Even today, they are still known as must-see travel destinations.

As for the private gardens in Luoyang city in the Northern Song's time, Li Gefei (about 1045 – 1105, a famous litterateur in the Northern Song Dynasty) recorded 19 famous private gardens in the city in his *Records of Celebrated Gardens in Luoyang* (洛阳名园记, *Luoyang Ming Yuan Ji*), most of which were accomplished on the base of the previous villas constructed during the Tang Dynasty (Fig. 20). Among them, six of them were enclosed in private mansions, ten were independent entertainment gardens, and two were pure botanic gardens.

Unlike those constructed during the Tang Dynasty, gardens built in this period were clearly independent and separated from living spaces. They served the purpose of entertaining the noble, powerful or rich guests, and were even regularly opened to the public. As for private gardens in the Yangtze River Delta, the book of *Meng Liang Records* (梦梁录, *Meng Liang Lu*) documented 16 famous private gardens, and *Stories of Old Time in Wulin* (武林旧事, *Wulin Jiu Shi*) documented 45. The most extraordinary of them were Great Wave Pavilion in the south Pingjiang (today's Suzhou), Yanshan Garden (砚山园, Inkstone Garden) built by Mi Fu (1051 – 1107, calligrapher and painter in the Northern Song Dynasty) in Runzhou (Zhenjiang), Mengxi Garden (梦溪园, Garden of Dream Pool) built by Shen Kuo (1031 – 1095, the greatest scientist and engineer in the Northern Song

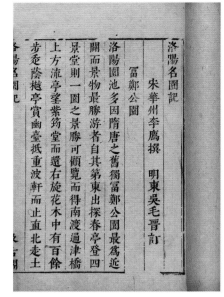

FIG. 20 *Records of Celebrated Gardens in Luoyang*

This book is an important historical document about private gardens in the Northern Song Dynasty. Though the listed gardens were confined to the territory of Luoyang, the book managed to reflect the artistic achievements, styles, fashions, and other essential characteristics of gardens in the Northern Song Dynasty, since most gardens introduced in the book were built by noble families, powerful government officials, or wealthy merchants, and thus, could be considered as the representative gardens of the time. We can have a clear view of it from the introduction.

Dynasty), and Shen Garden (沈园, Garden of Shen's Family) in Shaoxing, Zhejiang province. Shen Garden was especially known for witnessing the tragic reunion of Lu You (1125 – 1210, a famous poet in the Southern Song Dynasty) and his ex-wife Tang Wan.

In regards to the gardens constructed in the Liao and Jin dynasties (1127 – 1234, set up by Wanyan Aguda in Huining city), the predecessors of existing Beihai and Zhonghai in Beijing were recorded in more detail in historical documents. Since Liao and Jin's reign, this part of the capital suburb had become the center of imperial garden construction. In 936, Khitan (an ancient ethnic group from Northeast China) set up Liao Dynasty and renamed Youzhou as Nanjing (literally, the south capital located to the west of Beijing) the next year and started to build palaces and gardens there. In addition to the Linshui Palace (临水殿, Waterside Palace), Neiguo Garden (内果园, Interior Fruit Garden), Li Garden (栗园, Chestnut Garden), Liu Garden (柳园, Willow Garden), Changchun Palace (长春宫, Palace of Everlasting Spring), and other imperial gardens, a land where there was pond and islands (to the west of Liao's imperial city) was selected to construct Yao Chi (Jade Pond), in the middle of which an island named Yao Yu (or Jade Islet) was piled up and a palace named "Yao Chi Palace Hall" was built onto the islet.

Then in 1153, shortly after establishing its capital in Zhongdu (the southwest part of Beijing), the Jin Dynasty immediately mobilized a great deal of resources to construct palaces and gardens for themselves in the north suburb of Zhongdu, previously a piece of wetland. Once Emperor Hailingwang of Jin (i.e. Wanyan Liang, 1122 – 1161, the forth emperor of Jin Dynasty) chose this wetland as the site for his Qionghua Island (Jade Sparkle Island), he sent several painters to Bianjing (the capital of the Northern Song Dynasty) to make a copy of the official institutions and constructing methods of palace halls documented in the Song Dynasty, and especially, to paint a picture of the Shoushan Gen Yue (Gen Yue Garden on Wanshou Mountain) as a blueprint for imitation. Later, he even removed all the Taihu Lake Rocks displayed in the Gen Yue Garden to decorate his Qionghua Island.

At that time, Taiye Pond,

Qionghua Island, and Guanghan Palace (广寒宫, Moon Palace) on the island had already been completed. When the last element was in place, Taining Palace (太宁宫, Supreme Tranquility Palace) was established, then emerged a complete imperial garden in the style of Gen Yue Garden, presented the charm of a celestial island in paradise. The entire Taining Palace laid the earliest foundation of imperial gardens in Beijing. Subsequently, the prime time of imperial garden construction in the Jin Dynasty came during the reign of Emperor Shizong of Jin (1161 – 1189). One of the most renowned imperial gardens interior to the capital city during this time was the Xi Palace Garden (the Taining Palace) in Zhongdu. Located in the west corner of Jin's imperial city, the Xi Palace Garden had a number of lakes that were collectively referred to as Taiye Pond. Qionghua Island and Yao Yu Island were constructed inside the pond, supporting the Yaoguang Hall (Yao Guang Dian, Jade's Essence Hall), Yuzao Hall (Yu Zao Dian, Fish Algae Hall), and some others. In addition to the Xi Palace Garden, Zhongdu had other eight celebrated gardens that were collectively referred to as "Eight Scenery Gardens in Zhongdu."

In 1215, Mongolian army sacked Zhongdu, the capital of the Jin Dynasty, and renamed it Yanjing. In the winter of 1260, Kublai Khan (Emperor Shizu of Yuan, 1215 – 1294, the founder of the Yuan Dynasty) arrived at Zhongdu and chose Taining Palace in the northeast suburb of Zhongdu as his temporary residence since all imperial palaces inside Jin's imperial city had fallen into ruins

during the war.

By 1267, three palace complexes had already been built around the lake inside Taining Palace. Lying on the east and west banks of the lake, three building groups formed a triangle. The east bank belonged to Imperial Palace (大内, Da Nei, exactly where the Forbidden City is located in Beijing). To the north of Da Nei, there was a large green area named Ling Plant Garden (灵圃, Nimbus Plant Garden, located at present Mt. Jing), where some precious and rare animals were raised. On the west bank, there were two palace groups. One was Xingsheng Palace (Prosperous Sega Palace) for empresses or dowagers, and the other was Longfu Palace (Great Bless Palace) for the crowned princes.

Numerous flowers and trees surrounded these palace buildings, with rockeries scattered between them. Pavilions and corridors linked palace halls and towers together and made them a unity. A low wall of 20 li (10 km, 6.21 miles) surrounded these three complexes and defined the territory of the Imperial City. According to the description in *Chronicles of Beijing*, the Yuan Dynasty "rebuilt Qionghua Island in 1264 and set up the Guanghan Palace on its original foundation." The Taiye Pond of the Yuan Dynasty only consisted of today's Beihai and Zhonghai Gardens. Qionghua Island, Yitian Palace (仪天殿, Palace for Worshiping Heaven), and Xishan Platform (犀山台, Platform on Rhinoceros Hill) were built in the same Taiye Pond to complete the typical pattern of imperial garden, i.e. Three Celestial Islands in One Pond.

Of the three islands, two were

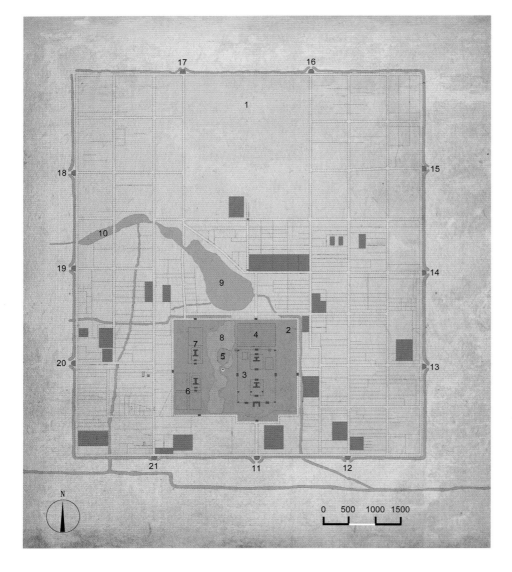

FIG. 21 Ichnography of Dadu city in the Yuan Dynasty
The overall planning followed the pattern passed down from the Tang and Song Dynasty, i.e. "Three One-inside-Another Sequential Square Cities" (Outer City, Imperial City, and Inner Imperial City, from outside to center). According to this pattern, the Inner Imperial City sits in the center of three square cities and everything is arranged symmetrically along a central axis. The Taining Palace was the center and the starting point of the overall planning. To its north, the Jishui Pond, a lake connected to Gaoliang River, determined the central axis of the overall planning of the Dadu. That is to say, the central axis started from a point on the northeast bank of Jishui Pond. Once the central axis was defined, the location of the Inner Imperial City was determined, i.e. to the east of Taining Palace Pond. Dadu was roughly a big square, inside which the Imperial City was situated slightly westward in the middle of the south half of it. In the Imperial City, Taiye Pond occupied the central area and the Inner Imperial City was located on its east bank. In order to highlight the importance of Taining Palace and the historical tradition of Qionghua Island and Yingzhou Island, a Xingsheng Palace and a Longfu Palace were constructed on the west bank of Taiye Pond to form a stable triangle with the Inner Imperial City. As a result, there appeared a beautiful landscape garden in the middle of magnificent imperial palace halls.
1. Inner City 2. Imperial City 3. Imperial Place 4. Ling Pu 5. Qionghua Island 6. Longfu Palace 7. Xingsheng Palace 8. Taiye Pond 9. Jishui Pond 10. Gaoliang River 11. Lizheng Gate 12. Wenming Gate 13. Qihua Gate 14. Chongren Gate 15. Guangxi Gate 16. Anzhen Gate 17. Jiande Gate 18. Suqing Gate 19. Heyi Gate 20. Pingze Gate 21. Shuncheng Gate

surrounded by water. The larger north island was first named "Qionghua Island" and then renamed "Wanshou Mountain (Mt. Longevity)," and later as "Wansui Mountain (Mt. Longevity)." Following exactly the pattern of traditional Chinese celestial islands, all constructions on Qionghua Island were symmetrically arranged along a central axis. On top of Wansui Mountain there was a Guanghan Palace, together with Jinlu Pavilion (Golden Dew Pavilion) to its left and Yuhong Pavilion (Jade Rainbow Pavilion) to its right. In front of Guanghan Palace, three palace halls stood in a row, the central one being Renzhi Hall (Ren Zhi Din, Hall of

Benevolence and Wisdom), the left one Jiefu Hall (Jie Fu Dian, Hall with Great Blessing), and the right one Yanhe Hall (Yan He Dian, Hall of Prolonged Peace) (Fig. 21).

The time of the Song, Liao, Jin, and Yuan dynasties was the first phase when Chinese classical garden construction matured. Especially in Song's time, its art and vitality reached the peak of perfection. During this time, Chinese classical gardening had gone through the transformation from the realistic reflection of the natural world to the recreation of the spiritual world. Poetic nuances and picturesque images were already accepted as key elements of garden design. The techniques of rockery creation

and arrangement, as well as water system arrangement, already advanced to a sophisticated level. During the Song Dynasty, we could find all types of garden architectures that will appear in later generations. Moreover, *Construction Method* (营造法式, *Yingzao Fashi*, compiled by Li Jie) and *The Book of Wooden Wares* (木经, *Mu Jing*, written by Yu Hao) were both published during the Song Dynasty.

Latest Prime Stage— Ming and Qing Dynasties (1368 – 1911)

After over 2,000 years of advancement in the field of garden construction, Chinese classical

gardens developed its mature stage in the Ming and Qing dynasties. The overall design, construction techniques, animal breeding approaches, and flowers and trees planting methods reached a very sophisticated level. In addition, talented designers and technicians continuously emerged in great numbers. What's more, the economic prosperity in Chinese feudal society provided garden construction activities with adequate material and technical supplies. Consequently, Chinese garden construction achieved its peak time in history in this late era of feudal society, leaving countless fantastic works for later generations. Most of the classical gardens which are still in existence were built during

Li Jie (Li Mingzhong) and His *Construction Method*

Li Jie (1035 – 1110) was a famous scientist and architect in the Northern Song Dynasty, known for a dozen of major large construction works completed under his supervision, and especially for being the chief editor of *Construction Method*. *Construction Method* was a book on a set of official standards on architecture design and engineering issued by the Northern Song government. It was the most complete monograph about architecture and architectural technologies in ancient China and a strong evidence of well-developed ancient Chinese architecture. The book was compiled based on *The Book of Wooden Wares* by Yu Hao.

Yu Hao and His *The Book of Wooden Wares*

Yu Hao was a construction artisan in Hangzhou in Zhejiang province during the late Five Dynasties and the early Northern Song Dynasty. Humble in origin, as an artisan he was keen on learning form others and diligent in thinking over every problem he encountered. Gradually, he acquired substantial constructing experience of wooden architecture, especially that of multilayer pagodas and towers. Regrettably, his three-volume book, *The Book of Wooden Wares*, was lost to history.

this period. In general, imperial gardens constructed in the Ming and Qing dynasties were masterpieces revealing the supreme accomplishment in the field of garden construction in all dynasties. The mature garden construction theories and techniques and the continuous appearance of prominent garden designers and artisans provided crucial elements for imperial garden constructions in Ming and Qing.

In 1402, Emperor Chengzu of Ming (Zhu Di, 1360 – 1424, the third emperor of the Ming Dynasty) seized the throne by force. The next year, he changed the title of his reign to Yongle (literally means everlasting happiness) and moved Ming's capital to Beijing. In 1421, he set out to build a new city in Beijing on exactly the same site where Dadu of the Yuan Dynasty was located (in fact, this is also the same site where Beijing is located today). However, instead of following the central axis defined by the Yuan Dynasty, he moved the central axis of his imperial city by about 150 meters to the east. Then, he moved the north city wall 5 *li* (2.5 km, 1.55 miles) to the south and the south city wall 2 *li* (1 km, 0.62 miles) further south, but kept the east and west city walls as they were in the Ming Dynasty. Thus,

FIG. 22 The Five Pavilions on the Five Peaks of Jingshan Mountain
This picture is extracted from *Beijing Scenic Spots*, published by China Nationality Art Photograph Publishing House.

the final overall planning of Beijing came into being and served both the Ming and Qing dynasties.

Ming's overall planning of Beijing is a clear demonstration of the fundamental principle of capital planning during the entire Chinese feudal age, i.e. "putting the imperial palace in the center of city planning." The central axis of Ming's imperial palace was perfectly aligned with the central axis of Beijing, the central axis was 7.8 kilometers in length from north to south, running through all the three city walls rings. Also on this central axis, a 50-meter-high artificial mound, Meishan Mountain (Mt. Jing in the Qing Dynasty), was piled up. This site was exactly where the previous Yanchun Belvedere (Yan Chun Ge, Belvedere of Prolonged Spring) was situated, which used to be the place emperors in the Yuan Dynasty met his officials and worshiped Buddha. It was for the purpose of suppressing the feng shui (also known as geomancy) of the previous dynasty.

After the entire city site shifted southward, the middle peak (the

highest peak) among the five on the Meishan Mountain took the place of Central Platform, the old geometric center of Dadu city of Yuan. Wanchun Pavilion (Pavilion of Ten Thousand Spring Seasons) sitting on the top of the middle peak was situated precisely on the central axis of Beijing and the middle point between the north and south walls of the imperial city (Fig. 22). Obviously, the symbolic meaning of the artificial mound is far beyond its functional meaning. From the symbolic perspective, it is there to demonstrate the supreme nobility and power of the emperors, serving the imperial city as a foundation to collect and accumulate good fortune.

The six imperial gardens

inside the imperial city, namely Imperial Garden, Garden of Jianfu Palace (建福宫花园, Garden of Constructing Blessing), Wansui Mountain, Xi Palace Garden, Tu Garden (兔园, Rabbit Garden), and Dong Palace Garden (东苑, Eastern Palace Garden), were given special attention. Among them, Xi Palace Garden occupied the largest site and was located exactly where the previous Taiye Pond in the Yuan Dynasty was situated.

Ming excavated the Nanhai, and therefore, expanded the water surface of Taiye Pond further to the south. In addition, the old wooden suspension bridge in front of Yitian Palace on Yingzhou Island was replaced with a nine-arch stone bridge (the Beihai Stone Bridge now). Together, these constructions defined the layout of Beihai, Zhonghai, and Nanhai that we see today.

Two other notable changes were: the island gardens previously surrounded by water became a peninsular garden connected to the east bank, and the old earth platform was enclosed with brick walls and became the Circular Wall. During the time of Tianshun (1457 – 1464), some new buildings were added to Qionghua Island

and along the north bank of Beihai. Later, during the time of Emperor Jiajing (1522 – 1566) and Emperor Wanli (1573 – 1620),

FIG. 24 Portrait of Emperor Qianlong, Qing Dynasty
Emperor Aisin Gioro Hongli, 1711 – 1799, was commonly known as Emperor Qianlong (reign title) but formally addressed as Emperor Gaozong of the Qing Dynasty (dynastic title). He maintained, built, and expanded imperial palaces and gardens in and around Beijing, such as Garden of Ningshou Palace and its attached gardens in the Forbidden City, the Qinian Palace (Palace of Prayer for Good Harvest) in the Temple of Heaven (to replace the original roof tiles with the new blue glazed tiles), Qingyi Garden (later renamed as the Summer Palace), three interior gardens in Old Summer Palace, Jingyi Garden in Xiangshan Mountain (Fragrant Hill), Jingming Garden (静明园, Garden of Peace and Brightness) in Yuquan Mountain, Mountain Resort, and Eight Outer Temples, as well as Mulan Hunting Garden, to name a few. None of them fails to be a splendid example of gardening in the Qing Dynasty.

more buildings and scenic places were established around Zhonghai and Nanhai, adding some human touches to the natural state of Taiye Pond. For instance, the Wulong Pavilion (Five-Dragon Pavilions), built in 1543, was actually a five-pavilion architecture complex connected by several diverse stone bridges (Fig. 23). Generally speaking, Xi Palace Garden was characterized by wide spacing between buildings. Individual buildings randomly scattered on a spacious land, giving visitors a clear sense of the wilderness. With Wansui Mountain and the Imperial Palace as its background, the Xi Palace Garden was the biggest scenic spot in Beijing.

During the reign of Emperor Jiajing and Emperor Wanli of the Ming Dynasty, driven by economic development and active commodity production and exchanges, capitalism began slowly but steadily developed. From Emperor Jiajing's reign in the Ming Dynasty to Emperor Qianlong's reign in the Qing Dynasty (1736 – 1795, the forth emperor in Qing) (Fig. 24) economic development had given birth to more and more cities, and more and more government officials and wealthy merchants, especially those in the Yangtze River Delta, began to build their private gardens. The Yangtze River Delta was the hub of Chinese capitalism. Because of the economic growth, education and culture activities in the local area took on a new look, which in turn contributed to the emergence of more talented literati. Apart from the human factor, warm and moist climate suitable for plant growing and the abundant resources of Taihu Lake rocks also provided a superior environment

Ji Cheng and His *The Craft of Gardens*

Ji Cheng (1579 – ?), also known as Ji Wufou, was a good painter from the city of Wujiang in the Ming Dynasty. He loved strange rocks and was good at designing and constructing gardens in accordance with the artistic conception of paintings. His *Yuan Ye* (completed in 1631 and first published in 1634) was the earliest and best monograph on gardening in Chinese history. The *Yuan Ye* has three volumes. The first volume contains six articles, i.e. "On Construction" and "On Gardening" (as a summary of theories), "On Situation," "On Layout," "On Building," and "On Non-structural Features." The second volume is "On Balustrade." The third volume also contains six articles, i.e. "On Doors and Windows," "On Walls," "On Paving," "On Rockery Piling," "On Selection of Rocks," and "On View Borrowing." The *Yuan Ye* is a theoretical summary of the mature Chinese classical gardening art. The garden design concepts and methodologies and the regularities of garden construction introduced in the book have general importance in guiding and inspiring later generations in their gardening practices. According to his theory, the "fundamental rule" of gardening is "to skillfully construct views in accordance with the surroundings and borrow the neighboring views, and to deliberately build the most suitable architectures in a particular circumstance and decorate them in the most appropriate way." As for mountain-piling approaches, he insisted on "piling up artificial hills based on the images of real mountains and making man-made mountains look like real ones." On the specific environment, the scale of space and the visual and psychological changes incurred in a visitor's mind during sightseeing, he categorized rockeries into several types, i.e. garden rockeries, rockeries in a hall and those in studies. He specifically emphasized that the key to a garden rockery is to "plan an area of foothills before piling up a hill" and the key to rockeries in a hall or in a study is to "capture steep and precipitous features of a mountain." As for selecting a site for a garden, he claimed, "No matter it is a site among mountain forest, or a site near a river and a lake, or a site in an uninhabited countryside or in a village, as long as the overall situation is suitable, it can be used to build a garden." His theories and experiences were widely applied by garden masters to various imperial gardens built in the Ming and Qing Dynasties. Even today, his book is still recognized as one of the most important references on Chinese ancient gardening arts.

Wen Zhenheng and His *Records of Superfluous Things*

Wen Zhenheng (1585 – 1645), also known as Wen Qimei, was a painter and garden designer in Changzhou (present day Suzhou) in the late Ming Dynasty. His *Records of Superfluous Things* is a series of literary sketches covering his reflection on life and his aesthetic criticism on different things. Of this book, four volumes, i.e. "On Buildings," "On Flowers and Trees," "On Water and Rocks," and "On Birds and Fishes," are directly related to gardening theories and techniques. In addition to that, fragments concerning gardening are here and there in other volumes. When summarizing "On Buildings," Wen made clear his garden design guidelines, i.e. "In all, manual works would be built in accordance with the natural conditions in the environment. Any subjective creation should echo with their corresponding objective views." And he put forward on his aesthetic principle—"3 Preferences and 3 Negations," i.e. "to prefer classical style to modern style, prefer the simple to the complicated, and prefer less design to mediocre design." In the end, he proposed his ultimate ideal for garden design, "a most charming garden should possess a simple elegance just as nature appears, yet such an artistic reach is not something one who couldn't understand the feeling could manage to discuss." Also, he listed 42 ornamental trees, shrubs, and flowers in the chapter of "On Flowers and Trees" and 18 water-bodies and rocks commonly used for a garden in the chapter of "On Water and Rocks." The *Records of Superfluous Things* touches extensively on topics concerning both macroscopic architecture and gardens and microscopic man-made everyday utensils and articles, overall planning and building requirements, and specific design and detailed instructions. One of its essences lies in its profound designing insights, truly elegant tastes, and spiritual quests.

for garden construction in this area. As a result, gardens in the Yangtze River Delta became the greatest representatives of Chinese classical garden construction in its prime. Among them, the most renowned projects built in the late period of the Ming Dynasty include: Ying Garden (影园, Shadow Garden), Xiu Garden (休园, Garden for a Rest) and Jiashu Garden (嘉树园, Garden with Beautiful Trees), Wumu Garden (五亩之园, Garden of Five Acres)

in Yangzhou by Zheng's brothers from a prestigious family, as well as Garden of Cultivation, Humble Administrator's Garden, Lingering Garden, Five Peaks Garden, Xi Garden (西园, Western Garden), Fangcao Garden (芳草园, Fragrant Grass Garden) in Suzhou; Jichang Garden in Wuxi, as well as Yu Garden in Shanghai.

As for theoretical achievement, Ming presented the world with several monographs on gardening, such as *The Craft of Gardens* (园

FIG. 25 Qingzhixiu Rock, a Taihu Lake rock in the Summer Palace
Mi Wanzhong (1570 – 1628) was a famous landscape painter in the Ming Dynasty known for painting garden views and rocks. Being an enthusiast for strange rocks, he was also an eminent rockery garden designer of his time. In his lifetime, he had designed quite a number of gardens, all located at the suburb of Beijing. The rock in the picture is an 8-meter-long Taihu Lake Rock that he discovered in the Fangshan Mountains, which he exhausted almost all his money to transport from the mountain to his private garden, not to mention all the troubles he encountered during the procedure. Later, Emperor Qianlong named it "Qingzhixiu" and displayed it in the courtyard in front of Leshou Hall (Hall of Happiness and Longevity) in the Summer Palace. Since then, the rock has stayed there as an evidence of Mi's gardening activities.

冶, *Yuan Ye*) by Ji Cheng, *Records of Superfluous Things* (长物志, *Chang Wu Zhi*) by Wen Zhenheng and *Illustration of Rocks in Suyuan Garden* (素园石谱, *Su Yuan Shi Pu*) by Lin Youlin. Besides Ji Cheng, Wen Zhenheng and Lin Youlin, the most reputable garden designers in the Ming Dynasty also include Gao Ni from Beijing, Mi Wanzhong (also a famous painter) (Fig. 25) and Rockery Lu (his real name was lost in history) from Hangzhou in Zhejiang province.

Thereafter, the time of Emperor Qianlong and Emperor Jiaqing (1796 – 1820) created another

peak in the later period of Chinese classical garden development. This period not only delivered glorious artistic achievements in imperial garden construction, but also a nationwide rush for private gardens that resulted in the establishment of three leading local styles, i.e. Jiangnan Style (prevailing in the Yangtze River Delta), Beifang Style (prevailing in Northern China), and Lingnan Style (prevailing in the area south of China's Five Ranges). The representative imperial gardens in the Forbidden City during this time included: Jingshan Garden (Mt. Jing Garden), Xi Palace Garden, the Imperial Garden, Garden of Cining Palace, Garden of Jianfu Palace, and Garden of Ningshou Palace (Qianlong Garden).

Xi Palace Garden was the largest of all imperial gardens inside the Imperial City. But as population in the area kept growing, the west boundary of Xi Palace Garden shrank gradually, with only a belt-shaped land along the bank of the three seas left untouched. Therefore, the Qing government conducted large-scaled

reconstruction and expansion so as to increase the architecture density. By 1651, Emperor Shunzhi built a lama pagoda on the site of the previous Guanghan Palace at the top of Qionghua Island and renamed Wanshou Mountain as Mt. White Pagoda. After that, he removed all palace halls on the south slope of Qionghua Island and replaced them with a complex— Yong'an Temple (永安寺, Temple of Everlasting Peace).

Situated on this slope, Yong'an Temple reached upwards yard by yard, hall by hall, just like layers of steps. Standing on the top of the Island, the neat and solemn White Pagoda was the highest point dominating the entire garden. Thus, to the interior views of Beihai area took on a completely new look, and Wansui Mountain was renowned for this Mt. White Pagoda thereafter.

Another scenic spot in the Nanhai area presented tranquil and secluded surroundings, and consequently, was purposely selected by Emperor Kangxi (1662 – 1722, the second emperor of the Qing Dynasty) as a place to handle daily governmental business and meet with his officials. Therefore, more palace halls, gardens, and facility houses were built here, and a wall was built along the north bank of Nanhai to make it a partly independent section. When it came to Emperor Qianlong's reign, with another wall built between Beihai and Zhonghai, the Xi Palace Garden was clearly divided into three separated gardens, namely, Beihai Garden, Zhonghai Garden, and Nanhai Garden.

In addition, in Emperor Qianlong's time, a lot of expansion work was done on Qionghua Island, especially on its east, north, and west slopes. New buildings on the west slope were Yuexin Hall (Yue Xin Dian, Heart-Pleasing Hall), Qingxiao Tower (Qing Xiao Lou, Tower for Celebrating Heaven), Linguang Hall (Lin Guang Dian, Jade Light Hall), and Yuegu Tower (Yue Gu Lou, Tower of Reading Ancient History).

The arrangement of the buildings had to be built in accordance with the steep terrain on the west slope, so the size of these buildings was generally smaller. Although there was a central axis, the overall design emphasized the winding flow of the up-down contrast between buildings, further creating a sense of a mountainous garden. Second, in regard to the north slope, it was further divided into two parts, the steep upper part and the gentle lower part. Based on the geographic features here, the garden designer added manual rockeries to the upper part to create rolling slopes and a variety of geographic features like cliffs, caves, hillocks, peaks, ravines, holes, valleys, and hollows.

This subsection was an epitome of natural mountain landscape. For instance, even caves could have different varieties like up-climbing caves, half-side caves, lighting caves, and stone rooms. The cave dug in this slop extended as long as 50 meters with five exits: two had spiral stairway for vertical traffic, two were natural egresses, and the last one was directly connected to a short corridor. From roof to floor, the cave had 8 lighting holes, each leading with light in a different way. One of these was like a natural window opening in the wall, inviting light from outside. Another one accepted light from above like a scuttle on the roof of this underground cave, though in reality it was a gap between two neighboring steps on the ground level. This design served two functions; letting both light and fresh air into the cave and serving as a rain shelter for the cave beneath. Furthermore, one of these two steps was the stone beam of the cave. Another feature of the north slope design was sharp cliffs, which gave the visitor a feeling "as if they were at the bottom of a deep valley surrounded by Alps."

Cliffs were purposefully designed to create an air of celestial dwelling in a mountain. For example, the 6-meter high (vertical height) cliff in front of Pan Lan Vihara (Curly Wind Vihara) was created with the idea of "looking up to a mountain to know its height." This building was placed quite close to the cliff so that visitors in the house were compelled to look up at an angle of elevation of 70°, yet no one could catch sight of the top of the cliff. Thus, a sense of being in front of a lofty mountain or a deep valley would definitely be felt.

Hangu Hall (Han Gu Tang, Hall of Indulging in Ancient Works) and Mujian Room (Room for Appreciating An Acre of Land) also had cliffs in front of them. The cliffs before Hangu Hall and Pan Lan Vihara were both mono cliffs. While the cliff before Mujian House was composed of two layers: a steep façade and a gentle back with a narrow trail winding in between. What's more, the lush ancient trees also presented diverse views, giving a picturesque sense to the entire environment. These rockery cliffs not only reproduced the dangerous and steep mountains, their true natural beauty, but also help to organize spaces in place of man-made walls or buildings. The waterscapes on the north slope is worth mentioning, too. Little creeks, waterfalls, ponds, and other waterscapes were constructed following the models of their counterparts in nature. Between perpendicular cliffs and inside thick woods, crystal clear stream of springs and roaring torrent of waterfalls created a sharp contrast of peace and turbulence, just as captivating as a creation by God.

On the lower or gentle part of the north slope, an extensive architect complex—a two-storey winding corridor extending as long as 60 spans—was constructed in imitation of Jiang Tian Yi Lan Complex (Complex of Beauty of River and Mountains in One View), a famous scenic spot located on Jinshan Mountain in Zhenjiang, Jiangsu province. Together, the cliffs on the upper part and the buildings on the lower part set off each other and unite to present a holistic picture featuring both the delicacy of the Yangtze River Delta gardens and the strength of the

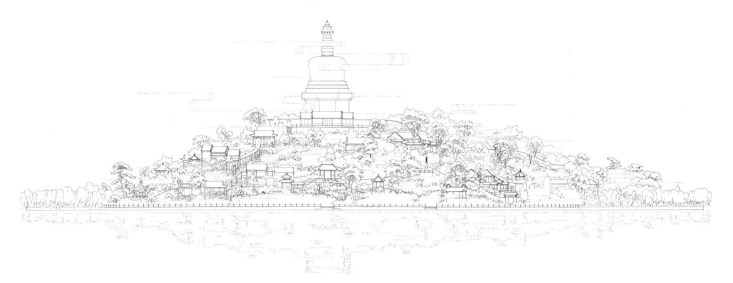

northern rockeries.

Turning to the east slope of Qionghua Island, it is by itself a beautiful place for its towering ancient trees and splendid blossoms. Seeing this, the garden designer kept the natural landscape of this slope as it was, and carefully arranged a small proportion of buildings, so that the natural landscape became the dominating element in this area.

In general, the four slopes of Qionghua Island were designed perfectly in their differences in concert with their geographical features in the natural surroundings. It is only fair to say that the planning and design of Qionghua Island were ingenious and creative. As a whole, the Qionghua Island is in perfect proportion. On a sunny day, together with its inverted reflection in water, the island simply shines from its background. Each building on the island is a meaningful existence, serving both as an

effective component of the entire view in the garden, and a place offering the best sightseeing.

In conclusion, Qionghua Island embodied the highest artistic accomplishment of Chinese classical garden construction that took thousands of years to develop. It is the complete quintessential summary of all important garden styles in northern and southern China, the typical example of Chinese celestial island tradition that has lasted for over 2,000 years, an artistic abstraction of natural landscape, and the outstanding representative of imperial gardens in Beijing (Figs. 26, 27).

During the reign of Emperor Qianlong, new buildings like Hao

FIG. 27 Partial elevation of the posterior hill of Qionghua Island (by Hu Jie)

Pu Jian Garden (Garden between Hao and Pu Rivers), Huafang Studio (Painted Boat Studio), and Can Platform (Silkworm Platform) were built along the east bank of Beihai Garden, and buildings like Jingxin Studio (Garden of Tranquil Heart), Xiaoxitian Temple (Minor Paradise), and Jiulong Wall (Nine-Dragon Wall) (Fig. 28), Ji Le Shi Jie Complex (Complex of West Paradise), Daxitian Temple (Major Paradise), and other Buddhist buildings were built along the north bank of Beihai Garden. Among them, Haopu Jian and Huafang and Jingxin Studios

FIG. 26 Qionghua Island, Beihai

FIG. 28 Jiulong Wall, Beihai
This screen wall, 25.52-meter long and 6.65-meter high, was located in Daxitian Temple in Beihai Park. On both sides of the screen, there is an exquisite mosaic rilievo of nine curling dragons, made with colorful glazed tiles and presenting diverse postures.

are relatively independent minor gardens inside the Beihai Garden.

Imperial Garden, Garden of Cining Palace, Garden of Jianfu Palace, and Garden of Ningshou Palace are the four imperial gardens in the Forbidden City. The former two were built in the Ming Dynasty and the latter two were built when Emperor Qianlong was in power. Garden of Jianfu Palace was located in the western section in the imperial garden. In contrast, Garden of Ningshou Palace was situated in the eastern section. Defined by their locations, these four gardens were closely integrated into the overall planning of the Forbidden City, and accordingly, they depicted similar construction features.

First, all of them were neatly arranged with an obvious central axis along which all scenic spots were symmetrically placed. In this regard, the most typical of the four is the Imperial Garden located at the north end of the central axis of the Forbidden City. The Imperial Garden was confined in a rectangular frame, with all buildings and scenic spots arranged in a symmetric pattern. The garden could be further divided into three sections: the central, east and west sections, where minor architectures

would set off the major ones.

Qin'an Hall (Qin An Dian, Imperial Peace Hall), the major architecture was precisely situated at the north end of the central axis. To its left and right sides, Yangxing Studio (Studio for Cultivating Temperament) and Jiangxue Hall (Jiang Xue Tang, Snow Hall), Qianqiu Pavilion (Pavilion of A Thousand Autumns) and Wanchun Pavilion (Pavilion of Ten Thousand Springs), Chengrui Pavilion (Pavilion with Pure Auspice) and Fubi Pavilion (Pavilion of Floating Greenery), as well as Yanhui Tower (Yan Hui Ge, Tower of Extending Brightness) and Yujing Pavilion (Imperial View Pavilion), were paired symmetrically. The symmetric pattern not only appears in their physical position in the garden, but also in the implications of their names and in their functions.

The second feature is that the terrain and site interior to the Forbidden City allowed very few natural landscapes, resulting in an extensive use of artificial constructions and rockeries. Consequently, rockeries were frequently seen as a means of view-managing, while water planning were only foils. In these

four gardens alone, there existed nearly one hundred rockeries, big and small. Third, all buildings in these gardens were luxurious, magnificent and utterly imperial.

Imperial gardens in the Forbidden City only accounted for a small part of imperial garden construction in the Qing Dynasty. The majority of imperial gardens were built in two locations: the northwest suburb of Beijing and Chengde in Hebei province. The northwest suburb of Beijing was known for its plentiful springs. After a few decades of recuperation, by the time of Emperor Qianlong, the Qing Dynasty was finally able to focus its resources on improving the condition of water source in the northwest suburb of Beijing. Such improvement works were for two purposes: to meet with the city's need for fresh water supply and the need for water transportation, and to improve the landscape in this area and build new gardens.

Gradually, the famous Three Mountains and Five Gardens (Fig. 29), the finest essences of Chinese imperial garden construction, were established one after another in this territory, each under the personal direction of Emperor Qianlong.

The center of the Three

FIG. 29 Panorama of Three Mountains and Five Gardens of the Qing Dynasty
The Three Mountains and Five Gardens include five imperial gardens, i.e. Qingyi Garden in Wanshou Mountain, Jingyi Garden in Fragrant Hill, Jingming Garden in Yuquan Mountain, Changchun Garden, and Old Summer Palace. The largest of them is Old Summer Palace, occupying an area of approximately 334 hectares. The smallest is Jingming Garden, occupying an area of approximately 65 hectares. This is a titanic garden group containing flat-land gardens, mountainous gardens and mountain-and-water gardens, and other garden types. Hence, the northwest suburb of Beijing became a world of imperial gardens centering on this five imperial gardens, the representatives of garden construction during the prime stage of Chinese classical gardens.

Mountains and Five Gardens was Yuanming Yuan or the Old Summer Palace, which had been in existence from the reign of Emperor Yongzheng, Emperor Qianlong, Emperor Jiaqing, Emperor Daoguang, and Emperor Xianfeng in the mid-Qing Dynasty, when it served as the critical political center and living space for emperors and empresses with the exception of the Forbidden City. It occupied an area of 334 hectares and contained over 150 scenic spots and more than 100 bridges. The construction area of all buildings in it was above 160,000 m². It took more than 150 years to complete this grandiose and extremely artistic garden, which won a reputation as the "Garden of Gardens." According to the *Postscript of Old Summer Palace* (圆明园后记, *Yuanming Yuan Hou Ji*) by Emperor Qianlong, "it can be acclaimed as the acme of perfection for its grand scale, deep and quiet valleys, bracing air, refreshing landscape, appealing plants, various architecture styles including both towering buildings and isolated houses. It has the blessing of the heaven and the earth. There is no better place for an emperor to enjoy a tour."

The construction of Old Summer Palace started in 1707. Initially, it was a gift from Emperor Kangxi to his fourth son, Yinzhen, Prince Yong (1678 – 1735, the next Emperor Yongzheng, the third emperor of the Qing Dynasty in power from 1723 to 1735). When Emperor Yongzheng took the throne, he officially announced the Old Summer Palace as one of his permanent residences to "avoid noise and focus on state affairs" and began the construction of the garden. Of all scenic spots in the garden, 38 were named and

autographed in person by Emperor Yongzheng. During the reign of Emperor Qianlong, the Old Summer Palace experienced the second wave of expansion; several scenic spots were added to the garden. As a result, the renowned "40 Scenic Spots in Old Summer Palace" were finally completed.

Satisfied with his garden, Emperor Qianlong ordered two imperial painters, i.e. Tang Dai (1673 – 1752) and Shen Yuan (1763 – 1795), to compose 40 colored paintings for these scenic spots on silk scrolls, on which the ministry of personnel, Wang Youdun (1692 – 1758) was entrusted to transcribe Emperor Qianlong's poetic odes to these scenic spots in the regular script (*kaishu*) on the scroll. The final result of all these efforts was the *Forty Scenes of Old Summer Palace and Their Notes* (圆明园四十景图咏,

FIG. 30 Zheng Da Guang Ming Complex in the Old Summer Palace
Zheng Da Guang Ming Complex, the first scenic spot in Old Summer Palace, was built for rites and ceremonies. Zheng Da Guang Ming Hall, the major construction in this yard, was relatively small in scale. Behind the palace hall, there was a piece of rockery named "Shou Mountain (Mt. Longevity)." In the northeast corner of the garden, a zigzag corridor winds its way to shelter the main hall. However, the northwest corner was left open to provide a wide view of rolling ridges of hills behind the palace hall. This opening served as a transitional space between the palace and the back lake scenic area, integrating the palace a part of the entire garden.

Yuanming Yuan Sishi Jing Tu Yong), which is now in the collections of the Paris Museum in France (Figs. 13, 30, 46).

In its early days, Old Summer Palace was simply a landscape garden built as a gift to a prince and had no more than a few buildings. Due to the fierce competition for the throne, Prince Yong (Yinzhen) had for a while escaped from the power struggle, and as a ruse, kept himself busy with the garden construction in the name of "Pochen Hermit (a hermit staying away from the earthly annoyances)." So, at that time, the Old Summer Palace was only a garden for him to reside, read books, observe crop growing, and enjoy himself in the beautiful wilderness. After he came to the throne, the garden witnessed a period of greater development. Garden design under his direction reflected Emperor Yongzheng's aspiration as the supreme ruler of the empire.

Subsequently, buildings typically functioning as the building to deal with administrative consultation, such as Zheng Da Guang Ming Complex (Complex of Justice and Forthrightness) (Fig. 30), Qinzheng Hall (Qin Zheng Dian, Hall of Industrious Administration), Wan Fang An He Complex (Complex of Universal Peace and Harmony), and Jiu Zhou Qing Yan Complex (Complex of National Peace), were built in the south section of the garden. Then, the Old Summer Palace had finally become an imperial garden, with the complement of some garden architectures.

During this time, its central sceneries were nine islands arranged in a *jiu gong* pattern (Sudoku, a bigger square being evenly divided into smaller squares) with buildings

on each of them. As a whole, they were named Jiu Zhou Qing Yan Complex, with *jiu zhou* (Nine Cities, a second name for the entire territory of China according to *Book of History*) and *qing yan* (peace) as an expectation for peaceful world. To its east, a pond named Fuhai (Sea of Blessing) was excavated to express "blessing as immense as the East Sea." In general, such arrangement highlighted the image of an imperial garden, i.e. "the entire territory of China is facing the sea to the east."

From this time forward, designers of the Old Summer Palace had begun to intentionally borrow from their European peers some elements of western gardens like the bottle-shaped handrails in Yu Yue Yuan Fei Complex (Complex of Fish Leaping and Bird Flying), the fountain in Gengzhi Gallery (Gallery of Farmers and Weavers),

as well as the European-styled yurt appeared in 1730.

In 1745, the 10th year of Emperor Qianlong's reign, he launched the construction of Changchun Garden (长春园, Garden of Eternal Spring), a garden with over 20 scenic spots like Hanjing Hall (Han Jing Tang, Tripataka Hall), Chunhua Gallery (Education and Civilization Gallery), Siyong Studio (Studio of Expecting Eternality), Scene of Hai Yue Kai Jin (Sea of Magnanimity Scene), and some other scenic spots in imitation of mini gardens of the Yangtze River Delta. In the 12th year of Emperor Qianlong's reign, he initiated the preliminary works for the Xiyang Lou Complex (Western Mansion), whose components were all symmetrically arranged along an axis line in imitation of the European gardens (Fig. 31). Representative buildings

FIG. 31 Relics of Xiyang Lou Complex in Old Summer Palace
Located in the north half of Changchun Garden, Xiyang Lou Complex was a suite of European style palaces and gardens, including six Western buildings, three large fountains, several courtyards, and a few small scenic spots. In contrast to the tradition of Chinese classical gardens, the Xiyang Lou Complex was characteristic of Le Notre Style, with all elements dominated by the axis and neatly symmetrically arranged. But, in general, Chinese garden construction techniques were also widely applied to its overall planning and detail designs.

of Xiyang Lou Complex included the Xie Qi Qu Fountain (Fountain of Harmonious Wonder), Fangwai Observatory (Observatory of the Outside), Haiyan Hall (Hai Yan Tang, Hall of National Peace), and Yuanying Observatory (Immense Ocean Observatory), as well as labyrinths and Dashuifa waterworks (Great Fountain). The architecture style adopted for these European buildings was a mixture of Baroque architecture art prevailing Europe at that time and Chinese traditional building techniques. As most of these buildings were built with stones, they would not easily fall victim to fire. That's why their remains are still standing there after two fires (in 1860 and 1900) set by invaders.

Large scale, absorbing diversified elements, and condensing the heaven and the earth in one micro-universe had always been distinctive characteristics of Chinese classical gardens. Yet it was only during the Ming and Qing dynasties that collective gardens welcomed their mature stage, enclosing a complete variety of the fine views of the whole empire into one garden and displaying perfect and exemplary gardening features absorbed from all renowned gardens, including the imitations of other famous gardens that already existed. Among the collective gardens, the large-scaled imperial gardens constructed during the reigns of Emperor Kangxi and Emperor Qianlong were the representative masterpieces. Both emperors had been on the throne for more than 60 years. As their reigns happened in the earlier half of the Qing Dynasty, the national political and economic foundation then were relatively healthy. Moreover, both

emperors had paid several visits to South China. Emperor Kangxi had arranged two official inspection trips, and Emperor Qianlong had visited the Yangtze River Delta six times. The charming landscapes, the appealing lake-and-mountain sceneries and magnificent gardens in Suzhou and Hangzhou areas left wonderful impressions on the two emperors, just as a poem indicated that "Who told you there is wonderful landscape in Jiangnan (the Yangtze River Delta)? It simply plants the heaven and the earth in your heart." In addition, emperors in the Qing Dynasty had great admiration for highly sophisticated culture of the Han nationality.

Therefore, the imperial gardens of the Qing Dynasty were largely imitations of sceneries in the Yangtze River Delta. For example, over 100 scenic spots in Old Summer Palace can find their archetypes in the Yangtze River Delta. Scene of Duan Qiao Can Xue (Scene of Lingering Snow on the Broken Bridge), Scene of Liu Lang Wen Ying (Scene of Orioles Singing in the Willows), Scene of Ping Hu Qiu Yue (Scene of Autumn Moon over the Calm Lake), Scene of Lei Feng Xi Zhao (Scene of Leifeng Pagoda in Evening Glow), and Scene of San Tan Yin Yue (Scene of Three Pools Mirroring Moon) were the imitations of landscapes in Hangzhou. Wenyuan Tower (Wen Yuan Ge, Tower of Source of Books), used Tianyi Tower (天一阁, One Sky Tower) in Ningbo as its model. And the scenic spot Wu Ling Chun Se (Spring in Wuling) represented the scenery in Peach Blossom Spring (Tao Hua Yuan). Ru Garden (Resemble Garden) was in imitation of Outlook Garden in Nanjing. Jian Garden (Garden of

Mirror) borrowed the landscape of Slender West Lake in Yangzhou. And the Lion Grove Garden in the Old Summer Palace originated from the Lion Grove Garden in Suzhou.

However, the reproduction work stuck to one principle that: "Go as close to the soul of the original design as possible, but make use of the natural conditions of new site to the best advantage. Do not ignore the favorable elements of the new site. It is acceptable to capture all their lingering charms, yet unnecessary to copy every detail of the original design. The only thing that matters here is to capture the soul of the original design." Therefore, such imitations were generally considered as artistic reinterpretation of the same idea, not as slavish copies. Please refer to Chapter Four for a detailed description of the temporary imperial gardens built in the Qing Dynasty.

Zhang Lian and Zhang Ran (Father and Son)

Zhang Lian (1587 – 1673) and his son Zhang Ran were two prestigious garden designers in the Qing Dynasty, known especially for their artistic achievement in rockery creation. Zhang Lian, also known as Zhang Nanyuan (literally Southern Wall), had been a painting student. He was an expert in portraits and landscape paintings, and designed gardens and pile rockeries in accordance with his rock-themed landscape paintings. For over five decades, he had been contributing to the construction of many wonderful gardens in the Yangtze River Delta areas. Years of experience allowed him to come up with a perfect construction plan in mind, so that he was capable of arranging rocks, flowers, trees, and other elements precisely where they need to be, just like they were situated in a working blueprint. His son Zhang Ran was an outstanding successor of his father's art and reputation, who had served the emperors for over 30 years. His creations included Yingtai Palace in Zhongnanhai (Middle Sea and South Sea Garden), Jingming Garden in Yuquan Mountain, and Old Summer Palace, as well as a lot of private gardens designed for noble families and high officials. Since Zhang Lian's entire family were in the business of garden making, they were called by the people of the time as "Rockery Zhang."

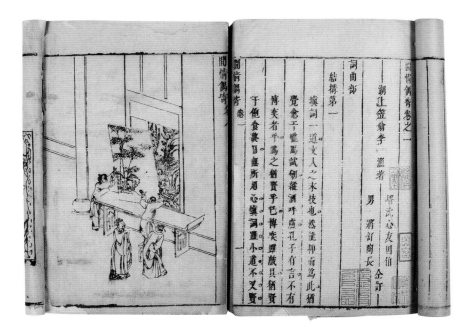

FIG. 32 Li Yu and his *Leisure of Soul* (閑情偶寄, *Xian Qing Ou Ji*)

Li Yu (1610 – 1680), from Qiantang (present day Hangzhou) in Zhejiang province, was an eminent playwright, litterateur, and artist in the late Ming Dynasty and early Qing Dynasty. Also known as Li Liweng (literally Senior in Bamboo Hat), he was good at poetry and painting, especially garden making. One of his creations, Banmu Garden (半亩园, Garden of Half *Mu*) in Gongxian Alley to the northeast of the Forbidden City, was a masterpiece of gardens in Beijing. In addition to Banmu Garden, he built for himself a Yishan Mountain Villa and a Jiezi Garden (芥子园, Garden of Mustard) in his later years. His *Leisure of Soul* has 8 volumes, with the forth volume, *Housing for Living*, devoted to architecture and gardening theories. The *Housing for Living* has five chapters, i.e. "On Houses," "On Lattice Windows," "On Walls," "On Plaques and Couplet Boards," and "On Rocks and Rockeries," and is a pithy and insightful explanation of gardening and architecture theories. Li's ideas of garden construction represented the professionalized tendency descended from the Ming to Qing Dynasties, attaching importance to techniques, construction processes and details, and staying away from rigid repetition of old patterns. This attitude highlighted a spirit of practical learning featuring the learning style in Emperor Kangxi's reign.

Ge Yuliang

Ge Yuliang (1764 – 1830), from the county of Wujin in Changzhou, was the greatest rockery designer in the history of Chinese classical gardens. He had a distinctive style that combined the natural arrangement style that was prevalent in the early Qing Dynasty of "more rocks, less earth" during the reign of Emperor Qianlong. He created numerous gardens in his lifetime, most of which were located in Suzhou, Yangzhou, Nanjing, and Yizheng, such as Xiaopangu Garden in Yangzhou, Mountain Villa with Embracing Beauty, Pu Garden (朴园, Simple Garden) in Yizheng, and Wusong Garden (五松园, Five Pines Garden) in Nanjing.

Ye Tao

After Zhang Ran, Ye Tao was another great garden designer from the Yangtze River Delta who served the royal families, and one of a few landscape painters in the Qing Dynasty who crossed the boundary and became a consummate rockery and garden designer. His creations include Ziyi Garden (自怡园, Self-Pleasing Garden) and Tong's Family Garden in Haidian district, Beijing. He also completed the painting of Changchun Garden under imperial order. Ye's talent in garden designing was in the daring use of rough and powerful cuts which left plenty of scars on the rocks as if they were hacked with a huge ax. While inheriting the "natural, desolate and distant" style of garden and rockery designing which was popular in the early Qing Dynasty, he borrowed the artistic conception of classical landscape paintings. As a result, he influenced the private gardens in Beijing in the reign of Emperor Kangxi.

Theories stem from practices and enrich practices in return. In the Qing Dynasty, garden design masters emerged in large numbers. Some of them even had detailed biographies in historical records. Famous garden designers in the Qing Dynasty include Zhang Lian and Zhang Ran (a father and son pair who were the most prominent imperial garden designers in the Qing Dynasty), Li Yu (an excellent garden and rockery designer in the end of Ming and early days of Qing Dynasty) (Fig. 32), Ge Yuliang (a famous garden and rockery designer in the Yangtze River Delta in the mid-Qing Dynasty), Ye Tao from Qingpu, Shanghai (the designer of Changchun Garden, or Everlasting Spring Garden in the reign of Emperor Kangxi), Dao Ji from Wuzhou, Guangxi province, Zhou Shilian from Huiji, Wang Song from Jiangxi province, Chen Yingqiu from Chaoyang, Guangdong province, Da Shan (1613 – 1705, a monk from Changshou Temple in Guangzhou), and Qiu Haoshi (1723 – 1795, a famous rockery designer from the town of Gaonian in Yangzhou). These garden design masters and artisans made immortal contributions to the development of garden construction in the Qing Dynasty. Most of their creations still exist today.

Gardening art in the Ming and Qing dynasties was actually the culmination of several millenniums' worth of experiences in garden construction in China. The primitive hunting and plant gardens constructed during the Yin and Zhou dynasties were created by merely enclosing natural land where there were mountains, waters, woods, animals, and birds, and downsizing the Qin and Han gardens that covered hundreds of square miles. Because hunting and plant gardens were so big it was impossible to maintain a number of buildings and plant flowers. In fact, wild mountains and natural vegetation dominated these early gardens, and palaces were simply scattered sparsely among them. The scenery of "only five strides away from the next tower, and only 10 paces away from the next pavilion" described in *Ode to E'pang Palace* by Du Mu (803 – 853, a famous literature in the Tang Dynasty) could be only seen along the arterial lines of a garden, instead of the whole garden. As for the imperial gardens built in Wei, Jin, the

Southern and Northern Dynasties, the Sui and Tang dynasties, which usually occupied more than 100 *li* (50 km, 31.07 miles), they were far inferior to the contemporary Summer Palace or Old Summer Palace in terms of the density of buildings, rockeries, and plants. In the Ming and Qing dynasties, the density of architectures within a garden had increased largely. As the art of rockery piling had reached a very high level, those huge gardens which took up large-scale wild land were rarely seen. This is an inevitable consequence of historical evolution, especially, an outcome of the development of garden construction art. Take rockery piling for example. From adopting real mountains to piling up rockeries, from piling a few rockeries sheer as decoration to imitating and downsizing real mountains, rockery piling achieved such artistic effects as "much in little," "forest within one foot," "seemingly remote landscape," "undistinguishable simulation," and "completely free of artificial hint." In other words, it is to use immense manual handicraft to create profound, imposing, spacious, and multi-scenery effects. Several large-scale royal gardens, such as Old Summer Palace, Qingyi Garden (清漪园, Garden of Clear Ripples, the predecessor of the Summer Palace), and Mountain Resort at Chengde were no more than 20 *li* (10 km, 6.21 miles) in width. Gardens in the Yangtze River Delta went even further in creating a larger universe and more scenic spots within a tiny space. The gardening artistic techniques like "view borrowing" and "changing views from different angles" matured in the Ming and Qing dynasties as well. In a smaller

territory, garden elements had to be arranged more densely, so designers needed to consider more carefully the interactive relationships between different scenic spots, either interior or exterior to the garden walls. Such transformation heightened Chinese gardening art to a supreme level.

2. Essential Genres

Based on kinships, purposes, functions, and artistic styles, Chinese classical gardens can be divided into six genres: imperial gardens, imperial mausoleum gardens, temple gardens, residence gardens, scenic spot gardens, and literati gardens.

Imperial Garden

Imperial gardens were private gardens belonging to emperors and royal families for sightseeing and

hunting. They were the earliest gardens recorded in historical documents, with the longest history and the largest scale, built in accordance with the most advanced architectural techniques, and representing the highest artistic achievements of China garden construction.

Their overall planning was mainly based on the Three Celestial Islands in One Pond pattern, and usually had imposing and spacious landscapes and complete sets of functional facilities (like buildings for residing, handling business, sighting, entertainments, and holding sacrificial services). Buildings inside an imperial garden are generally magnificent and spacious to demonstrate the power and nobility of royal families. These buildings, however, didn't intend to dominate the space, but instead, to integrate with their surroundings, so that they not only had a certain

FIG. 33 The Foxiang Tower (Fo Xiang Ge, Tower of Buddhist Fragrance) in the Summer Palace
Located behind the Duobao Hall (Duo Bao Dian, Hall of Treasures), sitting on a 20-meter-high white stone platform, this is a three-floor temple with eight elevation sides and a four-layer roof covered by yellow glazed tiles. Its powerful and magnificent 41-meter body makes it the main building in the front hill scenic area of the Summer Palace and the center of the mountain-lake scenic area of the Palace. Although it is based on a spot half way to the top of Wanshou Mountain, its roof is higher than the roof of Zhihuihai Hall (Zhi Hui Hai Dian, Sea of Wisdom Hall), which stands on the top of the mountain, adding more differences between the mountain and the buildings.

real function, but also served as a part of garden scenery that could offer the best perspectives of sightseeing (Fig. 33).

Imperial Mausoleum Garden

Imperial mausoleum gardens were the gardens attached to emperor tombs. In Chinese traditional culture, a man ought to respect the heavens, follow the teaching of their forefathers, carefully organize the funeral of his parents, and sincerely follow sacrificial rites in memory of his ancestors. Subsequently, elaborate funerals became a custom deeply rooted in Chinese culture. Imperial mausoleum gardens were exactly an outcome of such customs.

Before any imperial mausoleum garden was built, its designers had to carefully choose the favorable geographical feature as its potential site. After that, all plants and buildings had to be arranged in accordance with the strictest planning models to create an environment conducive to a memorial atmosphere.

Temple Garden

Temple gardens were the gardens attached to Buddhist or Taoist temples, including the courtyards inside and garden environment outside temples. Chinese temples were often intentionally situated in suburban areas where there were beautiful landscapes. Actually, in China, anywhere with appealing landscapes would be chosen as sites for temple construction.

Compared with other genres, temple gardens were unique in that they were open to the public. Temple

FIG. 34 Jin Ancestral Temple
Since it is situated at the foot of Xuanweng Mountain in Taiyuan, Shanxi province, the designer had to make reasonable changes in the overall planning to accommodate the different terrains of the mountain. From a function perspective, all buildings can be divided into two groups; religious buildings and scenic buildings. Vague as it is, the central axis leads to the main building, the Goddess Palace. All other buildings are symmetrically located along its sides, combined with the natural landscapes.

gardens function both as public and religious spaces. Accordingly, temple garden design was not confined to the ideal combination of buildings and natural landscape. Equal attention was paid to creating a sense of religious divinity (Fig. 34).

Residence Garden

Residence gardens, usually situated in urban areas, were private property belonging to nobles, government officials, and other persons who had high social status. As an attachment to a private mansion, a residence garden was usually used for daily activities, enjoying leisure moments, holding banquets, meeting friends, and reading books.

Generally small in scale, residence gardens were often adjacent to the back of private mansions, i.e. the "front yard for residence and back yard for garden" pattern, or "to one side of the residence as a side yard," in which its owner could live or enjoy himself in an artistic space (Fig. 35).

In densely populated cities that had little natural scenery, a residence garden was just like an urban natural world. Although

almost everything in a garden was man-made, they looked "completely free of artificial hint," thanks to the outstanding design and excellent skills of Chinese garden makers. In the hands of these garden masters, one rockery was enough to create the image of a mountain as high as Mount Hua (located in Shaanxi province, one of China's Five Great Mountains), one tiny pond as small as a spoonful of water a boundless river or lake. However restricted a garden space may be, they were able to accommodate infinite landscape in it by making creative use of diverse design techniques to break through space restriction.

Scenic Spot Garden

Scenic spot gardens were usually the results of unconscious or

spontaneous planning. They offered both the beauty of natural landscape and the charm of humanistic cultural sites. Therefore, they usually occupied a large area and were open to the public. In this type of garden, natural landscape often served as a background and man-made works played the role of accents in a tune.

Scenic spot gardens usually had so long a history that their development and protection could be dated back to hundreds or even thousands of years ago, and accordingly, are significant historic heritage.

Literati Garden

In general, the owner of a literati garden was either a civil official or a scholar-bureaucrat. Such owners were usually highly educated and knowledgeable men who built a garden to please his mind and eyes, express his aspiration, improve his temperament, and express his wish for a retreated life. What they expected from a garden was more than natural beauty. They wanted to abstract or distill the spirit of nature and integrate this spirit with

FIG. 36 A bird view of the Humble Administrator's Garden, Suzhou
This illustration is extracted from *Classical Gardens in Suzhou* by Liu Dunzhen, a book offering first hand data obtained through site survey and mapping.

FIG. 35 Garden of Pleasure in Suzhou
Garden of Pleasure, the latest of all classical gardens in Suzhou, was built in the reigns of Emperor Tongzhi and Emperor Guangxu in the Qing Dynasty. It was originally a private garden belonging to Gu Wenbing. Occupying a land of approximately 0.6 hectare, the garden is composed of two parts—the east part featuring courtyard architectures and the west part featuring landscape designs, which is also the focus of the entire garden. The designer adopted techniques like "opposite scenery" and "borrowed scenery" to arrange the rockeries, zigzag bridges, and buildings. Thus, the gardens views are tranquil, yet full of twists and turns. It is another typical example of "presenting more with less" and "producing giant with dwarf."

a particular cultural atmosphere to create a profound spiritual world.

Literati gardens usually had few scenic spots and focused on the overall effect, trying to arouse a feeling of elegance, implicit emotions, indirect expressions, ethereal and delicate touches, and gracefulness (Fig. 36).

Of all the six genres, imperial gardens and literati gardens possessed the greatest artistic accomplishment, and therefore, were the most critical components in Chinese classical gardens. In the following chapters, we will discuss in detail these two vital components of Chinese classical gardens.

FIG. 37 Yanyu Tower in Mountain Resort, Chengde, Hebei province

Chapter Two
Chinese Garden Culture

In Chinese culture, nature is a realm full of vitality, creation, and evolution. In Chinese philosophy, culture is considered not as a spiritual phenomenon independent of nature, but something spontaneously derived from nature or a creation that grows out of it. The very tenet of Chinese philosophy and culture is the "harmony of Heaven and Man." According to Ji Xianlin (1911 – 2009), a master of Chinese culture, "Heaven" represents both Heaven and Earth, "Man" is for mankind, and "harmony" is the construction of mutual understanding and friendship between the two.

This concept has a long history as it could be found in the teachings of Confucianism, Taoism, Mohism, and other schools of thinking. "Harmony of Heaven and Man" is the foundation of Chinese philosophy and constitutes the Chinese worldview. It reflects their simple view of nature when ancient Chinese people referred to construction activities, and represents their yearning for a harmonious and living environment of co-existence. The holy trinity of Heaven, Earth, and Man has been in the marrow of the Chinese nation for the past several millennia.

The Chinese culture of garden construction could be dated back to the 3 to 6 Century. It attributed great importance to such notions as the sense of liberty, "presenting more with less," and "environment should be stemmed from your state of mind and scenic spots should be designed in accordance with surroundings." A garden is not only a residence, but also more importantly, a place reflecting one's mind and soul. Even a mini-mountain no more than one foot in height or a tiny world downsized into one plate could bring about the feeling of an infinite universe. It can allow our imagination to transcend the limits of physical senses, fully activate our thought to broaden our vision up to the world and the universe, and finally help us reach the state of mind that "the universe is my heart, and my heart is the universe."

From the very beginning, Chinese gardens were not places simply for a relaxing walk or where people planted trees or prettified their environment. Those who lived in cities and were kept away from nature found a way to reflect upon their nostalgia and yearning for the natural world by constructing gardens. Gardens offered them a psychological compensation and an opportunity to purse an ideal spiritual and cultural life.

1. Philosophy

Chinese philosophy nurtures a genuine Chinese heart which is always absorbed in nature. Thus, Chinese gardens are closely related to the philosophy, always sticking to the principle of "learning from nature" and prioritize the natural beauty. The gardens were stemmed from nature but were not confined to their original natural state. They were constructed not to merely copy the formal beauty of nature, but to surmount the forms and explore the Tao embedded in it.

The Classic of Changes

The Classic of Changes or *I Ching* (周易, *Zhou Yi*) was the foundation of Chinese humanistic culture, and the philosophical source of various schools of thinking. The German philosopher Hegel (1770 – 1831) deemed it as "true oriental philosophy."

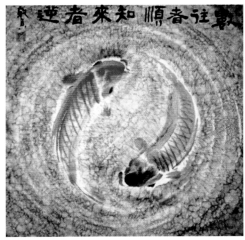

FIG. 38 Symbol for the concept of yin and yang
This figure with a pair of fishes nestling head to tail against each other represents a fundamental philosophy in *The Classic of Changes* that the principle of yin (the feminine, passive, and negative) and yang (the masculine, positive, and active) constitute the basic course of nature—Tao.

The basic viewpoints of *The Classic of Changes* emphasize on the trinity of Heaven, Earth, and Man, on the central role of man, on the harmony between man and nature, and on the harmony between men.

It deems the entire universe as nature and believes that the Limitless (*Wuji*) produces the delimited, and this is the Absolute (*Taiji*). The Absolute produces two forms, named yin and yang. The two forms produce four phenomena, named lesser yin, great yin (*taiyin* also means the Moon), lesser yang, great yang (*taiyang* also means the Sun). The four phenomena act on the eight trigrams (*bagua*). Eight eights are sixty-four hexagrams, which generates all (anything between Heaven and Earth, including mankind (Fig. 38).

Since mankind is a product of nature, the unity between them must be stressed upon. *The Classic of Changes* advocates both reforming and adapting to nature. Nature should be adjusted to meet the wishes of man, and man should neither subject himself to nature nor destroy nature. It is ideal to maintain harmony between man and nature.

In the meantime, human activities should correspond to the will of Heaven and Earth, not violating the time of a day and seasons of a year , and should accept good fortune or ill luck bestowed by supernatural beings—either the divine or the ghosts, and meanwhile, adapt to the natural principles.

In accordance with these teachings, a genuine Chinese heart is always absorbed in nature. Chinese gardens always stick to the principle of "learning from nature" and prioritize the natural beauty,

and always value the notions, such as "concealing ingenuity behind simplicity" and "real simplicity without exaggerated artificial ornaments," i.e. stressing on natural beauty while leaving no signs of the human touch. Hence, natural beauty between Heaven and Earth—such as the sun, the moon, the stars, the wind, the flowers, the snow, the rivers, the mountains—are in harmony with human architectures like pavilions, towers, terraces, or belvederes to create overall holistic "natural" environment, "a condensed mini-universe in human embrace."

Taoism

Laozi, one of the principal Chinese philosophers regarded Tao (universal laws) as the highest ideology, considering it as the origin of the universe. Laozi once said, "Tao produced two opposing principles in nature, which in turn functions on one another and produced an intermediate state, the third principle between these two. Subsequently, all creations evolved from these three principles." It clearly expresses an idea that human beings are only an organic ingredient of nature and not the dominators. The subordinate role that human beings play in nature will never be changed. Another representative statement of Laozi was that "Humans follow the examples of the Earth, the Earth follows those of Heaven, Heaven follows those of Tao, and Tao follow those of nature." It points out explicitly that nature is the origin of human spirit and values. The principle of Tao refers to absorbing inspiration from Heaven and Earth, all the creations and nature.

Early Taoist philosopher Zhuangzi (c.369 – 286 BC, also known as Zhuang Zhou) later further developed Laozi's idea that "Tao follows the examples of nature." He advocated achieving the "Harmony of Heaven and Man … without external interference." In other words, as for the relationship between human and nature, he insisted on allowing everything to take its own course without interfering with their natural practices; that is, sticking to and conforming to the original structure of everything. He had recognized natural beauty as the highest aesthetic criterion. "Grandiose beauty as Heaven and Earth possess, affirmative orders as the four seasons stick to, and mature laws as all creatures follow, they never explicitly suggested themselves."

This Taoist thought has great influence over the lifestyles of the later generations of Chinese. A strong evidence of such influence is that over thousands of years, Chinese people had constantly yearned for and sought out an idyllic lifestyle, expecting to enjoy their life in Shangri-La. Chinese classical gardens were stemmed from nature but were not confined to their original natural state. Gardens were constructed not to merely copy the formal beauty of nature, but to surmount the forms and explore the Tao embedded in it.

Confucianism

Confucian philosophy, with Confucius (551 – 479 BC) as its representative figure, was the pioneering thought that decimated human worship of nature. It aimed to realize "harmony of Heaven and Man" through proactive action. Confucius put forward the idea that "the wise likes water, while the benevolent likes mountains" in *The Analects of Confucius* (论语, *Lun Yu*). The mountain is distinguished as benevolent, silent and everlasting, while the water as wise, flexible, and joyful. Water and mountains are infused with human personality and inspire human thought. The idea that nature is part of human morality and wisdom unlocked the direct physical contact between human beings and nature. Nature serves as a spiritual carrier of human expectations. Such idea entitled spirituality to nature, and connected nature with the moralities of noble people, bridging nature with humanity for the first time.

This philosophy of "personalized nature" aroused the Chinese respect to natural landscapes, and further developed into a unique landscape culture, in which human spiritual experience and moral performance, such as "morality analogy," are included. Thus, in composing works on the theme of landscapes, literal, poetic, and painting works were no longer confined to landscape per se, but expressed feelings that were more human.

Similarly, in constructing gardens, such an aesthetic ideology of "personalized nature" was reflected in the activities of re-creating natural landscapes with manpower, as well as in the "personifying" every garden element. The purpose of garden construction is to endow human feelings to nature and express personal feelings towards natural landscapes.

With such a philosophy, "harmony of Heaven and Man," as guidance, Chinese garden construction activities expressed a constant longing for nature. In the eyes of Chinese ancient philosophers and artists, all visible phenomena available in nature represent the principle of Tao. And only when they represent the principle of Tao can they become the objects of art and have artistic value.

Thus, the "nature" in Chinese gardens is not a simple miniature of real mountains and waters, but a world having experienced human construction, such as generalizing, processing, and refining, which physically and spiritually surpasses their prototypes in the real world. This personalized nature is not limited to finite space but extends to the entire universe and strives for infinite inclusiveness. Therefore, the Chinese art of garden represents the supreme spiritual realm of the natural world.

2. Painting and Poetry

The Chinese garden, poetry, and painting were descendents of the same aesthetic consciousness. Landscape poetry and painting had great impact on the construction of detailed sceneries and holistic artistic conceptions in gardens. It is largely attributed to the profound literary and artistic heritage that Chinese landscape garden was able to achieve a high artistic reach. The numerous poetic stanzas and paintings that depict the beauty of natural landscapes would serve as references for garden designers and artisans to seek inspiration. Many poets and painters were even directly involved in the planning and designing of gardens.

FIG. 39 *Nymph of the Luo River*, by Gu Kaizhi, Eastern Jin Dynasty
This is a colored painting made on a 27.1 cm long and 572.8 cm wide silk scroll. It has four copies, which are now collected by the Palace Museum, Beijing, Liaoning Provincial Museum, Shenyang, etc.

Landscape Painting

In the period of the Wei, Jin, and Southern and Northern dynasties, Chinese landscape painting shrugged off its original auxiliary status as background picture setting of the human images in figure paintings, and developed into an independent painting type. From some parts of background landscapes in the two figure paintings composed by Gu Kaizhi

(c.345 – 409), *Nymph of the Luo River* (Fig. 39) and *Admonitions of the Instructress to the Palace Ladies* (both were facsimiles composed by later painters), we are able to grasp a rough idea about landscape paintings at that time.

When painting rocks, only contour lines and dyeing were adopted, while the technique of light ink strokes (*cun*) to highlight the texture or shade of rocks were not applied. When describing water, contour lines were more frequent and when painting trunks and leaves, contour lines with dyeing was the basic method, and the leaves were usually fan-shaped leaves on ginkgo trees. Defects still existed at the time though.

In some paintings, the landscape still served as a foil to figures, which led to a discordant proportionate relationship between human images and their background landscapes, where "the size of the figure in a painting is bigger than that of a mountain, and stream does not present the splendor of surging tides." What's Furthermore, in some paintings, trees and stones were exaggeratedly outlined in pursuit of adornment effects. Defects as these still existed; the theories of landscape painting were immature. They either emphasized on philosophical realization, or on emotional expression.

The *Preface to Landscape Painting* (画山水序, *Hua Shan Shui Xu*), composed by Zong Bing (375 – 443), a landscape painter of the Southern Dynasty, was a representative among these theories of early Chinese landscape painting. He stressed that when composing a piece of landscape painting, a painter intended to unveil the charm of artistic conception via describing natural images. Thus, he promoted the Chinese painting theory further ahead, based on the original understanding that "spiritual charm can be composed by physical views." The practice of Chinese landscape painting had a profound impact on the appreciation and construction of landscape gardens later.

By the middle of the Tang Dynasty, landscape painting had fully matured. Landscape painters had exceeded the pure naturalism (sheer realistically representing the natural settings), and had formed certain regular approaches to summarizing the landscapes, associating the natural beauty with the poetic beauty.

As a famous poet and painter of the Tang Dynasty, Wang Wei (c.701 – 761) stated clearly in his theory of painting that "whenever painting landscapes, painters should organize an artistic conception in mind before putting the views down."

In Wangchuan Villa (辋川别业, Wangchuan is located today's Lantian, Shaanxi province), a garden he constructed, there were 20 scenic spots. Every individual scenic spot had its own particular features yet all were threaded together as an organic unity. As to the layout of the spaces and arrangement of sceneries in the villa, he made a clear distinction between the major ones and the minor ones, and focused on mutual contrast effect between different spots. Therefore, he managed to produce a rhythmic alternation with scenic spots varied in scale of spaces and in density. In terms of the general layout of the villa and the contrast and balance among various garden elements, he fully reflected his artistic theory in painting that "the hill-peaks and the tree-tops in one picture should not look alike. Trees are overcoat for hills, and hills serve as skeleton supporting trees. Trees should not be too crowded to fully veil the beauty of hills, and hills should not be too messy to highlight the vitality of them."

Wang Wei also proposed a mode of landscape painting in which "the main peaks should be towering and their surrounding mountains should look as though they are running toward the major peaks. Temples can be embraced in the arms of mountains. The human residences should be placed aside a river bank. A number of trees ought to be sitting around the village to construct an image of a forest whose branches should hold fast to their trunk. Streams should flow together at the edge of a cliff and dash downhill like a waterfall, and the springs should not flow turbulently … When painting the typical human residential buildings like towers and platforms built on a plain, tall willows should be added to echo the residence. While drawing Buddhist or Taoist temples constructed on renowned mountains, unusual cedars are most suitable woods to set off lofty towers. The distant scenery should be partly visible in mist. The cliffs far away should be hidden in clouds. The flag of a tavern should hang high by the side of a road and the sail of a passenger boat should swing low above water."

Landscape paintings, poetries, and gardens were components of Wang Wei's life and aspiration. His painting *Wangchuan Villa* and *Anthology of Poems Composed in Wangchuan* (辋川集, *Wang Chuan Ji*) came out at the same time, which indicated the close relationship among landscape paintings, poetries, and gardens. Wangchuan Villa reflected an intriguing charm of poetry and painting, exactly like his paintings. By melting and mixing the poetic charm and painting verve, Wang Wei strongly expressed his aesthetic ideal.

The Song Dynasty was the golden time in the history of Chinese painting. Landscape paintings in this period presented a variety of styles. In this heyday of imperial fine arts, royal artistic achievements reached their peak and achieved unprecedented artistic fruits. With a well equipped imperial art academy, master painters emerged continuously, and a multitude of masterpieces were created. Representative painters of the time included Dong Yuan (? – c.962), Ju Ran, Li Cheng (919 – 967), and Fan Kuan, Guo Xi, Mi Fu (1051 – 1107) and his son, as well as the Great Four Painters in the Southern Song Dynasty, Li Tang (1066 – 1150), Liu Songnian, Ma Yuan, and Xia Gui.

Guo Xi, a prominent landscape painter in the Northern Song Dynasty, opened a new era of landscape painting when ink-painting made unprecedented progress in techniques, such as *cun* (light ink strokes, using dry light ink to highlight the texture and grains of a rock or a tree), *ca*

FIG. 40 *Early Spring*, **by Guo Xi, Northern Song Dynasty**
This is an ink and color painting made on a 158.3 cm long and 108.1 cm wide silk scroll. Guo Xi is a native of Wenxian, Henan province. In the years 1068 – 1077, he was put in charge of painting matters in the imperial court. He was one of the founders of the Northern style of landscape painting. This painting depicts a misty mountain range in early spring dotted with pavilions and circled by winding streams that exhibits spatial depth in a small flat painting surface.

(wiping, complementary painting technique after using *cun* technique to make the rock of trunk look heavier), *dian* (dotting, using only ink or color dots to create visual images without lining out the profiles of the images), and *ran* (dyeing, going together with rough bark or dot strokes), that stress the appealing artistry of applying ink and brush.

Extant paintings composed by Guo Xi include *Early Spring* (Fig. 40), *Snow in Spring on Guanshan Mountain*, *Extensive Remoteness with Bush and Stone*, *Profound Valley*, and *Ancient Trees on Remote Mountain*. The aesthetic focus of this period turned gradually from political education and religious spirit to humanistic spirit, the latter of which was the source from which traditional Chinese aesthetic culture originated.

In his book on painting theory, *Gracious Taste in Woods and Springs* (林泉高致, *Lin Quan Gao Zhi*), Guo Xi emphasized that the purpose of the landscape painting was to "enable you to fully enjoy the natural beauty without leaving your dinner party" or to satisfy your wish for retreating into woods or beside springs by appreciating a painting. Guo Xi ranked landscape into four levels, where people can "roam, watch, reside, and amuse themselves," and pointed out that

the essence of the landscape lied in its functions as a place to "reside and amuse yourselves."

He also analyzed the essential elements of natural landscape and proposed "three qualities of remoteness" to represent the beauty of mountains, i.e. "extensive remoteness, lofty remoteness, and profound remoteness." He further interpreted that "on one hand, to a mountain, rivers are her blood vessels, trees and grass are her hair, and mist and clouds are her charming expressions. Accordingly,

a mountain with streams is lively, a mountain with woods is luxuriant, and a mountain with misty clouds is charming. On the other hand, to a river, a mountain is her face, pavilions are her eyes and eyebrows, and fishing activity is her vitality. Consequently, a stream with a mountain looks graceful, a stream with pavilions appears sprightly, and a stream with a fisherman proves boundless." Another statement is that "a mountain without mist and clouds is no less boring than a spring season without flowers and plants. A mountain without clouds is not elegant, that without a river is not graceful, that without paths is not lively, and that without trees are not vivid. A mountain without depth is shallow, that without breadth is narrow, and that without height is low." These theoretical statements became the guiding principles of landscape garden designing.

Southern Song Dynasty was content with occupying half its original territory in the Yangtze River Delta, and its incompetent rulers always submitted to the ruling of Jin, a kingdom set up by a northern minority. Seeing this, patriots in the Southern Song Dynasty felt heavy and burning bitterness. Similarly, righteous blood rushed ferociously in the ardent painters' hearts. This unique political environment had a tremendous impact on landscape painting.

The landscape painting in the Southern Song Dynasty utterly differed from that of the Northern Song Dynasty in artistic style and mental attitude. In the Northern Song Dynasty, panoramic landscape paintings had already reached its peak, yet when it came to the Southern Song Dynasty, it was more fashionable to present only a fragment of the landscape instead of an overall picture. In other words, painters tried to "present more with less," abstracting the essence of the entire view into a tiny patch half hidden behind the surroundings. Then, landscape painting accomplished the stylistic transformation from "capturing the general magnificence from afar" that was typical of the panoramic painting style to "capturing details from aside" that was typical of the partial perspective,

from reproducing the substantial beautiful images to uttering the unpredictable implicit beauty, and from emphasizing on regional characteristics to stressing on expressing emotional atmosphere.

These changes led by Li Tang (one of Great Four Painters in the Southern Song Dynasty) were inspired by an innovative spirit. The new style of ink paintings featured freedom and simplicity, adopting powerful ink strokes, rigid and tough lines, and violent rough grains as if made by a sharp ax. The drawing techniques reflected by *Fisherman Hermit beside Clear Brook* were unprecedented; its composition courageously gave up the most part of the environment, leaving only a small section of the scenery, and leaving no vacancy either on the top or at the bottom. This was a drastic change of composition method, creating a completely novel feeling and leaving endless space for imagination.

Ma Yuan (Fig. 41) and Xia Gui, two figures among the Great Four Painters in the Southern Song Dynasty, possessed a more vigorous and concise painting style than Li Tang, which earned them such nicknames like "Corner Ma" and "Half View Xia."

In the Southern Song Dynasty, the pursuit of artistic conception and implicit beauty in painting played an important role on the development of Chinese freehand landscape painting. In general, the landscape painting of the entire Song Dynasty showed strong regional features, focused on describing natural scenery from an objective perspective and, by means of such description, created a certain artistic conception, namely "state of physical surroundings."

FIG. 41 *Dancing and Singing (Peasants Returning from Work)*, by Ma Yuan, Southern Song Dynasty
This is a colored painting made on a 192.5 cm long and 111 cm wide silk scroll. In this painting, all mountains and rocks were drawn with thin, solid, and powerful lines to bring out their outlines and internal structures. The painter used the technique of *cun* to highlight the texture and grains of the rocks. In dealing with huge rock pieces, he used the side surface of his paintbrush and started a swift touch with a heavy strike, and ended it with a gentle leaving. Then he intentionally left blank spaces between every two touches. All outline strokes were rough and harsh, seemingly without careful planning. When it came to bamboos, he also used hard lines to bring out their outlines. As a result, the resilient bamboo leaves look like heavy iron nails. The entire painting created a concise, sturdy, and vigorous scene.

In the Yuan Dynasty, when the political situation became more and more stable, people gradually recovered from the trauma of war. In the history of Chinese landscape paintings, those composed in the Yuan Dynasty accomplished the supreme achievement in creating artistic conception.

FIG. 42 *The Studio of True Appreciation*, **by Wen Zhengming, Ming Dynasty**

The most striking features of these paintings lie first in the works composed by literati and high officials that became the center and core of painting activities and the mainstream in this domain of art. Second, for the first time in history painting serves the subjects as a means of releasing their temperaments and interests. And third, painting methods had changed greatly, i.e. the aesthetic tendency or the focus shifted from the objective reproduction of nature to subjective representation and free-hand-style expression.

The works of the Yuan Dynasty clearly expressed the literati's state of mind and their interests in life, focusing on the expression of subjective temperament and the performance of ink style. For this reason, a weighty stylistic transformation from reproducing the "state of physical surroundings" that was typical of the Song Dynasty to presenting the "state of mind," which characterized the Yuan Dynasty. At the same time, the integration of poetry, calligraphy, and painting grew to a higher level. Painters gave special attention to subjective intention and taste as well as their styles of

using ink and strokes. The aesthetic taste for painting had undergone a fundamental change. And landscape painters highlighted the significance of painting forms.

The objects presented in the Chinese landscape painting had been of mountains and rivers, yet later themes rarely displayed any specific landscape environment. When it came to the Ming and Qing dynasties, Chinese landscape paintings, to some extent, reflected the situation of Chinese art of garden construction.

Qiu Ying (c.1501 – 1551) in the Ming Dynasty was the man with the greatest achievement in this subfield. The proportion of human figures in these paintings was reduced gradually, serving the main pictures as non-essential foils.

In the Ming and Qing dynasties, there appeared a great multitude of garden-themed landscape paintings. The literati of this period differed from those in the Southern Song Dynasty in that they seldom travelled or painted of life in nature, and so developed a habitual painting activity of directly describing the garden views instead. Especially in short sketches, painters either copied the existent landscape

painting composed by former painters or presented entirely artificial sceneries.

The majority of the protagonists who were responsible for the construction and improvement of the most famous gardens in the Yuan, Ming, and Qing dynasties were prominent landscape painters of the time. The painters who participated directly in the garden construction included Ni Zan (1306 or 1301 – 1374) in the Yuan Dynasty, Shen Zhou (1427 – 1509), Tang Yin (1470 – 1523), Wen Zhengming (1470 – 1559) (Fig. 42), and Qiu Ying in the Ming Dynasty. They usually applied the concepts of Chinese landscape painting to the garden construction art. A garden is a three-dimensional painting while a painting is a flat garden. The interaction between gardens and Chinese paintings never stopped.

Landscape Poetry

Chinese poetry and Chinese classical landscape gardens were two descendents of the same artistic root and dependent on each other, shining side by side as two pearls in the treasury of Chinese ancient culture. Chinese poetry is not only the foundation and cultural content of landscape gardens, but also the artistic carrier describing the physical sceneries and scenic spots in gardens, enabling the landscape gardens to possess an artistic conception both rooted in real physical nature and higher than the nature. It has played an irreplaceable role in the development of Chinese classical gardens.

Since the time of *Book of Songs* (诗经, *Shi Jing*), every generation had contributed poems and essays describing and extolling the natural landscapes in China. Landscape poetry did not welcome its self-conscious stage (when it became an independent genre in literature) until the Wei and Jin dynasties, when numerous literati good at landscape poems emerged. Tao Yuanming (365 or 372 or 376 – 427), Xie Lingyun (385 – 433), and Xie Tiao (464 – 499) were the most renowned poets among this group.

Featuring a fresh and natural writing style, Tao Yuanming's poems focused on the theme of pastoral life. His 5-piece serial poem *Retreating to Pastoral Life* (归田园诗, *Gui Tian Yuan Shi*) had been regarded as the representative work of pastoral poetry. His 20-piece serial poem *Drinking* (饮酒, *Yin Jiu*) had also been considered as the model work among all natural landscape descriptions. For example, the two lines in the fifth piece of the 20:

While picking asters neath the Eastern fence,

My gaze upon the Southern mountain rests.

(Translation by Yang Xianyi and Gladys Yang)

His ideal garden, Peach Blossom Spring, was a universe integrating nature with humanity, which not only evokes in readers infinite yearning for the place but also sets up an ideal mode for garden construction. The entrance of Humble Administrator's Garden in Suzhou vividly reproduced the entire process of how a fisherman of Wuling discovered this Peach Blossom Spring. Another example is the Scene of Wu Ling Chun Se (Spring in Wuling), a scenic spot in the Old Summer Palace, which

was also built according to *Tale of the Peach Blossom Spring* (桃花源记, *Tao Hua Yuan Ji*) by Tao Yuanming (Fig. 43).

Another significant figure, Xie Lingyun, who lived in the late period of the Eastern Jin Dynasty, was the first poet in Chinese history to have composed a large number of landscape poems. His poems were based on careful observation of natural landscape and reproduced distinctive images and tranquil artistic conceptions, which marked the birth of new

FIG. 43 *Peach Blossom Spring—A Celestial World*, **by Qiu Ying, Ming Dynasty**
This is a colored painting, collected by the Tianjin Art Museum, was made on a 175 cm long and 66.7 cm wide silk scroll. This painting takes its subject matter from a famous literary work *Tale of the Peach Blossom Spring* by Tao Yuanming, which tells of the accidental discovery of a hamlet cut off geographically and temporally from the world for ages. The distant view in the painting is of rolling mountain ranges standing upright above clouds and mists, stressing on the lofty remoteness of the mountains. A temple, platform, pavilion, or tower appears and disappears among the mountain, just like a scene from paradise. The front view section in the painting is a vivid portrait of an elegant landscape composed of twisting pines and a running creek under a wooden bridge.

aesthetic standards and tastes, and promoted landscape poetry to be an independent aesthetic object.

Another poet, Xie Tiao, wrote poems that were refreshing in content and fluent in form. His work was so elegant that the Emperor Wu of Liang would "feel that his breath would become foul after a couple of days without chanting poems by Xie."

These landscape essays and poetry uncovered how people in the Wei, Jin, and Southern and Northern dynasties appreciated and enjoyed nature. The aesthetic value of natural landscapes was unprecedentedly and fully developed. Meanwhile, influenced by its contemporary aesthetic fashion of appreciating natural landscapes, the landscape garden construction made a great progress.

In the Tang Dynasty, Chinese landscape poetry arrived at a prosperous and matured stage. At such a period when literati had an ever-increasing influence on society, they actively contributed to garden construction activities, combining the sentiments in poetry and paintings with garden sceneries. They would create scenic spots according to the description of a poem or a piece of painting.

Bai Juyi is a case in point. A large proportion of his work, as many as over 3,000 pieces, were poems to natural landscape gardens, while poems on natural sceneries and gardens accounted for a majority of all the poems (nearly 50,000 in total) composed in the Tang Dynasty. At present, when studying the gardens built in Chang'an and Luoyang, researchers couldn't neglect the related Tang poems praising the two capitals. Likewise, investigation on

Wangchuan Villa built by Wang Wei had primarily relied on more than 30 poems in his *Anthology of Poems Composed in Wangchuan and Prologue* (辋川集并序, *Wang Chuan Ji Bing Xu*).

In general, of all landscape poems in the Tang Dynasty, literati's landscape poetry was the most influential ones, which could be classified into three groups. In the first group, poets directly described the artificial garden elements, such as pavilions, platforms, halls, bamboos, brooks, and pools, expressing their leisure and relaxed feelings when they indulged themselves in the scenery. In the second, poets indirectly exposed his real aspiration or ambition primarily by extolling the natural scenes in gardens. The third group of poems was written to record a tour, or as a courtesy, replied to another poet's work, where gardens served as the background or settings of the poem. Such poems usually contained insightful ideas about garden construction. The development of urban gardens and suburban villas granted officials and literati an approach to real waters and mountains in the boundless universe. While garden construction promoted the development of landscape poetry, poetry elevated the artistic reach of landscape gardens. Poetry is to garden construction as water is to fish.

Landscape poetry remained prosperous during the period of the Song Dynasty, both in earlier Northern Song and then later in Southern Song. At that time, the free-hand-style landscape garden containing artistic verve came into being, as a fruit cultivated by the

literati's painting theories, poetic sentiments, and artistic conceptions of poetry and painting. Since the Song Dynasty, gardens with inscriptions on garden architectures emerged in large number, such as Great Wave Pavilion built by Su Shunqin (1008 – 1048) and Dule Garden (独乐园, Garden of Solitary Enjoyment) by Sima Guang (1019 – 1086).

Poetry at that time played a role in elevating physical images to a spiritual level, extending the artistic conception embedded in a garden. Once inspired by the poetic names or inscriptions entitled to a scenic spot, travelers would naturally extend their imagination, and diverse sentiments would arise spontaneously. Hence, "image beyond present image," "sight beyond present sight," and "music remained after the instrument stops playing" were naturally produced. This approach of applying poetry to a garden to deepen its artistic conception had been passed down from generation to generation since. For example, because a building on a rockery island in the Humble Administrator's Garden in Suzhou was named as Xue Xiang Yun Wei Pavilion (Pavilion of Fragrant Snow and Luxuriant Clouds), plum trees planted on the island had been compared to fragrant snow, luxuriant woods and flowers to piles of clouds. Such an inscribed name would naturally evoke a poetic sentiment of seeking and enjoying plum blossom in flying snowflakes.

In the Yuan, Ming, and Qing dynasties, landscape poetry made further progress and flourished extensively. Mountain images and water images were more diversified and widely used during the period.

FIG. 44 Complex of Tian Yu Xian Chang in Mountain Resort at Chengde

Landscape images were everywhere, used as a poet's alias, or appeared in collected works, or showed up as a landscape-related hobby. Therefore, literati were motivated to whole-heartedly make a vivid description of landscapes in this social environment. Mi Wanzhong, Wen Zhengming, and Wen Zhenheng (1585 – 1645) in the Ming Dynasty, and Shi Tao (1642 – c.1718), Zhang Lian, Zhang Ran, and Li Yu in the Qing Dynasty directly engaged themselves in garden construction. While directing the garden construction activities, they referred to the incisive free-hand-style landscape poetry and paintings, and created beautiful living surroundings in accordance with the artistic conception typical of such artistic compositions. Their activities contributed to the emergence of new garden construction patterns.

3. Cultural Conceptions

The Chinese gardens represented the desires and ideas of the emperors, literti and ordinary people. The specific garden architectures, plants and general layouts in gardens are artistic symbolic entities, which conjured up the splendid cultural conceptions.

Three Celestial Islands in One Pond

Originating from celestial myths, the pattern of Three Celestial Islands in One Pond first appeared at the end of the Zhou Dynasty and became popular in the Qin and Han dynasties. It was a fruit cultivated by Taoism, primitive worship to celestials, and worship to mountains.

Emperor Qin Shihuang was obsessed with celestial magic and sent his men to search for celestial islands many times in vain in the hopes of finding immortal elixirs. Therefore, this emperor made a big pond and piled up rockeries in his imperial gardens after the images of sea and celestial islands to compensate for his desire for visiting paradise in person. Furthermore, such constructions indicated that he expected to receive the celestials and worship them there. During the Qin Dynasty, a pond and an island

(Penglai Island) were constructed in Lanchi Palace, with the pond symbolizing a sea and the island symbolizing a celestial island. This was the start of setting out to apply Three Celestial Islands in One Pond as the major theme to garden constructions.

When it came to the Han Dynasty, excavating "seas" in palace gardens came into fashion. Three celestial islands, i.e. Penglai Island, Yingzhou Island, and Fangzhang Island, were piled up in the Taiye Pond to the northwest of Jianzhang Palace. Since then, a new view-making pattern took shape. However, the technique adopted during the process of constructing Three Celestial Islands in One Pond in Lanchi Palace and Jianzhang Palace was relatively concrete in the instance of the stone whale sculpture.

Emperor Wen (407 – 453) of Liu Song Dynasty also built three celestial islands—Fangzhang, Penglai, and Yingzhou—in Xuanwu Lake located in the north of Leyou Plain. In the Northern Wei Dynasty, similar pattern reappeared in Hualin Garden in Luoyang, only with more buildings added to the islands for the Emperor to know what it was like being in a celestial world. Therefore, the Wei, Jin, and Southern and Northern dynasties started constructing the celestial paradise of a sea and three islands with a free-hand artistic technique.

In the Sui and Tang dynasties, the Xi Palace Garden, an imperial palace garden, which was renamed Dongdu Palace Garden (东都苑, Palace Garden in East Capital) in the Tang Dynasty, also adopted this pattern, and built architectures on the three islands. But its essential ideas of "a place to welcome and receive celestials from Heaven and to achieve longevity" remained the same.

In the Northern Song Dynasty, Qujiang Pond (Winding River Pond) was excavated in Gen Yue Garden, an imperial garden. Penglai Hall was built on the island which was piled up in the pond. Likewise, in the Jin Dynasty, a huge lake was excavated in Daning Palace (大宁宫, Palace of Great Peace) in the northwest suburb of Zhongdu city. Similarly, a hall named Guanghan Palace was built on Qionghua Island in the pond. In the Yuan Dynasty, Qionghua Island was renamed Taisui Mountain and two more islands, Yuanchi Island and Pingshan Island, were piled up in the pond. In the Ming Dynasty, the water area between Yuanchi Island and the east bank was filled and leveled up with earth, and the peninsula was renamed the Circular Wall. Then the water surface of Taiye Pond was further expanded when Nanhai was excavated to the south of this pond. Consequently, the three seas came into existence, i.e. Beihai, Zhonghai, and Nanhai, which remained the same ever since. Afterwards, the Nantai Platform (南台, South Platform) was built in Nanhai. In the Qing Dynasty, Nantai Platform was renamed Yingtai Platform (瀛台, Yingzhou Platform).

Since the Song Dynasty, this view-making technique (Three Celestial Islands in One Pond pattern) had accomplished three transformations: 1) from physical simulation to liberal expression, 2) from seeking immortal lives in the Qin and Han dynasties to enjoying landscape with a celestial paradise as their central theme, and 3) from satisfying the emperors' individual desire for immortal life to offering them an illusory artistic beauty.

In the Mountain Resort, Scene of Tian Yu Xian Chang (Joy and Freedom from Heaven and Earth), the 18th scenic spot among the 36 scenic spots named by Emperor Kangxi located on the central platform on Jinshan Island to the east bank of Chenghu Lake. The major construction on the platform, Shangdi Tower (Shang Di Ge, Tower of Supreme Deity), stands magnificently where True Warrior Grand Emperor and The Jade Emperor was enshrined. With various buildings scattered on the slopes and with misty ripples weaving around, the whole island appears exactly like a paradise (Fig. 44).

As to the Old Summer Palace, three islands were closely situated right in the center of Fuhai (Sea of Blessing), the largest water area in the garden. One island was bigger and the neighboring two smaller. Pengdao Yao Tai, the bigger one, was placed in the center, while its south neighbor Mountain of Sea Celestials on Yingtai stood to its right and its north neighbor Yu Yu Island to its left. Fuhai and the three islands made up the layout of Three Celestial Islands in One Pond.

In regards to the Summer Palace, the West Causeway separates the entire water surface into three sections, with Kunming Lake sitting to its east and Yangshui Lake and West Lake to its west. Each lake has one island. The Dragon King Temple was constructed on the island in Kunming Lake (Fig. 45), Zhijing Tower (Zhi Jing Ge, Tower of Making Mirror) on the Island in West Lake, and Zaojian Hall (Zao

Jian Tang, Hall for Appreciating Algae) on the Island in Yangshui Lake. They formed a stable triangle across the entire water surface.

Unifying the Country and Dominating All Life

The Chinese imperial gardens represented the desire of the emperors to bring the universe under their control, as they were the temporary supreme dominators of the state. Both the specific images and general layouts in imperial gardens were artistic symbolic entities, which conjured up the ideas of "interaction between Man and Heaven," which indicated that all kings in the earthly world behaved in accordance with the principle of Heaven and therefore, they represented the wills of the celestial deity and were righteous dominators, and "supreme imperial authority" so as to consolidate the emperors' dominance and ruling.

Some gardens were laid out to symbolize the *jiu zhou* (Nine Cites) in ancient China, indicating the entire Chinese territory. In some gardens, the name or inscription of a scenic spot would bestow high praise to the virtues of the emperors and to the peaceful and prosperous world under their rule. Some gardens even combined the buildings in a garden with their surrounding sceneries to represent some historical events, religious teachings, myths, and legends.

For instance, Jiu Zhou Qing Yan Complex (Fig. 46), the central scenic spot in Yuanming Yuan, was composed of nine islands with architectural complex on them, representing the country. And *qing yan* represents an emperor's expectation for a peaceful world.

FIG. 45 Longwang Temple (Dragon King Temple) on Kunming Lake in the Summer Palace

FIG. 46 Jiu Zhou Qing Yan Complex in Old Summer Palace
This was one of the largest building complex in Old Summer Palace, located to the north of Zheng Da Guang Ming Complex, on the central axis of the entire landscape area, between the front lake and the back lake. The island of Jiu Zhou Qing Yan was the largest among nine islands surrounding the back lake.

While Chengde Mountain Resort was designed together with the architectures around the resort, all of them as a holistic construction complex symbolized that Qing was a great multi-ethnic feudal empire.

Peach Blossom Spring and Pastoral Scenery

As ancient China was an agricultural society, emperors put high emphasis on agriculture. "Good harvest" became an important criterion to judge the achievements of local officials. The emperors participated in the farming activities with their officials and duly worship Heaven and Earth in all seasons for a good year and good weather. Farmlands and cottages in the imperial gardens not only provided the emperors with foods and services, but also met their needs of displaying agricultural rituals.

FIG. 47 *Gathering at the Orchid Pavilion, by Wen Zhengming, Ming Dynasty*

In the literati's gardens, farmlands and cottages reflected the literati's expectation to be removed from politics and material pursuits. Because of social and political turbulences, a large number of literati chose to escape from reality and return to pastoral life.

Tao Yuanming, a litterateur in the Eastern Jin Dynasty, described a pure paradise not yet polluted by secularity in *Tale of the Peach Blossom Spring*, a sharp contrast to the dark officialdom. Under his pen, the local residents enjoyed a tranquil, peaceful, and happy life. This fictional Eden in the agricultural society, a real Shangri-La, soon became a canon for literati who wished to abandon themselves to the landscapes. They started to build huts, humble cottages, and pastoral sceneries in their own gardens, after the models of farmhouses, and follow the hermit's life style. This was referred to as "retreating to gardens." Since then, Peach Blossom Spring had been a tireless theme of garden

construction for generations, such as Scene of Wu Ling Chun Se in Yuanming Yuan, Scene of Hu Shan Zhen Yi (Real Charm of Lake and Hill Pavilion) in the Summer Palace, Humble Administrator's Garden in Suzhou and He Garden in Yangzhou.

Floating Wine-Cup in Winding Channel

The entertainment of floating a wine cup in a winding channel (*qu shui liu shang*) originated from the ablution activities in the ancient Shangsi Festival (the third day of the third month of Chinese calendar). Every year on the Shangsi Festival, people meet their friends along the river, picking orchids or lighting incense, and washing themselves of bad luck. Composing poems, dancing, and praying for future children were also major activities during the celebration. Ever since celebrities like Wang Xizhi and Xie An gathered in Orchid Pavilion and completed the *Poems Composed at the Orchid*

FIG. 48 Scene of Qu Shui He Xiang in Mountain Resort at Chengde
This is a square pavilion structure standing in the middle of rugged rockeries. The artistic conception it constructed resembles that of floating a wine cup in a winding channel. Emperor Kangxi and Emperor Qianlong used to host government officials and Mongolian nobles here.

Pavilion (兰亭集, *Lan Ting Ji*), ablution activity and floating wine cup in a winding channel became elegant activities when literati and celebrities recited their poems and expressed their sentiments and ambitions (Fig. 47).

Floating a wine cup in a winding channel could be played in two ways. One way was to sit along a winding stream on the ground with a wine cup filled with liquor set on the water surface and allowed to flow downstream. Wherever the cup stopped, people in the front would finish the cup. Thus, the term as "floating wine cup channel." The other way was to construct a building over a stream, introduce water into the channel inside the building, and then float a wine cup inside the architecture. The building was called floating cup pavilion or floating cup hall. The former was to entertain literati among themselves while the latter was for emperors to entertain their officials in banquets.

Floating a wine cup in a winding channel gradually developed into cultural activities, containing such elements as touring, sightseeing, and assembly. It was frequently seen in many gardens, such as Scene of Qu Shui He Xiang (Lotus Fragrance upon Winding Stream) in Chengde Mountain Resort (Fig. 48), Zuo Shi Lin Liu Complex (Complex of Sitting on Rock in Front of a Stream) in Old Summer Palace, Xishang Pavilion (Pavilion of Benediction and Enjoyment) in Qianlong Garden in the Forbidden City, and Scene of Hong Qiao Xiu Xi in the garden attached to Prince Gong's Mansion (Fig. 49).

FIG. 49 Stone carving of floating a wine cup in a winding channel in Qinqiu Pavilion in Prince Gong's Mansion
Qinqiu Pavilion (Pavilion with Oozing Autumn Taste) is a pavilion with only single eaves and six corners pointing to the top. Water is poured into the groove from an inlet located on the top of a rockery to simulate the celebration activity of "floating a wine cup in a winding channel" in the ancient festival dating back to the Jin Dynasty.

4. Gardening Principles

Learning from nature, integrating into nature, following nature, and representing nature, the Chinese gardens embody their culture of "harmony of Heaven and Man," and reflect three important artistic ideals: eco-system scenes, picturesque scenes, and artistic scenes. They are the fundamental reasons why Chinese gardens always maintain their artistic vitality.

Nature Priority

The basic principle in designing Chinese classical gardens is to keep "harmony of Heaven and Man." This principle manifests nature, magnifies nature, and artistically reproduces the natural beauty. It stresses that nature and mankind are harmoniously coexisting and that "all creatures and I are in one unity."

This statement was initiated as early as the Warring States Period by Mencius, which was later developed into a characteristic of ancient Chinese philosophy. The concept emphasizes the unity of natural laws and humanity, which is contrary to the Western belief that man dominates the world. On the other hand, it emphasizes that natural beings and human activities should coordinate with each other harmoniously, which indicates that human activities should comply with the law of nature. Moreover, the doctrine of "interaction between Man and Nature," the philosophical foundation of the traditional Chinese feng shui theory (also known as "geomancy"), claims that unusual astronomical phenomena and strange changes in nature can predicate the coming of social evolutions or revolutions, and vice versa.

The concept of "harmony of Heaven and Man" is not only a Chinese cosmology and general cultural principle, but also our aspiration. It is thus entitled with a profound humanistic implication: nature and man coexist side by side instead of opposing each other, share prosperity instead of being alien to each other. Wen Zhenheng said, "Residence sites between mountains and rivers are supreme choices, sites in villages rank second, and sites in suburbs rank third."

The proposal unveiled the ideal in ancient Chinese hearts when choosing their residential sites. Chinese landscape poems and paintings were full of respect to and passion for nature. According to such "landscape art works," mountains and forests were not only shelters for people, but also land to pursue spiritual consolation and entertainment. Ji Cheng in the Ming Dynasty put forward in *The Craft of Gardens* the theory that "man-made as the gardens are, they appear natural," which expressed the highest aesthetic ideals in the Chinese culture of garden construction.

The Overall Principle

The Chinese garden construction puts emphasis on an overall principle that is "ingeniously coordinating with local geographical condition and borrowing views, while exquisitely designing the most appropriate element in the right location. In *The Craft of Gardens*, Ji Cheng classified view borrowing technique into five categories: "remote borrowing," "neighboring borrowing," "downward borrowing," "upward borrowing," and "seasonal borrowing."

Remote borrowing means adopting natural sceneries outside the garden, for which designers should create a perspective line so as to clear up the visual obstacles blocking your views upon the sceneries. Remote borrowing can be further classified into several sub-categories: borrowing mountains, waters, sky, architectures, plants, etc.

Neighboring borrowing is to adopt sceneries adjacent to or in the vicinity of the garden. And the techniques of downward, upward, and seasonal borrowing are applied in line with changes of season, climate, time, and weather.

The two most prominent examples of remote borrowing

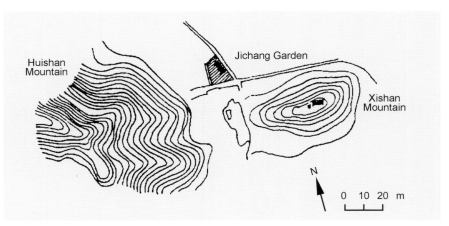

FIG. 50 Location of Jichang Garden

are Jichang Garden or Garden for Lodging One's Expansive Feelings in Wuxi, which borrows sceneries of Xishan Mountain and Huishan Mountain; and the Summer Palace in Beijing, which borrows the scenery of the pagoda on the top of Yuquan Mountain.

Regarding the Jichang Garden in Wuxi, mountainous views exterior to the garden are purposefully involved. Extending your sight to the west while standing on the east bank of a pond, you will enjoy the gracious landscape of Huishan Mountain, which leisurely approaches, appears at one moment and disappears at another, as if it were originally a part of the garden. Turning to the southeast direction from the west bank of this pond, you would find that the figures of Huishan Mountain and Longguang Pagoda are within your sight. Consequently, the spatial arrangement achieves infinite variety (Fig. 50).

Another example was located in the northwest suburb of Beijing, a rarely seen prestigious imperial garden area in history. Quite a few renowned gardens are scattered on this site like men on a chessboard, among which the most well-acknowledged were known as the Three Mountains and Five Gardens, (Fig. 51) which cover all the forms of Chinese landscape gardens: artificial landscape gardens, natural landscape gardens, and natural mountainous gardens. Therein, when Qingyi Garden (the former Summer Palace) was designed, the Three Mountains and Five Gardens had been entirely taken into consideration as a whole. Kunming Lake and Wanshou Mountain inside Qingyi Garden and neighboring Yuquan Mountain constructed an organic holistic

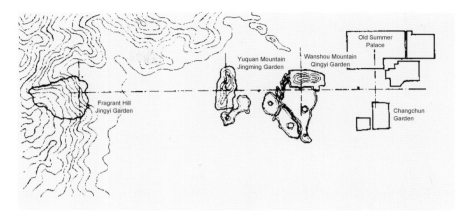

FIG. 51 Panorama of Three Mountains and Five Gardens, extracted from *The History of Chinese Classical Gardens* by Zhou Weiquan
In this book, Zhou divided the history of Chinese classical gardens into budding stage, transformation stage, bloom stage, and matured stage. Then, he further divided the matured stage into three sub-stages. By reviewing this evolution process, he introduced the fundamental laws of the development of Chinese gardening and pointed out the directions for its future development.

FIG. 52 The Summer Palace borrowing the scenery of Yuquan Mountain

landscape. Moreover, no fences or walls had been constructed around this garden, leaving no dividing line to seclude any space inside. Thus, it became an extensive sea of gardens (Fig. 52).

A case of neighboring borrowing is Great Wave Pavilion in Suzhou, which borrows the waterscape at its front door, and mixes views from inside and outside of the garden. An earth hill was piled up on the bank of this stream,

and trees were planted to shelter the rockery, composing an air of the wild mountain woods. The Canglang River winded its way, hugging the garden in its embrace. The stream approaches to the pavilion from the west and extends eastward along its south side, and then departs. Both riverbanks were lined with rockeries and shadowed by ancient trees. Pavilions, terraces, and gazebos were built near the water, therefore, once tourists are

FIG. 53 Guanyuchu Pavilion (Pavilion for Watching Fishes) at the northeast corner of Great Wave Pavilion is embraced by water from three sides.

inside these architectures, they would see their own reflections on the water surface, leaving them feeling as if they were inside the garden even though in reality they are outside. Along the water is a winding double-pavement corridor, whose arc points to the pavilion, rolling up and down. This internal side leans against the hill, while its external side faces to the stream. With the leaking windows on the wall inside the corridor, sceneries inside and outside the garden seem to be partially blocked and partially connected, and are naturally combined together (Figs. 53, 54).

Borrowing views is an important technique in the Chinese garden construction to break spatial limit, to expand space, and to enrich the sceneries. We can not only adopt natural landscapes and humanistic scenes, but also borrow seasonal views like flowers in wind and moonlight in snowy days. Besides, by uncertain borrowing, such as seasonal and temporary changes like morning glows, drum playing at dusk, the imagination of tourists can also produce abundant views and boundless garden space.

Site Choosing Principle

Site choosing is a prerequisite to garden construction. "Adjusting measures to local conditions" is one of the basic principles of gardening art.

Gardens are considered the ideal living environments. Therefore, above all, their locations must be carefully selected. Then, designers should conduct a detailed analysis

FIG. 54 Layout plan of Great Wave Pavilion in Suzhou

Guanyuchu
Pavilion

in order to make full use of the original geographic features and conduct the fewest earthworks. The existing trees should be left untouched as much as possible. The environmental characteristics of the garden site should be taken into account.

Natural conditions of the site should be brought into play during the garden construction, accordingly, gardens built in different environments such as mountain forests, rivers and lakes, uninhabited countryside, urban sites, and villages, are sure to stage different artistic conceptions.

Mountain forests usually present appealing natural environment with rugged terrain and luxuriant trees, so gardens constructed here should capture an air of primitive simplicity and tranquil spaciousness.

In contrast, gardens attached to urban mansions should be located in a remote site which could offer a quiet environment. Since urban sites feature even ground with little charming natural condition, keeping existing trees and managing vertical designs will be very crucial. As to small-scale gardens, rockeries are not necessarily lofty, but instead, exquisitely piled up with "every miniature hill being delicate, and every rock piece being expressive" so as to present a grandiose sense of a mountain with a few rock pieces. Gardens in urban sites are usually built on even land with limited space, so it is more appropriate to leave more vacancy for water. With sufficient water surface in a pond, the sky and surrounding sceneries could be reflected in the water, and garden space seems to be expanded and elegant freshness and serene tranquility is expressed accordingly.

Gardens in the village sites enjoy spacious open fields, so an extensive water surface is not necessary. Riverbank and lakeside gardens are advantageous in borrowing the open, clear, and extensive scenery of river areas including the natural scenery of lakes, mountains half-veiled in clouds, water surface in mist, flying birds, and fishing boats. Gardens in inhabited countryside, however, make the best of geographical features to take form.

Examples of Chinese classical gardens of this kind are numerous. For example, the famous Old Summer Palace was situated in a low-lying swamp area, where no natural mountain is available. Giving play to low-lying area, the designers excavated a huge lake, and piled up continuous slopes and hills with the soil unearthed. The designers did not expect a lofty and precipitous mountain, but instead, wished to construct a landscape with a mountain and a lake hugging each other. The tiny streams would pool into a lake, and then wind their way farther into brooks or rivers. And all the picturesque sceneries merged into this macroscopic physical environment, this water network, forming a unique artistic conception.

The ancient Chinese garden construction also paid particular attention to feng shui. The ancients preferred to introduce a stream of water to flow from northwest to southeast, and considering the general topography of China, the northwest rises up high while the southeast lies low.

"Water in embrace" was defined as a pond or a river in front of a house which looked like a half moon or an extending hug, functioning to collect and

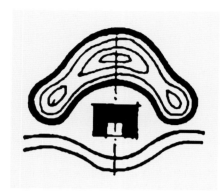

FIG. 55 The best location for a residence (painted by Wang Qiheng)
The house should be located to the south of a mountain or on its south slope and embraced by a golden belt (river).

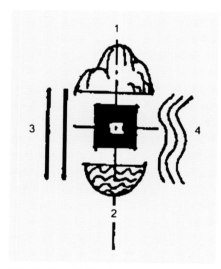

FIG. 56 The relationship between residence and the Four Spirits (painted by Wang Qiheng)
1. Mountain (Black Tortoise and Snake)
2. Pond (Vermillion Bird)
3. Road (White Tiger)
4. River (Azure Dragon)

FIG. 57 The best location for a town based on feng shui theory (painted by Wang Qiheng)

keep the vitality in the house site (Fig. 55). Those concepts had a crucial impact on water planning in a garden, including their external forms, direction, pooling, distribution, etc. The Four Spirits of feng shui were materialized into four environmental elements —mountains (Black Tortoise and Snake), rivers (Azure Dragon), roads (White Tiger), and ponds (Vermillion Bird), corresponding to the four directions. The site in the middle of Four Spirits with the Azure Dragon to its left, the White Tiger to its right, the Vermillion Bird in its front, and the Black Tortoise and Snake at its back would be the ideal environment (Fig. 56).

The feng shui theory reflected the Chinese people's environmental awareness, which accorded with ecological environment, namely, "human should adapt to the natural conditions, and vice versa." This was in reality a theory on how to choose the right site and make the ideal environment out of natural geographical features. Its central principle was to maintain and collect good luck from the site, so a closed, complete, and balanced environment was much favored, which was facing south, sitting in front of water, and set against a hill. An ideal place should have natural superior conditions like sunshine, ventilation, water source, drainage, waterlog prevention, traffic convenience, cold-proof, soil, and water conservation, etc. Surrounded by mountainous ranges, winding and clean water, and lush and verdant trees, people in such a natural environment and harmonious landscape would naturally enjoy a sense of beauty (Fig. 57).

The Emperor Huizong of Song in the Northern Song Dynasty built Gen Yue Garden according to alchemist's advice that "the northeastern corner of the capital enjoys great geomancy except for the slightly low-lying altitude, which, if heightened, would be favorable for royal offspring."

Therefore, Emperor Huizong of Song commanded the construction of Gen Yue Garden in the low-lying area of the northeastern part of Kaifeng. In the Qing Dynasty, the Emperor Qianlong had Jingyi Garden built in the valley of the Fragrant Hill in the northwest suburb of Beijing. The garden was embraced in mountain ranges from the north, the west, and the south. Layers after layers of garden architectures were built on the slope of the hill, naturally integrating with the surrounding landscapes— verdant pines and cypresses, clear brooks and waterfalls, steep cliffs and rocks—as if they were created by a deity.

The Chengde Mountain Resort was located in the natural scenic area to the north of the Great Wall. Wulie River winds to its east and Luanhe River lies to its south. Embraced in the arms of majestic mountains, you are able to enjoy elegant peaks and gentle weather in the resort. It is a promising geomantic site chosen by the Emperor Kangxi after his travels all through Chinese territory in search of favorable places (Fig. 58).

Pursuits for Artistic Conceptions

In Chinese garden construction, the pursuits for artistic conceptions can be categorized into three types, namely "eco-system scene,"

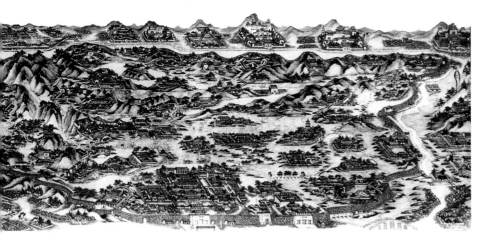

FIG. 58 Panorama of Mountain Resort at Chengde
Of all the imperial gardens, this was the largest natural landscape garden built in the Qing Dynasty, occupying an area of 5,640,000 m². It was composed of four landscape areas, i.e. Palace Area, Lake and Island Area, Flatland Area, and Mountain Area. It had altogether over 180 scenic spots, was a perfect combination of southern and northern garden construction styles in China, and collected the best elements of all Chinese classical gardens. It was a perfect example of Chinese classical gardens that had great scientific and artistic values. This illustration is selected from *Prominent Scenic Spots in Chengde City* by Xiao Tian.

"picturesque scene" and "artistic scene."

Sun Xiaoxiang, the great Chinese master of garden construction, painting, flower gardening, and a professor of architecture designing, considers "eco-system scene" as the first aesthetic ideal of garden construction. That is to seek for artistic prototypes for a garden from nature and life. "Eco-system scene" mirrors the beauty in life and nature through a realistic approach. During the Chinese classical garden design, designers should try to create appealing natural beauty featuring "lush and thriving woods by the side of trickling spring water," as well as a nice social environment full of the beauty of life featuring the "pleasantness of sharing intimate words with kinsfolk, feeling relaxed, and taking pleasure in music and books," in order to make the garden an appropriate place where people can "roam, watch, reside, and amuse themselves."

"Picturesque scene" is the second ideal of garden construction, a recreation process based on the artistic prototypes obtained from the first scene. To achieve a picturesque scene is to place the prototypes into the local space, order and arrange them to appear successively according to space and season. "Picturesque scene" reflects the artistic beauty. Chinese classical gardens are three-dimensional paintings and silent poetry, because most gardens were arranged on the basis of landscape painting composition and relative theories. However, they are not mechanical imitation of nature, but an artistic summary of it after abstracting and choosing the essence. This is a process of selecting one out of a million. This "one" represents the essence of "a million," and in this way a garden could reach the ideal of "coming from nature but going beyond it."

"Artistic scene" is the third ideal of garden construction, which aims at raising the visual and auditory images created by the second stage to the ideal, romantic, and spiritual level. "Artistic scene" reflects the ideal beauty, the romantic passion evoked by the eyes. Chinese traditional garden construction and the art of classical poetry and paintings attach great importance to the pursuit of artistic conceptions. Landscape paintings strive for "spiritual appreciation of objects instead of sensory contact with them." Herein, "objects" doesn't refer to the objective images, nor things seen and heard, but those integrated with human emotions and will after psychic contact. Artistic creation is not limited to objective description or realistic reflection of the objects, but actively seeks for "images beyond images, ideals beyond ideals, charms beyond charms." Chinese classical gardens can stimulate the yearning of tourists and the pursuits for good feelings, beautiful aspiration, great personalities, and harmonious society, when they enjoy the grandiose artificial lofty mountains and running streams, refreshing winds, bright moon, and man-made architectures, and subsequently, "inviting old memories at familiar sights." Without "in-depth appreciation of sights," designers will never create perfect gardens.

Professor Sun Xiaoxiang

Mr. Sun Xiaoxiang (1921 – today) is a professor in Beijing Forestry University. The global landscape garden construction community knows him as "the father of the Academic School of Chinese Modern Landscape Garden." Sun is a winner of many international academic awards. His garden design work include: Hua Gang Guan Yu Park, Hangzhou city, the overall planning of Hangzhou Botanical Garden, the overall planning of Beijing Botanical Garden (South and North gardens), the overall planning of South China Botanical Garden, Guangzhou city, the overall planning of Fairy Lake Botanical Garden, and the city of Shenzhen, as well as Zhuge Liang's Thatched Cottage Theme Park, a Chinese literati garden in Boise, Idaho, U.S.A.

FIG. 59 Xiaofeihong Bridge in the Humble Administrator's Garden, Suzhou

Chapter Three
Art of Classical Garden Construction

Chinese art of classical garden construction is a highly developed system that boasts splendid artistic achievements and a unique style. It always tries to break through the spatial limitation to reproduce the beauty of natural landscapes within a small space, creating limitless scenes within a limited space. Consequently, it has earned itself a vital position in the world gardening history as the essence of Chinese classical gardens.

1. Layout

Every individual Chinese classical garden is a holistic artistic creation, whose layout best represents Chinese art of garden composition. The first step of laying out a garden is to determine a theme, which is the soul of a garden. Then based on this theme, a designer carries out planning how to start, to develop and to conclude the theme. All the composing sections should distinguish themselves from other sections. When it comes to detailed arrangements, the designer must keep a delicate balance between oppositional pairs such as highlighting vs. understatement, sparseness vs. denseness, front vs. back, and twist vs. straightness.

Exquisite layout is the key to a successful garden design (Fig. 59).

Static and Dynamic Layouts

Gardens have a dual nature. That is to say, a garden is an artistic work where both time and space should be taken into consideration. Based on how the time-space relationship is presented in garden compositions, garden layouts can be classified into two types: static layout and dynamic layout.

The smallest aesthetic unit in a garden is a static spatial arrangement a man sees from a fixed viewpoint, which is intentionally defined in a local static composition. It's just like a piece of spatial painting, where only things within sight shall play a role in a layout. All the other things, as long as they are not within the sight, can be totally ignored. From this perspective originate various compositions like opposite scenery, leaking through scenery, borrowed scenery, enframed scenery, vista line, wide open space and enclosed space and other variations (Fig. 60). Opposite scenery is a relative term since architectures in a garden are themselves the scenic spots for visitors to appreciate and spots from where visitors could appreciate the surrounding sceneries. In other words, one building can serve as the opposite scenery for another one and vice versa. This is how a complicated net of opposite sceneries emerges.

Dynamic layout reflects the power of time over a garden. Common dynamic layout includes continuous layout, layout of seasonal views alternation, and layout of future and recent plant growth. In a garden composed of a number of regional sections, when a visitor moves from one section to another, the scene in his sight is replaced by another. To put it in another way, scenes shift constantly as the viewpoint of a visitor rises,

falls or turns. This is so-called "changing views from different angles," a concept in Chinese classical gardening theories. That is why whenever a Chinese garden maker is planning landscape areas or scenic spots, he would always put the best viewpoints at the best places for sightseeing, such as main halls, platforms, towers, balustrades, and covered corridors to bring about more changes into a sightseeing route.

Protagonist and Foil Views

A garden can be divided into many independent static layout units, or

FIG. 60 A view outward from a window opening in Garden of Autumn Vapors
The framed scenery is also known as a "one foot painting." A window frame on a solid wall serves as a frame presenting the garden view on the other side, where visitors could figure out the remarkable view in the opposite side from this epitome.

scenic areas. These units are interconnected, yet meanwhile, each has its own unique theme and features. In every scenic area, there is always a protagonist view (or main view) and one or more foil views. A protagonist view must definitely differentiate itself from its foil views. In some gardens, mountains or hills are their dominant views, such as Mountain Villa with Embracing Beauty and Great Wave Pavilion (Fig. 61); while in others, water is their advantage, such as Master of the Nets Garden and Humble Administrator's Garden. Either option is able to achieve unique attraction.

As to dynamic layout, the initial view, climax, and final view in a garden are sequenced in a dynamic way. Of the three components, the climax must be highlighted, while the initial and final views work together to set off the climax. Take Foxiang Tower architectural complex in the Summer Palace for example. The initial view in this continuous composition is Paiyun Hall (Pai Yun Dian, Hall of Dispersing Clouds). Then, Foxiang

FIG. 61 Rockery in the Great Wave Pavilion

Tower constitutes the climax of the composition. In the end, serving as the final view, Zhihuihai Hall concludes the entire continuous layout. The climax functions as the protagonist view in a continuous layout, intensively expressing its main theme, while the initial and final views serve as foils, setting off and contrasting with the protagonist view.

In Chinese classical gardens, the following methods are often adopted to highlight the theme of a composition, namely placing the protagonist view at a higher or central position, arranging garden elements symmetrically, and highlighting the protagonist view by contrasting it with foil views. For instance, Foxiang Tower in the Summer Palace and the White Pagoda in Beihai Park, the centerpieces in their respective overall layouts, are both lifted to a higher position to strengthen their dominant roles. Generally, a series of transitional spaces which are usually small but full of rhythmical changes and contrasts will be arranged in front of any larger-scaled scenic area, so that the entire view will not be exposed to visitors completely. The transitional spaces narrow down the vision of the visitors and sense of dimensions so that at the moment when he enters the larger area, he would find himself suddenly in a bright open environment and greatly delighted. The Humble Administrator's Garden is a typical example of this kind. When a visitor enters its middle gate, he would find a big rockery standing right in front of him. Yet, after he passes through the rockery, a totally different picture would unfold before his eyes. In the case of a large garden

design, the technique of "minor gardens inside a bigger garden" can also achieve the same effect.

Be it a big or small garden, as long as the protagonist view can be effectively highlighted and the foil views can set off or contrast with it, playing a positive role in composing the garden so that it will leave a deep impression with every visitor in spite of all the weaknesses or shortcomings in other areas.

Contrast and Harmony

Chinese classical gardens strongly resist plain or bland scenes. Therefore, contrast and harmony are indispensable tools for garden designing activities. These two approaches come hand in hand to help to clearly differentiate the protagonist view from its foils, and to produce more artistic charm with less construction.

The first approach is to select the landscape embodying two sharply contrastive geographic features as the main theme in a landscape garden. Yet, such contrast is feasible on condition that no one basic function of a garden is compromised. Also, when creating such contrast, a garden designer has to consider the local conditions, focusing on how to make the best use of original landscape and modifying natural condition only when absolutely necessary. For example, both the Mountain Resort at Chengde and the Summer Palace in Beijing successfully and ingeniously group water and mountain as contrastive pairs, which present appealing landscapes. Likewise, small residential gardens Lion Grove Garden, Lingering Garden, and Humble Administrator's Garden

also produce contrastive landscapes with varied geographic features.

The second approach is to intensify contrastive effect by growing plants. A designer can avoid tedious stiffness in the composition in two ways, either growing tall trees at higher places and bushes and grasses at lower places, or planting two plants side by side that are clearly different from each other in terms of physical looks and growth habits. As to the latter, the designer could pair an evergreen tree with a deciduous tree, a tall and thin twisted wood with twisted but out-stretching branches, or a coniferous tree with a broad-leaved tree.

The third approach is to create contrast between different waterscapes. Spacious and narrow water surfaces, running and still streams, and varied water bodies can constitute pairs of contrast and diversify sightseeing effects.

The forth approach is to focus on the harmony, the major method to smooth the relationship among buildings, natural landscapes, and plants. In general, building complexes are asymmetrically laid out in accordance with natural terrains, to achieve the harmony between man-made buildings and nature.

An exemplary case is the contrast and harmony between the Mt. Longevity and the Kunming Lake in the Summer Palace. The water surface of Kunming Lake is as smooth as a mirror, forming a remarkable contrast to the pagoda on Mt. Longevity. Meanwhile, the horizontal lines of the pagoda eaves create harmony by paralleling the water surface of Kunming Lake. The harmony in the composition could not be accomplished if the pagoda was replaced by a cone one without eaves. In terms of scale and size, the vertical size (height) of Mt. Longevity and the horizontal size (width) of Kunming Lake form a gigantic contrast while the rippling reflections in the water surface and the wavy skyline of Mt. Longevity constitute a tuneful harmony to a large extent (Fig. 62).

2. Waterscape

When designing the waterscapes, it is essential to elaborately shape the water surface and exquisitely manage the territory of its banks. The success of water arrangement in a garden depends on the available water sources, water forms, and the subsequent bank planning and constructing. The rivers, lakes, creeks, and waterfalls in natural landscape all have their own specific appearances and characteristics, providing much inspiration for water arrangement

techniques in Chinese classical garden construction. Water is the most important element to garden designing, just like the saying goes: "A garden without water is not a real garden."

Searching for water source is a very important step in site survey, planning, and designing process. The condition of a water source determines the scale and artistic form of a garden. Natural water source is of course the best option. A number of existing famous Chinese classical gardens were designed and built primarily because of the supreme water conditions in the sites. The Summer Palace, for instance, was built at the bank of the Kunming Lake, a large water body accumulating the springs from Xishan Mountain (Western Mountains). For another, the Mountain Resort at Chengde was built at its site only after Emperor Kangxi finally selected the Rehe River (Hot River), the shortest river in the world as the water

source of this imperial garden after he carefully surveyed the natural conditions of several potential sites. From all these examples, we can clearly see the importance of searching for appropriate water source to garden construction.

If a garden has to be built at a site where natural water source is scarce or unavailable, a garden maker would turn to excavating water source manually. In Chinese garden history, there were quite a few such examples. Man-made water source is usually created in two ways: excavating a pond or lake and drilling a well. It must be pointed out that when excavating water source, the inlets and outlets must be designed as those of natural water sources, and they should present natural water forms like creeks, rivers (Hao River and Pu River as described in legends), deep ponds and so on. As to an artificial pond, it should take an irregular shape just like the natural ponds, and then its boundary

FIG. 62 Kunming Lake and Mt. Longevity in the Summer Palace

should be lined with Taihu Lake rocks, yellow stones, or gray stones, so that such man-made ponds are able to coincide with architectures in the garden space.

Water Surface

Lake and pond. Lakes and ponds are all terms for closed water bodies. Such terms could be used alternatively to meet the needs of artistic taste in garden construction and do not necessarily indicate the size of their water surface. Sometimes, even a spoonful of water is deemed as a lake or a sea. The only trait they share is that they are water surfaces enclosed by rock banks or earth causeways.

Closed water bodies present various forms, generally categorized into two types: naturally curving shape and geometrical shape. Naturally curving lakes or pools are enclosed by winding banks, appearing like a cove or a bay, and subsequently, create the feeling of spaciousness. It seems that you cannot catch sight of another end of it. A neatly geometrical-shaped water surface is more likely to be artificial lakes and ponds, usually appearing in smaller gardens. No matter whether a water surface is spacious or narrow, geometrical-shaped or natural-shaped, a Chinese classical garden designer tend to divide it into smaller parts with islands, causeways, piers, bridges, corridors, and stepping stones to break the solitude hovering above the water surface, to increase its spatial layers, and to inspire a sense of extensive remoteness (Fig. 63). For example, in spacious water surfaces like the Kunming Lake in the Summer Palace, islands and causeways were purposefully

built to add more scenic spots and landscapes. In small water surfaces like Beihai Lake, a covered corridor—Qinquan Corridor (Corridor of Oozing Springs) and several zigzag bridges and arch bridges in Jingxin Studio were built to multiply its spatial depth.

Deep pool. Deep pools are another type of closed water surface. Centralized and deep space, tall cliffs, low water level, and isolated environment enclosed by dense woods are their typical features (Fig. 64). Because of their depth, people believed they are where Chinese dragons haunt and are therefore more popularly called "dragon pools," for instance, the Heilong Pool (Black Dragon Pool) and Bailong Pool (White Dragon Pool) in Beijing. Even some private gardens would also reproduce the artistic concept of deep pools, for example the small pool in front of Bingli Hall (Bing Li Tang, Courtesy Abidance Hall) in the Jichang Garden, whose the artistic effect is superb.

Brook, ravine and "scene along the Hao and Pu Rivers." Unlike the closed water surface such as pools, ponds, and lakes, brooks, ravines, and "Scene along the Hao and Pu Rivers" are used for presenting belt-shaped water surfaces like rivers and creeks. Curves and twists are popular in brooks and ravines to extend their flowing range, which gives an artistic conception that "a river flowing from a remote origin continues its journey to somewhere far away." Brooks and ravines can be either directly adopted from nature or manually made. The former is running water. Many famous scenic spots, gardens attached to temples, or private

FIG. 63 Stepping stones on a water surface in Five Peaks Garden

FIG. 64 A bird view upon the pool in Winding Water Garden
Built in 1745 and occupying an area of 30 *mu* (2 hectares, 4.94 acres), the garden was confronting the moat of Qingpu in Shanghai, known for the 24 scenic spots in the garden.

academies benefit a great deal from them. For example, the "Nine Brooks and Eighteen Ravines" in Hangzhou is a natural landscape consisting of rock banks, a gravel riverbed, and crystal clear shallow water for travelers to wade in, to count swimming fishes, to roam along the bank, or to enjoy a moment on the stepping stones. The green branches shade both banks, where mountain and water embrace each other. Another case in point is the Bayin Ravine (Eight Tones Ravine) in the Jichang Garden, which produces rising and falling sounds when a small torrent runs through an exposed rocky riverbed. Sometimes if there is no natural brook or river available at a garden site the garden maker would have to excavate one. The brooks and ravines to the south of the Huo Po Po Di Gazebo (Gazebo of Lively Place) (Fig. 65) in the south part of the Lingering Garden is a typical example of man-made water scenery. Aside from the previous examples, a winding canal is also a type of brook and ravine. The game of floating a wine cup in a winding channel in Lan Pavilion (Orchid Pavilion) in Shaoxing was an excavated brook decorated with natural rocks.

The "Scene along Hao and Pu Rivers" is a special form of belt-shaped water. The idea of this view-making technique came from a famous dialogue between two great philosophers, i.e. Zhuangzi and Huizi, when they met on a bridge across Hao River. Zhuangzi said, "Look at the way that fish swims, it must be a happy fish." Hearing this statement, Huizi asked, "You are not a fish. How do you know if it is happy?" Zhuangzi answered, "You are not me. How do you know whether I know if it is happy?" In a scenic spot in this form of water, an elevated stone slab bridge or a "water-touching" bridge is usually built to indicate this philosophical conversation based on such a historical account. The Hao Pu Jian Garden (Garden between Hao and Pu Rivers) in Beihai Park and the Hao Pu Pavilion (Pavilion upon Hao and Pu Rivers) in the Lingering Garden are exemplary works of this idea. This particular form of water scenery reflects an ideology in Chinese ancient philosophy (Fig. 66).

Bank

Natural banks in plain area tend to be gentle earth slopes, while those around creeks or deep ponds in mountainous areas are usually stone crags, huge rocks, broken cliffs, or scattered reefs. A garden designer must select suitable bank forms for different water forms. Varied bank forms could appear collectively along the same water surface, adding diverse changes to the water scenery.

Rockery bank. To build a successful rockery bank, either with Taihu Lake rocks or yellow stones, a designer must make the best use of the original texture and shape of material rocks. Rocks of different sizes are placed alternatively, textures on the rock surfaces are consistent, and rocks with inward and outward curving surface are paired to make rhythmic rolling ranges. Here and there, some places must be left for soil to plant

FIG. 65 Gazebo of Lively Place and the brook and ravine to its south in Lingering Garden

FIG. 66 Hao Pu Jian Garden in the Beihai Park

FIG. 67 Stone jetties in the Humble Administrator's Garden

flowers, vines, bushes, and trees. The south bank and northwest bank of the pond in the Master of the Nets Garden are good examples of rockery banks with yellow stones. In all, rockery banks should guard against stiffness and, especially, any exaggerated height. If the bank is towering compared with the water level, visitors seem to look into a well and the expected artistic effect of an excavated pond would be lost.

Stone jetty. Stone jetties are very frequently seen decorations along the banks in Chinese classical gardens, which were termed as *shi ji*, and could be classified into two types based on their sizes. Smaller-scale stone jetties are simple plate stone slabs supported by a few pillar-like rocks slightly above water, e.g. the stone jetty at the north bank of the pond in the Master of the Nets Garden and the dock rock close to the He Feng Si Mian Pavilion (Four-Sided Pavilion in the Lotus Breezes) in the Humble Administrator's Garden. The larger ones usually have cliffs or a stone stair road as their backgrounds. The horizontal stone slabs that look like a waterside platform form a striking contrast with the vertical cliff. Thus, the cliff scenes are spontaneously extended to the water surface. Good cases in point include the stone jetties to the south of the Xue Xiang Yun

Wei Pavilion (Pavilion of Fragrant Snow and Luxuriant Clouds) in the Humble Administrator's Garden (Fig. 67) and the ones in Five Peaks Garden.

Revetment. Revetments, either piled up with stone or earth, consider their harmonious relationship with neighboring garden elements as the critical point. Thus, revetment arrangement is undoubtedly an inevitable part of pond excavation and waterscape creation. Along the riverside beside a room or a platform, stone revetments are more popular. As for their shapes, piling stone slabs would be a good choice. It would be better if the interstices between two pieces of slab stones are horizontal and go perfectly well with water surface and the building. Nevertheless, the problem of piling stone slabs is that although it is a better choice over irregular pattern and tiger skin pattern, it requires much more labor.

To avoid soil erosion, earth revetments are compelled to be built into a gentle slope, and as a result, usually occupy a larger area. That's why small gardens seldom employ earth revetments. If earth revetment is designed in a proper way in a large-scaled garden, it can produce remarkable artistic effect as well. The earth hillsides piled up interior to a pond located in the central part of the Humble Administrator's Garden are rare and precious examples among the existing Suzhou classical gardens. The bulrushes along both banks and the dense woods at the north bank successfully reproduce the natural and lively water scenery of the Yangtze River Delta. A rockery piled up with one or

two layers of stones randomly decorate its southeast earth revetment, with a few clusters of trees or bamboos escorting the rock pieces and some wisteria hanging over the water surface. The rockery not only protects the revetment from collapse but also adds more mountainous beauty to the surroundings, achieving two positive results from the effort.

Waterfall and fountain. Waterfalls and fountains are the two most important elements in the water arrangement art of garden construction. The brooks and ravines within a great multitude of temple gardens, villas, and large landscape gardens were created by nature, attracting many visitors. If a request to make a waterfall in gardens situated on a plain in either urban or suburban areas, a garden maker would have to first draw water to a higher altitude so that it can fall down. For example, in the Lion Grove Garden in Suzhou, water is stored in water tanks hidden inside the wall copings and

FIG. 68 Waterfall in Lion Grove Garden

roofs, and then released to create a waterfall (Fig. 68).

The waterscape opposite to a waterfall is a fountain. However, Chinese classical gardens cherished natural taste, elegance, tranquility, and wild flavor more than any other feature. Therefore, when making water arrangement for a garden, a designer would first pay close attention to reproducing the natural water scenery with artistic approaches. Subsequently, fountains, obviously man-made dynamic waterscapes, seldom appear in Chinese classical gardens. In 1747, under the instruction of Emperor Qianlong, three fountains, i.e. Xie Qi Qu Fountain, Haiyan Hall (Hai Yan Tang, Hall of National Peace) fountain, and Dashuifa waterworks, were built in the Xiyang Lou Complex in the Old Summer Palace. Inside Dashuifa waterworks, ten bronze dog sculptures spewed water through their mouths to a bronze deer, which gave the fountain another name, "hounds hunting after a deer." The Haiyan Hall fountain had twelve bronze sculptures molded into Chinese zodiac symbols in arhat gowns. Each can eject water to "strike" the hours. The water was supplied by a manually operated machine—Dragon Tail Machine—which lifted water up to a higher place for the zodiac symbols to discharge in turn every two hours. When noon came, they'd discharge water together.

Floating cup pavilion. Of all the water arrangement patterns in Chinese classical gardens, this water scenery is a typical reflection of literary taste. This idea originated from a moment described by Wang Xizhi, a prestigious calligrapher over six hundred years ago, in his *Preface to the Orchid Pavilion Collection* (兰亭集序, Lan Ting Ji Xu). According to Wang's description, "along a winding water channel in which water runs, people sit and wait for the coming of a floating wine-cup. Even without appealing music, a single cup of wine with an instant poetic composition is enough to express our feelings at this moment." Such gracious literati activities were naturally indispensible to any garden, and were organized repetitively by later generations of Chinese literati. In the *Construction Method*, Li Jie, an architecture scholar in the Northern Song Dynasty, made a clear introduction to the construction methods of a floating cup pavilion. There are two construction methods, "mode of excavating channel" and "mode of laying brick on slab-stone." The former refers to cutting a winding canal on the surface of a big flat stone, and the latter by first placing a big stone slab as foundation and then placing smaller stone pieces on it to create a channel.

3. Rockery

As early as the Western Han Dynasty (206 BC – 25), man-made hills and rockeries had already appeared in Chinese landscape gardens. And rockery construction techniques kept on developing ever since the Eastern Han Dynasty (25 – 220) and Three Kingdoms Period (220 – 280). In the era of Han and Wei Dynasties (220 – 265), Chinese classical gardens had outgrown the stage of simply imitating the natural mountains, and begun to reproduce natural mountainous

sceneries in a given area to meet with specific needs. During the two Jin dynasties (265 – 420) and the Northern and Southern Dynasties (420 – 589), Chinese literati turned to Taoism to "escape from reality." Dedication to strange-looking rocks, peaceful idyllic life, and beautiful landscapes were widely accepted as "elegant taste." As a result, natural wildness came overwhelmingly into fashion in the garden designs of that time. This fashion was a gradual step forward after centuries of generalizing and abstracting the essence of natural landscapes, and a progress made on the base of landscape garden constructions during the Han and Wei Dynasties. In the Tang (618 – 907) and Song (960 – 1279) Dynasties, along with social, economic, and cultural developments, gardens multiplied in quantity, and designers had accumulated much more experiences, both theoretical and practical. Years of experiences in observing and producing cliffs, valleys, caves, hollows, and various stone combinations enabled Chinese garden artisans to sum up the special features of "earth-stone combination" in a rockery. Then, they were able to produce rockeries with diversified artistic concepts— masculine and powerful, steep and precipitous, deep and quiet, and broad and extensive—after years of mental digestion and physical practices (Fig. 69).

At the same time, under the influence of Chinese landscape painting, rockeries gradually absorbed the artistic features of them, which later became one of the most important approaches in Chinese classical garden construction over time. Such

FIG. 69 Rockery in Humble Administrator's Garden

rockery combinations are rich in variations and allowed great room for innovation, which subsequently made Chinese rockery a unique artistic form in the world garden arts.

Types of Rockery

Rockery in Chinese classical gardens can be classified into three types according to their building materials—earth hill, stone rockery, and earth-stone rockery. Whether soil and stone are properly combined, what rock materials are used, and who takes part in the rockery construction will definitely influence the style of a rockery.

As to the rockery structure, earth collapses when exceeding a certain angle or a certain height. Therefore, it is impossible to use earth alone to create a masculine, precipitous, or any complicated images, which makes earth-stone combination the essential technical option. Comparatively speaking, caves, valleys and cliffs, or high rockeries built in a small area require more stones. On the other hand, when stone proportion rises, so do the material and labor costs of quarrying, transporting, moving, and building, not to mention the time consumed in these works. Consequently, the

proportions of earth and stone in a rockery must be appropriate.

Earth hill. The approach of piling up a hill only with earth is the most primitive way of creating rockeries. An earth hill is more of an imitation of natural views and appears similar to the natural hills. The advantages of earth hills include: less manual work, readily available materials, and easier to grow plants so that it would be easier to arrange woods, creeks, hills, and valleys together to present a beautiful landscape and offer visitors a delightful experience. The earth hill situated in the northwest corner of the Xue Xiang Yun Wei Pavilion in the Humble Administrator's Garden is one of the best earth hill works that still exist today, with its original appearance basically remaining unchanged. Seeing the problem of earth hills, i.e. easy to collapse, Li Yu put forth in his *Leisure of Soul* a principle of rockery building—"use earth for large hills and stone for small rockeries."

Earth-stone rockery. Earth-stone rockery is one step forward from primitive earth hills in the history of rockery development. Judging by artistic effects, earth-stone rockeries are better carriers of higher artistic tastes. In *Craft*

of Gardens, Ji Cheng stated that "rockeries piled up half with earth and half with stones could present the most elegant tastes." There are two types of earth-stone rockeries, i.e. "stones in earth" and "earth in stones." The former means to bury stones in earth with only sharp points exposed to the air, just as several stone bones hidden in a natural earth hill rise up from soil. This method is very popular in Japan. The latter indicates enclose earth with stones, which can be further divided into two sub-types in accordance with the order of piling up earth and stones, namely "first piling up earth hill and then enclosing it with stones" and "first defining rockery shape with stones and then filling it with earth." The method of enclosing earth with stones was widely applied almost all through Chinese history.

A multitude of excellent earth-stone rockery works still exist in China today, for example Jinshan Island (Gold Hill Island) at Mountain Resort and Mt. Longevity in the Summer Palace in Beijing. Rockeries with more earth than stones are uncommon among gardens in the Yangtze River Delta. The very few larger examples of this type include the rockery in Great Wave Pavilion and the rockery in the west corner of Lingering Garden (Fig. 70). Rockery makers piled up about a meter-high stone embankment for both of them to protect their foothill and another two stone embankments to protect both sides of the winding stone stair roads inside the hill. Smaller examples of this type include the hill which supports Xiuqi Pavilion (Beauty Pavilion) and the two small isles inside the pond in the Humble Administrator's Garden. These three rockeries look much closer to nature than the larger-scaled hills, though their piling techniques are basically the same, with only one difference; that smaller rockeries are more economical in using stone pieces.

In contrast, rockeries that have more stones than earth are more popular in China. And based on structure, it can be further classified into three sub-types. As far as the first sub-type is concerned, the surface and caves of the rockery are completely made of stone. This sub-type tends to have more caves or holes in the rockery and keep a thin layer of earth on top. The Lion Grove Garden is a typical example of this type. The second sub-type also has rocky surface and caves, though fewer caves and holes, and thicker earth layers on top and at the back of the rockery, for example, the rockery in the Garden of Cultivation. The third sub-type has stone surface and stone top but leaves no room for any cave or hole at the bottom section. In other words, it is a complete "earth-in-stones." A typical example of this type is the rockery to the north of the pond at the central part of Lingering Garden.

FIG. 70 Earth-stone rockery in front of the Wen Muxixiang Gallery (Osmanthus Fragrance Gallery) in Lingering Garden

Stone rockery. Stone rockeries, totally piled up with stones, appeared slightly later than earth hills and earth-stone rockeries in the history of rockery development. Unlike the previous two types, stone rockeries are smaller in size, yet require more sophisticated piling techniques to vividly realize the unity of form and spirit. Some are "rocky caves under a pavilion" or "caves under a platform," while others look like a screen or a peak standing in a courtyard or beside a walkway. Still, others lean against walls and function as stone stair roads leading visitors to a higher place (Fig. 71). Mi Fu, one of the greatest painters in the Song Dynasty, made a brilliant summary of the aesthetic values of rockery stones based on their forms and texture and put forth an aesthetic criteria with four rhyming Chinese characters—*shou* (thin), *zhou* (crumpled), *lou* (leak) and *tou* (holey). According to his criteria, any stone or rock which could meet all these four criteria is a top-rank stone.

There are two types of stones that are commonly used for rockeries, i.e. mountain rocks and lake rocks. One type of mountain rocks, collected from mountains, has many sharp edges and corners or appears spiky and straight. Another type of mountain rocks, collected from waterside, is neatly square or roundish because of years of water erosion after rising up from water. The mountain rocks collected from Mt. Huangshan in Anhui province, Mt. Yaofeng in Suzhou, and Mt. Chuanshan in Zhenjiang are usually called

FIG. 71 Rockery and walls in Yu Garden

yellow stones because of their yellowish brown color. Yellow stones are widely used in gardens in the Yangtze River Delta. The mountain rocks popular in gardens in northern China are gray stones that are quarried from the suburbs of Beijing. Because of its slab-like shape, gray stone is also called "gray cloud slab." Lake rocks refer to the rocks fished up from the bed of a river or lake. Among those, the ones produced from Taihu Lake, called Taihu Lake rock, are the most renowned. Taihu Lake rocks are characterized by the exquisite caves and holes that give views of the other side, hollows on rock surface that look like it has been riddled with bullets, and graceful and charming shapes. Most Taihu Lake rocks are limestone or sandstone. From the Yangtze River Delta gardens to the private and imperial gardens in northern China, almost all Chinese classical gardens were competing with each other for their collection of Taihu Lake rocks. In the Song Dynasty, Emperor Huizong even set up a special organization, Bureau of Strange Flowers and Marble Shipment (*hua shi gang*) to collect and transport Taihu Lake rocks for his Gen Yue Garden on Wanshou Mountain.

Layout of Rockery

When creating a rockery, a rockery maker must determine the position, shape, size, and height of the rockery according to the natural conditions around it. Its size must go well with the space provided. Its shape must be "lower in front and higher at back." Its profile must change when viewed from different angles.

In small gardens that are confined to their narrow spaces, a rockery is usually placed opposite to an architecture, and flowers and other plants would be planted on or around the rockery to add liveliness to the scene. When designing rockeries for a medium or large garden, a rockery maker must first determine the protagonist scene in the overall layout, i.e. rockery-centered or pond-centered, before he could consider the size and shape of the rockery. In either case, he'd pay close attention to the coordination of the rockery and its surroundings, or the harmony between rockery and pond. If a pavilion, a tower, or a hall is built opposite to the rockery, he also needs to consider the proper proportion of the rockery to the building, and whether their external profiles match each other well. If a pavilion is to be built on a lofty hill, instead of being located on the hilltop, it would be better to lower its altitude and place it somewhere at the hillside, applying the main peak as its background view. One thing must be avoided by all means is to place a lofty hill and a high tower in one scenic spot, which consequently makes one section of the garden too gigantic and unnatural.

Setting-off technique is an important concept in the art of rockery construction. Specifically speaking, it is about how to use different components of a rockery, e.g. cliffs, peaks, ridges, valleys, ravines, terrace, roads, bridges, and waterfalls, to set off the main peak. Meanwhile, these components must set off each other in a right way based on their heights, sizes, and shapes, to create contrast between imaginary scenes and actual scenes, add more layers of views, extend spatial depth, and add more changes and dimensions to the profile of the rockery. The one piled up in Yu Garden in Shanghai is a typical larger rockery. The designer put its main peak at the back and arranged winding stair roads, platforms, valleys, ravines, waterfalls, and cliffs on the front hill to create a complicated layer-after-layer façade that naturally sets off the steep main peak. It is better to arrange the main peak slightly sideways instead of on the central spot, especially those relatively long mountains.

Construction Technique

A thorough knowledge about the images of real mountains and the shapes, textures and colors of rockery stones is the prerequisite for rockery construction. A rockery must be built with the same type of stone materials. Or, to put it another way, it is improper to mix different types of stones on one rockery. It is contrary to the real world to pile up a yellow stone hill with Taihu Lake rocks, pile up typical Taihu Lake rockery with yellow stones, or mix the two kinds of rock materials in the same work.

Ideal lake rocks must at least have swirls, crumples, and holes.

FIG. 72 Rockery in Garden of Cultivation

FIG. 73 Yellow stone cave in Autumn Hill in Individual Garden

Big or small, a swirl is relatively shallow. Some swirls overlap part of another, while some have a hole in them, although a hole is not necessarily inside a swirl. Holes on the rocks present pretty varied shapes. The surfaces of holes, brushed and eroded by water, are usually very smooth, with roundish edges. Sometimes, a big hole is accompanied by a few smaller ones and the smaller holes are usually interconnected by hidden tunnels. Whether broad and shallow, deep and serried, or skew or vertical, crumples mostly appear collectively on one aspect of a rock piece.

Cliff. Cliffs on natural mountains are eye-catching scenes themselves and, therefore, are the most significant scenes reproduced by a rockery hill. How to set up a cliff depends on visitors' expectation for sight-seeing from different perspectives. Sometimes, a cliff could lean against a wall to save land, space, labor costs, and reduce the difficulty of construction. The rockery in Pian Shi Shan Fang (Rockery Built

with Pieces of Stones) in the He Garden in Yangzhou is a good case in point. If a cliff is placed at waterside, its reflection in water would make it more precipitous and lively (Fig. 72).

Cave. A cave is the best stage for a rockery designer to demonstrate his best art and skills. Based on existing caves, we can divide them into two types, i.e. common caves, including dry caves and water caves, and tunnel-like winding caves that are widely used in gardens constructed in Suzhou. In some caves, the rockery makers would prepare a few tables and chairs for visitors to rest their feet, play a chest game, or simply enjoy cool air. A cave can be big or small, depending on the size of the rockery in which it exists. Larger-scaled examples include the one in the front hill of Mt. Longevity in the Summer Palace and the caves in the back hill of Qionghua Island in Beihai Park in Beijing. Pacing through the hill in these caves, you are inside the hill at one moment and outside it at another. It turns

and twists constantly, adding to its attraction. A distinctive feature of rockery caves in the gardens of the Yangtze River Delta, e.g. the yellow stone cave of Autumn Hill in Individual Garden in Yangzhou is the way the roof structure is handled (Fig. 73).

There are three kinds of cave roof structures. The first and the simplest is lintel structure, a stone bar or an irregular huge rock, or a stone bar with several pieces of rocks on it that is placed above the cave mouth. The second is corbel structure, an ancient brick-laying technique used in masonry buildings. More specifically, it is to lay layers after layers of bricks, stones, or timbers to make the entire structure incline to project outwards or shrink inwards, to support a structure above it. The third is arch structure. An arch cave is built with a number of irregular stones. But sometimes, stone beams are used to reinforce the internal side of the arch. Anyhow, in any case, the key point is to conceal any part of the man-made structure. Only such works could be considered as masterpieces.

Valley and waterfall. To add more liveliness to stone rockeries, designers tend to construct valleys and waterfalls in the rockeries, considering the conditions of water sources available. For instance, in Jichang Garden in Wuxi, running spring water produces various musical sounds and thus creates an engaging scenic spot—Eight Tones Ravine. In addition to the brooks and valleys at the bottom of a rockery, we could take advantage of the height of the rockery and create waterfalls or other down-pouring water scenes on the hilltop or at hillsides. Imperial gardens and private gardens built for powerful officials or rich citizens usually set up a structure to collect raindrops and then let it pour down in a natural way. In the gardens of southern China, rainwater collected by eaves would be led to a rockery to create a "spring waterfall." In *Craft of Gardens*, Ji Cheng specially introduced how to use high walls and eaves to catch water and create flying springs or dashing waterfalls. First, build gutters on the top of the walls of a high building to catch rainwater and lead it to a small water tank on the roof of the rockery. Then, when the water tank is full, the water will overflow through a projecting stone outlet and create a waterfall.

Courtyard rock. Courtyard rocks refer to individual rocks or small rock combinations placed in a courtyard or a square. Courtyard rocks must meet with the aesthetic criteria for artistic rocks—thin, crumpled, leaky, and holey. Or, at least, they must have unique looks or some kind of special values. Courtyard rocks should

have appeared later than rockery piling in history. From the most exquisite rockeries, we can sort out some individual rock pieces solely for appreciation. Quite a great quantity of individual art rocks still exist today, for example, Yulinglong Rock (Exquisite Jade Rock) in Yu Garden in Shanghai, Qingzhixiu Rock (Azure Glossy Ganoderma Rock) in the Summer Palace in Beijing, Guanyunfeng Rock (The Cloud-Capped Peak), Xiuyunfeng Rock (Cloud Peak), Yitiyun Rock (Cloud Ladder Peak) in Lingering Garden in Suzhou, as well as Yiyunfeng Rock (Peak Against Cloud) in Outlook Garden in Nanjing.

Construction. Piling rockery with natural stones is a process of five steps, i.e. rock selection, rock examination, foundation, base-making, middle layer piling, and capping.

As for rock selection, the best option is to use local rocks to bring out its local characteristics. Either real rock pieces available in nature or ancient and famous rocks found in dilapidated gardens can both be adopted. As to natural rocks, any regular and symmetrical cubes, full and plump rounds or ovals, straight and upright peaks, rocks with unusual textures, and those simulating real life images all could be chosen as rockery materials. Otherwise, reusing rocks in abandoned gardens helps not only to reduce the consumption of mountain stone resources and cut down various related costs, but also to avoid repetitively constructing similar rockeries everywhere.

Rock examination is also termed as "rock reading" or "rock appreciation." Before a construction activity, a rockery maker must

carefully examine the raw materials on the spot, distinguish their texture, colors, and sizes, and classify them in accordance with their planned position on the rockery and the design requirements. It is suggested to mark out those rocks used for key positions or frameworks to avoid confusion. Ancient Chinese rockery artisans attached particular importance to this step. They believed that the first and foremost thing in rockery building was to have a full understanding about every rock at hand. This would enable them to find the right places for each and every rock and achieve better artistic effect with half the effort.

Foundation here means to lay foundation for the planned rockery. The depth of a foundation depends on the height of the rockery and on the real condition of the earth foundation at the site. Commonly used foundations include wooden stake foundation, stone foundation, lime-soil foundation, and reinforced concrete foundation which appears only in contemporary time.

Also known as foot-raising, base-making means to reinforce the base layer of the rockery and define its planar contour. It is suggested that stones are only applied to enclose the foothill and support the main peak, while the rest of the base layer should be stuffed with soil to save rock materials.

The so-called middle layer refers to the main massif beneath the top layer and above the base. The construction work of this part, consequently the major part, collectively represent how exquisite and creative a rockery designer is able to unite his hill-molding techniques with his engineering measures. Ancient Chinese rockery

FIG. 74 Bridging rockery in Lion Grove Garden

artisans summarized their rockery piling experiences into a 30-word pithy formula, that can be paraphrased as follows: To begin with, when making arrangements and layouts, one must pay equal attention to creating fascinating but artistically justifiable images and maintaining structural stability. When arranging stones, one must take all sides of a rock into consideration and prepare a good base for the next layer. Secondly, the key to stone combination is to engage stones with each other according to their shapes and align their texture to the same direction. What's more, an arch, seemingly flying high above in the air, should make the inside and outside a unity. Still, top rocks ought to stick out as a slant, project sideways, and/or hang over people's head. And the rocks that bridge two cliffs must slope down instead of being hung vertically (Fig. 74).

As to the next point, a rockery maker must have a thorough knowledge about diverse attributes of stones concerning efflorescing, decomposing, breaking or cracking, erosion, stone species, and texture, before he is able to combine different rocks into a unit that present a natural overall texture and a proper holistic structure. Additionally, when trying to achieve the illusion of flying rocks or drifting clouds, he can make one layer of stones slightly projecting forward and leaning backward on the base of another. In addition, he can insert a small stone into the gap between two bigger pieces to seize up the two. Or he can intentionally stuff a big stone between two cliff walls to create a thrilling effect and a sense of crisis in the visitors. Such a technique is not only a good way

to reinforce the structure but also a fantastic approach to produce a good artistic image. During the process of piling up a suspending rockery, he also has more than one options—either hang a piece of rock at one side of the rockery or simply hang them overhead in the front.

As far as reinforcing stone combination is concerned, both cramps and iron welding could be applied. When joining two or more stones together, a rockery maker can fasten these pieces with lead wires, steel wires or coil ropes together either by punching holes first or not; then fill the openings and joints with adhesives immediately, and then, stack two or three layers of stones onto this layer. When the adhesives set, those wires or ropes can be removed and he can proceed to handle the seams. Two seam handling methods are available for artisans to choose from: apparent seams and hidden seams. The apparent seams should be in line with the surface features, colors, and textures of material rocks. As to the hidden seam process, the stones are stuck together by adhesives applied to their backs so that the gaps in the front can remain natural and unchanged.

Capping is also called conclusion. The top layer is extremely important to the overall effect of a rockery. In China, different regions have different capping styles. In general, the style popular in northern China is masculine, in central China graceful, in southern China fancy, and in western China precipitous. There are over 20 types of top layer forms available, such as peak, ridge, spring, and hole. Even the peak can be further divided into more sub-types. Peak rock requires the perfectly well-shaped material

rocks. A peak can be a single rock, or a pair of rocks, or a group of rocks, or a stone combination. When establishing a peak, the best option is to let rocks stand on their own and keep balance by themselves, with supporting or binding approaches used only when absolutely necessary. The pose of peak rocks must be aligned with the tendency of the main body but not to the extent of losing the solid foothold of itself. Even with a group of peak rocks, each should distinguish itself from others, playing varied roles in the group—protagonists, foils, affiliates, and accessories. And they should be purposely located irregularly to achieve special charm. Rockery makers must avoid at all costs symmetrical frames like a brush rack, a structure with a sea of sharp knives, or sword all over the hilltop. On the other hand, bare-headed ranges completely covered with tasteless hard rock pieces should be avoided as well. A better option is to create an earth-stone unit with plants adorning them.

4. Architecture

With the "harmony of Heaven and Man" as the utmost pursuit

of Chinese classical gardening art, garden architecture, as one of the four essential elements of Chinese classical gardens, must unite itself perfectly with the other three essential elements, namely rockery, water, and plants into an organic whole. Garden architectures adopt wooden framework and attach emphasis on dynamic interaction between inside and outside spaces. Garden architecture is usually a complex composed of more than one individual building that scatter in the corners of a garden. Consequently, the sophisticated and diversified functions and needs can be broken down into smaller components and assigned to individual buildings of the complex. In addition, the garden architectures can be freely arranged, either leaning against a hill or perching beside a stream, being strewn at random with some suspending high while others resting low. There could be hundreds and thousands of variations. Consequently, garden buildings are able to play practical roles as well as aesthetic roles, both as a place for visitors to have a rest and as a decoration to the natural landscape in the garden, and thus, they physically realize the philosophy of "Tao follows the example of nature."

Architecture Type

The size of a garden architecture and the number of views attached to it depend on the scale and role assigned to each building. Garden architectures can be categorized into two types: buildings built for residing and living and buildings built for sightseeing and resting. Neatly symmetrical patterns are more commonly used for the former, and free and lively patterns are more popular in the latter kind. Sometimes, buildings of these two types would keep distance from each other. At other times, they are integrated into one group. Some imperial gardens were separated from imperial palaces, serving as the temporary palaces outside the capital. Some imperial palaces were simply built inside imperial gardens. For instance, both the Old Summer Palace and the Summer Palace in Beijing have an independent scenic area in which palaces were built for emperors to handle governmental affairs and to live. In the Mountain Resort at Chengde, palace area was specially located in the key area of the resort as an independent scenic area, where buildings were placed in a neat symmetrical layout to create a solemn and orderly atmosphere. Being the crucial focus of garden construction, buildings for

FIG. 75 Yuanxiang Hall and Yiyu Gallery (Leaning Against Jade Gallery) in the Humble Administrator's Garden
Yuanxiang Hall is a four-sided hall structure sitting right in the center of the central area of the garden. To the north, across the water, there are a rockery and Xue Xiang Yun Wei Pavilion and Daishuang Pavilion (Pavilion of Expecting Frost). To the northeast, there is Wu Zhu You Ju Pavilion (Pavilion of Phoenix Tree and Bamboo) that is famous for deep and far views. To the northwest, there are He Feng Si Mian Pavilion and Jianshan Tower (Jian Shan Lou, Mountain-in-View Tower). To the southwest, there is Xiaofeihong Bridge (Little Flying Rainbow Bridge). To the east, there are Xiuqi Pavilion, Pipa Pavilion (Loquat Pavilion), and other buildings. To the south, there are pond and rockery functioning as obstructive scenery. In all, each and every side of the hall offer unique scenery.

sightseeing and resting could present almost all the techniques, concepts, and arts in garden construction. Therefore, garden architectures include a variety of types and forms. You'd find introductions to several usual types as follows.

Hall (*ting* and *tang*), gallery (*xuan*) and lodging (*guan*). Halls, the principal buildings to be considered in garden designs, are mainly used for formal occasions like receiving friends and guests and, sometimes, for enjoying beautiful views as well. As an integral component of a garden, halls can take on flexible and varied styles. From the structural perspective, they can be divided into two types, i.e. *ting*—halls using rectangular beam and pillars—and *tang*—halls using round beam and pillars. A lotus

FIG. 76 Furong Gazebo in the Humble Administrator's Garden
It is situated at the bank of a pond in the east section of the Humble Administrator's Garden. Being an important architecture in the east section, it faces west and offer deep and far views. With peaches and willows adorning the banks of the pond, the scenery in this area is very beautiful. It was named "lotus" because it is the best place for people to enjoy lotus in summer. Half of its foundation stands in water and the other half rests on the bank. The half above water is supported by a stone beam and pillar structure. There is a lady stay lining around four sides of the waterside pavilion for visitors to rest.

hall is one type of larger-scaled hall built at waterside with a spacious platform in front of it for people to enjoy waterscapes, e.g. Hanbi Mountain Hall (Hall of Green Water) in Lingering Garden. A lovebirds hall is another kind of hall, whose internal space is separated into a front part and a back part with a partition screen, an indoor umbrella, or a gauze screen. As for internal structure, if one part uses rectangular beam and pillars, then the other will use round beam and pillars. As a result, a lovebirds hall looks just as if a *ting* and a *tang* were stuck together. That's why it was named "lovebirds hall." Its south half is a genial space for people to stay in winter and spring, while in contrast, its north half is refreshing and suitable for visitor to stay in summer and autumn. A typical example of a lovebirds hall is Yanyu Hall (Yan Yu Tang, Hall of Swallow Fame) in Lion Grove Garden. As for a four-sided hall, all the four walls are replaced by partition boards for the convenience of sightseeing. Meanwhile, the architecture looks so exquisite and provides wide, open, and spacious views. A four-sided hall usually has around itself a winding corridor with hanging fascias decorating the eaves in each span and preparing a belt of balustrade with seats for people to rest. It must be pointed out that four-sided halls are the most sophisticated and exquisite among all garden architectures. A typical example of four-sided halls is Yuanxiang Hall in the Humble Administrator's Garden (Fig. 75).

Xuan and *guan* are variations of halls, but not as important as halls. They are smaller buildings built mainly as scenic spots, e.g. Zhu Wai Yi Zhi Gallery (Gallery of a Few Bamboos) in Master of the Nets Garden, the Qingfengchi Lodging (Lodging of Breezes and Pond) in Lingering Garden and the Yiyu Gallery (Gallery of Agreeable Rains) in Individual Garden.

Gazebo (*xie*) and stone boat (*fang*). Both gazebos and stone boats are waterside buildings. To achieve harmony between the building and water surface, all the lines on the building from its overall contour to its detailed parts, like doors, windows, balustrades, and goose-neck chairs are horizontal. Most *xie* are waterside belvederes, but their specific structure depends on their environment. Usually, half of the foundation of a waterside pavilion stands in water and another half sits on a bank. The half above water is usually supported by a stone structure. The façade facing water is often left open with balustrades sheltering the side. Most of them have a gable and hip roofs that are supported by exterior pillars, for example Furong Gazebo (Lotus Gazebo) in the Humble Administrator's Garden (Fig. 76).

Stone boat, also called "boat on land," is a kind of boat-like structure built by the waterside. A stone boat is composed of three sections—front, middle, and back. The front part is the highest of the three and the middle part is the lowest. The back part is usually a two-floor structure from which one could take a look at the distance, just like the tail of a real painted boat in Suzhou. Most staircases in stone boats are concentrated in a section between the middle

and the back part where there is also a door leading to the lower deck. The front part usually has an open façade. Low walls are built at either side of the front and middle part, and a series of long windows would be fixed to the low walls above them. Contrary to the front and middle parts, the back part usually uses whitewashed walls to create a visual contrast to the other two. Exemplary works include Xiangzhou Stone Boat (Fragrant Isle Stone Boat) in the Humble Administrator's Garden and Buxizhou Stone Boat (Anchorless Stone Boat) in Warm Garden (Fig. 77).

Tower and belvedere (*lou* and *ge*). Towers and belvederes are outstanding parts of a garden because of their superior sizes and heights. They stand either on top of a hill or rockery, providing visitors with a bird view, or at the back of a garden as the climax that concludes the entire garden layout, e.g. Foxiang Tower on Mt. Longevity in the Summer Palace and Shangdi Tower on Jinshan Island in Mountain Resort at Chengde. If used as foil sceneries, towers, and belvederes are usually placed in a secluded location, e.g.

Tianxiang Belvedere (Tian Xiang Ge, Belvedere of Fragrance from Eden) in Nearby Garden (Fig. 78), Yuancui Belvedere (Yuan Cui Ge, Belvedere for a Far View of Green Wood), and Huan Wo Du Shu Chu (Tower of Returning to Reading) in Lingering Garden.

Pavilion (*ting*). Pavilions are built to provide visitors with a place to rest and extend their views to the remote places. In addition, they are also important decorations to the garden landscapes. A saying that "A garden without pavilions is not a real garden" indicates the status of a pavilion to a garden. Pavilions could be ranked into two kinds,

FIG. 77 Buxizhou Stone Boat in Warm Garden
First built in 1410, it was located at Changjiang Road in Nanjing. When Emperor Chengzu of the Ming Dynasty conferred the title of Prince Han on his second son, Zhu Gaoxu, Warm Garden was the west garden of the prince's residence. It was built on an irregular site and the pond, like a narrow and long trench, runs from south to north. The Anchorless Stone Boat is situated on the south side of the pond with two stone bridges connecting it with both sides of the pond.

FIG. 78 Tianxiang Belvedere in Nearby Garden
Nearby Garden is located in today's Changzhou Hotel, Changsheng Lane in Changzhou. It is a classical garden in the late Ming architectural style, built in the early Qing Dynasty that still exists in the Yangtze River Delta.

FIG. 80 Fan-shaped pavilion in Garden of Autumn Vapors
The planar layout of this pavilion looks like an unfolded fan, with its large arc extending outward and its small arc inclining inward. It is a distinct style of its own.

FIG. 81 Fang Zhu Lin Liu Pavilion (Pavilion on Fragrant Isle Confronting a Stream) in the Mountain Resort
It is the 27th spot among the 36 scenic spots named by Emperor Kangxi in the Mountain Resort. Built in 1703, it is a waterside square pavilion with double eaves. With three sides facing water, it erects on a natural stone bank. Taking a rest here and watching the running water, a visitor can easily calm his heart and refresh his mind.

FIG. 79 Jishan Pavilion (Pavilion Close to Hill) in Garden of Autumn Vapors
Built in the Ming Dynasty, Garden of Autumn Vapors was located in Jiading, Shanghai. The pavilion is built at a site half way to the top of the rockery. When a visitor stands at the foot of the rockery and looks up at it, it gives an eye-catching scenic spot of the entire landscape. When a visitor stands in the pavilion and take a look at the scenery around the pavilion, he will enjoy a broad view.

half pavilion and independent pavilion. The former kind is named because they are usually attached to covered corridors or leaning against a wall. Independent pavilions usually stand beside a pond, on the top of a hill, or in dense woods or flowers, accordingly, their positions and shapes match their surroundings fairly well (Fig. 79).

Pavilion styles vary a lot. Based on their planar layouts, they can be classified into triangle, square, rectangular, diamond and double diamond, round, half-moon, fan-shape (Fig. 80), and double-ring pavilions. Based on their façade designs, they can be ranked into single-eave pavilions, which are more popular, and double-eave pavilions. As for their roofs, pavilions absorb every kind of roof that has ever appeared in Chinese architectural history. The specific structure of a pavilion depends on its planar and façade designs.

Generally speaking, as far as single-eave roof is concerned, a square pavilion has four or twelve pillars to support it. A six-cornered pavilion requires a six-pillar structure and an eight-cornered pavilion requires an eight-pillar structure. As far as a double-eave roof (Fig. 81) is concerned, a square pavilion can use sixteen pillars at most. Six-cornered and eight-cornered pavilions should double the number of pillars in a single-eave pavilion, using twelve and sixteen pillars. Doors or windows are not available anywhere between two pillars, but it is permitted to use a low wall or a section of low balustrade between two pillars.

Corridor (*lang*). Among all garden architectures, a corridor helps to link different buildings together and often serves as a sightseeing route. Corridors could twist and turn, rise and fall in accordance with the geographical features. They add more changes to the landscape and from a functional perspective, divide spaces into subsections and improve the depth of views.

Based on their external shapes, covered corridors can be categorized into four types; straight, zigzag, wavy, and double-pavement. According to their physical locations, they can be ranked into wall-side corridor, independent corridor, winding corridor, two-storey corridor, climbing-hill corridor, and waterside corridor. A corridor can be located anywhere, embracing a pond or a wood, climbing up a hill, running through a dense green

shade, or flying across water, linking other buildings, rockeries, and ponds as a whole, granting more beauty to garden architectures and scenic sports. As far as zigzag corridor is concerned, they are full of twists and turns. And except for a small section built against walls, most part of a zigzag corridor extends away from the walls while winding its way outward and create a series of smaller courtyards of different shapes between the wall and itself, where flowers and rock pieces could be arranged (Fig. 82). A double-

FIG. 82 Zigzag corridor in Garden of Zeng's and Zhao's Families
The beauty of this corridor lies in its zigzagging shape. Usually, a zigzag corridor can twist and turn, rise and fall in accordance with the geographical features. Sometimes, it couches in the waist of a mountain like a curling dragon. Sometimes, it stays at the remote end of a stream. It links different landscapes together with its zigzagging route, brings more depth to the garden space, and adds more attractiveness to the garden itself.

pavement corridor can be regarded as two corridors combined together side-by-side with only one partition wall in between. Usually, this partition wall is decorated with window openings. Both pavements are smooth for travelers (Fig. 83).

Two typical examples of double-pavement corridors are the one in the southwest corner of Great Wave Pavilion and in front of Lixue Hall (Li Xue Tang, Hall of Standing in Snow) in Lion Grove Garden. As the name suggests, a two-storey corridor has two floors and is often built near a tower or a hall, e.g. the two-storey corridor beside Jianshan Tower in the Humble Administrator's Garden (Fig. 84). A climbing-hill corridor can only be built on a rolling slope, connecting buildings at the foothill and on the hill top. Meanwhile, the corridor would be a scenic spot in itself,

FIG. 83 Double-pavement corridor in Garden of Pleasure
Originally, there was no Garden of Pleasure but two neighboring gardens. The garden in the east was a residence belonging to Wu Kuan, a minister of the Ming government. The garden in the west was the private garden of Gu Wenbin. Later, Gu's family took over the east garden and integrated the two into one. The double-pavement corridor is the partition wall separating the east part and the west part. Each part has independent landscapes and charms. The east garden is dominated by a building complex, while the west garden is particularly known for waterscapes.

FIG. 84 Two-story corridor beside Jianshan Tower in the Humble Administrator's Garden
The two-story corridor was exquisitely designed and constructed. The architecture echoes with its own reflection in water, forming a delightful contrast. Looking out through the carved windows of the corridor, a visitor could capture some vague but beautiful views of the other side. The entire corridor delivers a far-reaching artistic conception.

adding more charming views to the garden. A good case in point is the one on the back hill of Qionghua Island in Beihai Park (Fig. 85).

Paving

Paving of roads, courtyards, and squares, a very critical element to a good garden, is in fact more artistic than indoor paving. Generally, mountain and slope roads are paved with regular or irregular stones or bricks. More often than not, rocks and plants are scattered along both sides for decoration. In some imperial gardens and even some private gardens, colored pebbles, broken brick chips, and tile rubbles, as well as pottery and porcelain fragments were adopted to patch up animal, plant, or geometrical mosaics, adding more artistic elements to roads and courtyards. These mosaics physically demonstrate the wisdom and creativity of ancient Chinese garden makers. Except for the slab-stone pattern, paving patterns are

FIG. 85 Climbing-hill corridor on the back hill of Qionghua Island in Beihai Park
On the north slope of Qionghua Island, there are several building complexes linked together with rockeries and the climbing-hill corridor, e.g. Mujian Room and Kanhua Corridor (Corridor for Appreciating Paintings).

FIG. 86 "Live as long as pines and cranes" decorative paving in the Lingering Garden

FIG. 87 "Plum Flower" decorative paving in the Garden of Pleasure

FIG. 88 "Fan" decorative paving in the Master of the Nets Garden

FIG. 89 Partition boards in Yan Bo Zhi Shuang Hall (Yan Bo Zhi Shuang Dian, Hall of Refreshing Mists and Ripples) in the Mountain Resort

generally called "decorative paving (*hua jie pu di*)." Exemplary paving works can be found in the Imperial Garden in the Forbidden City, the Summer Palace, the Humble Administrator's Garden, and Lingering Garden (Figs. 86, 87, 88).

Decoration, Furniture, and Furnishing

The key to Chinese classical garden decoration is to integrate garden landscapes and garden architectures into an inclusive environment to make the garden views more enjoyable for sightseeing. For instance, doors, windows, partition boards, as well as grill headers, hanging fascias, balustrades, screens, curtains, windows, and indoor umbrellas must serve two purposes, i.e. dividing spaces into smaller sections and keeping the connection between different spaces (Figs. 89, 90). There is a variety of patterns and forms available for a designer to choose from according to their specific positions and environments. Another distinctive feature of garden decorations is their demands for high quality materials and craftsmanship. For example, garden furniture is usually made of such valuable materials as red sandalwood, rosewood, boxwood, and nanmu. To achieve a sense of simple elegance, the craftsmen would not conceal the original timber colors with paints.

Elegance, natural taste, and uniqueness are the essence to garden furniture and furnishing, so that they can meet with their functional needs—living, guest receiving, banqueting, and resting, and meanwhile play a decorative role. They set off the contrastive relationship between protagonist scene and their foil scenes and supply empty spaces so that such spaces won't appear too vacant or void. In addition, they reflect the lifestyle and ideology that the previous garden owner had. There is a great multitude of furniture and furnishing, for example, beds, low beds, tables, chairs, tea tables, stools, cabinets, cupboards, antique shelves, lamp stands, flower pots, fishbowls, bird cages, bronze caldrons, incense burners, music instruments, swords, antiques, calligraphy works, paintings, and the four treasures of study (writing brushes, ink stick, ink slab, and paper). One advantage of furniture and furnishings is that they are mobile and may be moved or replaced on different occasions or for different seasons (Fig. 91).

FIG. 90 Swan-neck-shaped armchairs and hanging fascias attached to Sheya Corridor (Duck Shooting Corridor) in the Master of the Nets Garden

Inscription Board

Inscription boards (*bian e*) can be classified into two kinds. The horizontal ones are called "*bian*" and the vertical ones "*e*." They are usually displayed above the lintel of the entrance of a building, on the door-facing wall of a hall, or right below the main beam of a hall (Fig. 92).

Inscription boards are a unique component of Chinese classical gardens. Although they are not and indispensible structural parts of any building, they do add more specialties to a garden, effectively broadening the cultural connotation and heightening the decorative art of a garden. Almost all important buildings in the Summer Palace, Beihai Park, and the Mountain Resort at Chengde, and the private gardens in Suzhou, Yangzhou, and other Yangtze River Delta cities have inscription boards to bring out the theme and describe the physical sceneries, cultural connotation, artistic conception, and special features of the hosting building and its surroundings, which usually can motivate visitors to associate the building and its surroundings with their feelings and emotions.

Wall, Window and Door Opening

In Chinese classical gardens, the wall is an important factor of space composition used for separating spaces, setting off scenes, and blocking eyesight. But too many

FIG. 91 The view inside Wufengxian Lodging (Celestial Lodging of Five Peaks) in Lingering Garden

Fig. 92 Inscription boards and couplets on front pillar in Dianchun Hall (Dian Chun Tang, Hall of Counting Spring) in He Garden

FIG. 93 Carved windows in Lingering Garden

FIGS. 94 — 97 Four examples of carved windows with patterns of musical instrument, chess, book and painting in Lion Grove Garden

FIG. 98 Carved windows and a door opening in He Garden

walls in a garden would definitely result in a sense of tedious boredom. To solve this problem, garden makers began to arrange carved windows, door openings, and window openings on these walls to create various contrasts—like light vs. shade, imaginary scenes vs. actual scenes, to bring more lively changes to walls (Fig. 93).

Carved windows are also called "decorated wall openings." Carved windows can bring some changes to a dull and boring wall. And more importantly, views behind the wall with carved windows are "partly hidden and partly visible," and thus, more scenic layers are supplied to the space seemingly separated by the wall. In addition, when lit by sunlight from different angles, the patterns in the carved windows will bring about changing and diversified shades. This effect could bring more liveliness to garden scenery. There are many different carved window patterns which generally can be categorized into two groups—geometrical patterns and animal and plant patterns. The geometrical patterns include zigzag pattern,

cross pattern, pattern (Swastika), hexagon pattern, octagon pattern, diamond pattern, pen shaft, interlocking ribbon, linked squares, ice cracks, wave pattern, and their combinations. The animal and plant patterns consist of deer, phoenixes, bats, cranes, pines, bamboos, plum flowers, orchids, banana leaves, lotuses, guavas, and peaches. In addition to the above two categories, there are patterns like Chinese characters, the four treasures in a study, antiques, and patterns based on eminent persons and story plots (Figs. 94 – 97).

Gates without door planks (door openings) or windows without window sashes (window opening) are usually fixed to the garden walls, corridors, and pavilions walls. In addition to their basic functions—enabling passengers, sunlight, and fresh air to pass through, they are often used as frames for visitors to capture vivid images during their sightseeing tour. With door openings and window openings, views in different

spaces are able to enter or merge into each other to achieve the effect of expanding space both in depth and in width (Fig. 98).

Door openings can take many different shapes. Square, rectangular box, oval, polygon,

FIG. 99 The door opening in Yu Shui Tong Zuo Gallery (Gallery of "With Whom Shall I Sit") in the Humble Administrator's Garden

flowers, fruits, leaves, and even daily utensils are the most frequent patterns (Figs. 99, 100). Window openings have even more options, e.g. squares, vertical and horizontal rectangular boxes, hexagon, octagon, round, half moon, crescent, fan-shape, vase, bodhi-leaf, gourd, and plum flower. Some gardens were even assigned a wall to display different patterns just like a painting exhibition held in a gallery, so as to add more features to the garden scenery (Fig. 101). In Individual Garden in Yangzhou, an extremely novel wall—holey ventilated wall with a matrix of holes—was made beside Winter Hill. When winds blow through these holes, it sounds just like the roaring winter gale, bringing a special attractiveness to the garden (Fig. 102).

The exact shape and proportion of a door opening and a window opening depends on the detailed designs of rooms, walls, and spatial condition of the local environment. For instance, larger and simple-styled moon gates and octagon openings are better choices for a wall which separates a major scenic area into two halves for travelers to pass through. Smaller and intricate openings with diversified patterns are more suitable for covered corridors and small courtyards. Similarly, because of the inherent conciseness and simplicity, vertical and horizontal rectangular boxes and square patterns are the most suitable patterns for halls, pavilions, and waterside pavilions. Since window openings are built for people to see views in the distance, they should offer convenience for human eyes to extend their sight.

FIG. 100 A door opening in Lion Grove Garden

FIG. 101 Window openings in the Rockery Built with Pieces of Stones of He Garden

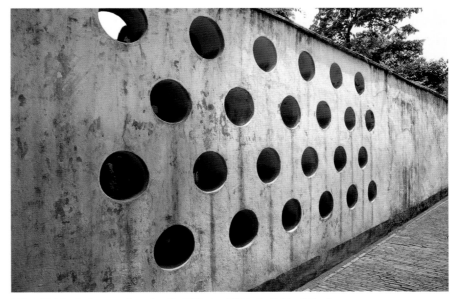

FIG. 102 The holey ventilated wall of Winter Hill in Individual Garden

5. Plant Arrangements

View making with plants is one of the essential elements in Chinese classical gardens. Based on the physical attributes of plants, e.g. pose, color, reflection, and shade, plants can join up with buildings, rockeries, and water bodies in the garden to create a unique landscape. On a windy, rainy, or snowy day, plants can produce tuneful sounds in a garden, which will not only add more brilliance to the landscape, but also offer people inside the garden a special aesthetic experience. Moreover, a good garden maker can endow plants with personified moral connotations such as integrity, nobleness, or a free and easy personality, and with more fairly poetic concepts.

There are plenty of species of garden plants available, basically classified as arbores, bushes, flowering shrubs, vines, herbal flowers, bamboos, and aquatic plants.

In Architectural Spaces

In addition to providing shade, fragrance, colorful views, and space partition, plants can enrich the scenic composition as an escort to buildings. A building and plants around it can bring out the best of each other if the contrast, interpenetration, transition, setting off, and similar relationships between them are handled properly. Such relationship can best reflect the combination of man-made beauty and natural beauty and bring more content into the scenic spot.

Small plant ornaments, e.g. one or two banana trees, bamboo, or bonsais, are meant for single or

FIG. 103 **Plants outside a carved window in the Master of the Nets Garden**

piecemeal spaces in, for example, a courtyard to break up the monotonous boredom in the garden, achieve interaction between imaginary scenery with realistic scenery, and realize the effect of "changing views from different angles." Arbores like phoenix trees or scholar trees are good choices for open and spacious courtyard. Areas in front of and at back of a room are good locations for trees with vivid colors, fragrance, and elegant poses, e.g. plum trees and bamboo. It must be pointed out that if too

many trees are planted around a building, the physical beauty and lighting of the building itself will be compromised, and that a proper space should be kept between a building and the trees around it.

The window openings, carved windows and door openings are built for traffic and communication, for expanding spaces, and for enjoying garden scenes (Fig. 103). In such places, it is ideal to plant trees that grow slowly, and thus are able to maintain their appearance for a long period of time, and have elegant poses and bright colors. The obscure image of a green twig, or a banana leaf, or a few bamboos stretching at a slant outside a half-closed window is absolutely picturesque. A few sword-like rocks or Taihu Lake rocks settled aside would balance the image and maintain a relatively long-lasting composition featuring the conflict between calm rocks and lively plants. Outside those windows which introduce daylight into room, it is better to grow a few red maples, camellias or azaleas. The red flowers, leaves or fruits in front of a white wall, simply like dancing flames, constitute an extraordinary visual effect When handling the stiff and rigid lines in the corners of a building, a garden maker could soften and mitigate the hardness with a small delightful ornament by arranging some plants together with a few rocks. When

it comes to waterside buildings, any plant that could block the eyes from waterscape must be resolutely removed. Pavilions are good places to arrange a larger wood. Or, it is possible to plant a few tall arbores beside the pavilion and accompany them with some lower flower shrubs. Typical works of this kind include Xiuqi Pavilion in the Humble Administrator's Garden and the fan-shape pavilion in Lion Grove Garden.

On Hill and Rockery

Prior things to consider before arranging plants on a hill are the species, position, density, pose, and growing speed of plants. In general, deciduous trees with sparse branches are the best options for a flat slope, though they are not supposed to be too closely planted. If it is a larger-scaled hill ridge, it is better to mix deciduous trees with evergreen trees. In this case, the span between trees could be

relatively smaller. If it is a cliff or cliff valley, pines with twisting branches reaching out of the valley are preferable over tall deciduous trees. It would be even better if those pines can be accompanied with some flower shrubs that grow slowly but present better poses, integrating coarse simplicity and gracious elegance together.

As far as rockeries with more earth than stones are concerned, the combination of taller deciduous trees and lower evergreen trees usually takes up the main body of the rockery. Then, under the crown of these trees, bushes are escorting them as the middle layer of plants and then flowers and grasses as the bottom layer. Such three-layer arrangement can accommodate more species of plants, among which the number of deciduous trees usually exceeds the number of evergreen trees. To enhance the wildness of a mountainous forest, it is better to allow the plants to grow freely and compete with each other in terms of height and prosperity. As far as rockeries with more stones than earth are concerned, a garden maker should plant fewer trees around the rockery, arrange them in a sparse layout, and accompany them with fewer bushes and grasses, to highlight the steepness and abruptness of rocks to the maximum extent. Lion Grove Garden and Lingering Garden are exemplary works of this style (Fig. 104).

The combination of evergreen trees and deciduous trees can be handled in a free way. Yet, there is not any definitive rules as to

FIG. 104 Plants outside Xiuzhu Belvedere (Xiu Zhu Ge, Belvedere of Slender Bamboo) in Lion Grove Garden

how many trees should be chosen from each species, either evergreen or deciduous. They tend to be arranged at the designers' will. The best options for trees on cliff walls are the pines or other trees that have twisted trunks and branches. Usually, these trees will try every means to stretch their branches outward for more sunlight. So, they'd naturally grow out of the cliff edge aslant, and consequently present very gracious images if trimmed appropriately.

On Water Surface

Plant arrangement beside water surface (e.g. ponds and pools) is very important to enriching the waterscape composition. Beside a pond, a few larger-sized deciduous or evergreen trees, which are rich in changes in their appearance, are usually planted. For one thing, these trees can substantiate the waterside space and serve as the transition between the gentle water surface and the hard revetments. For another, if a building or several buildings stand beside the water surface, these trees can set off the building(s) and tie the architectures of varied shapes together into an organic whole. For example, the pond in the Master of the Nets Garden has only a few trees along its bank, which effectively set off the entire garden landscape.

It is important to keep a wider span between every two trees at the waterside road and prevent them

FIG. 105 He Feng Si Mian Pavilion in the Humble Administrator's Garden

from blocking the sight of the waterscape.

Lotuses, water-lilies, duckweed, or other aquatic plants are frequent vegetation to add another layer of view on the water surface. But, some measures must be taken to prevent them from occupying the entire water surface and covering reflections in water. For example, in the Humble Administrator's Garden, when lotus on the water surfaces in the garden bloom in summer, the entire scene of green lotus leaves and pink lotuses, and the heart-touching fragrances that gentle breezes bring to noses offer visitors a very delightful experience (Fig. 105).

FIG. 106 Zhichun Pavilion, Summer Palace, Beijing
If you stay in the pavilion, your vision can be extended up to 2000 meters away. All scenic spots will thoroughly be within your sight.

Chapter Four
Living Examples of Chinese Gardens

Though China has over 3,000 years of garden construction, the well-preserved classical gardens so far were mainly built in the Ming and Qing dynasties (the last two feudal dynasties) due to dynastic alternations in history and other political reasons. And those well-maintained gardens in northern China are basically royal gardens, while those in the south are private gardens assembling in the Yangtze River and Pearl River basins. This chapter will introduce 20 representative living examples selected from all the gardens available, the majority of which are royal gardens, and gardens attached to temples, and literati gardens.

1. Gardens in Northern China

Gardens in northern China are mainly imperial gardens. A great multitude of imperial gardens constructed in Beijing and its suburban areas during the Ming and Qing dynasties were fortunately well preserved and passed down through history. These imperial gardens could be divided into two

FIG. 107 The upturned eaves on the roof of Chengguang Hall, Beihai Park

categories. One is natural landscape gardens which directly adopt the natural mountains and streams, such as the Summer Palace in Beijing and the Mountain Resort in Chengde. The other is artificial landscape gardens on plain land, like the Old Summer Palace in Beijing. In general, these imperial gardens occupy larger spaces than private gardens, and their general arrangements are relatively more complex. Furthermore, as gardens were possessed by the ruling class, they also present complex and diversified symbolic features, serving to extol the royal hierarchy. The following examples are typical gardens in northern China which are relatively well-preserved up to now.

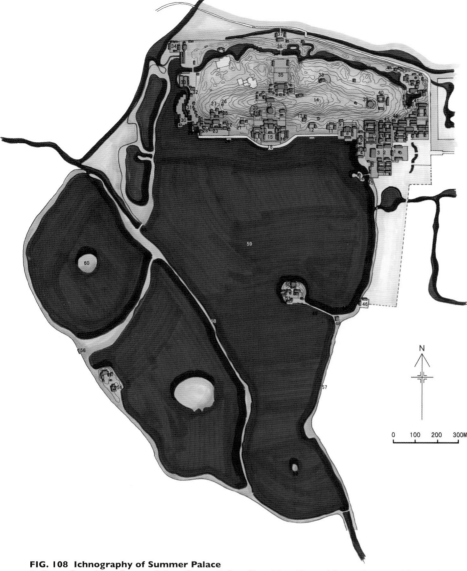

FIG. 108 Ichnography of Summer Palace
1. Dong Gong Men Eastern Palace Gate 2. Ren Shou Men Gate of Benevolence and Longevity
3. Ren Shou Dian Hall of Benevolence and Longevity 4. Yu Lan Tang Hall of Jade Waves
5. Yi Yun Guan Lodging Suitable for Ruta 6. De He Yuan Garden of Virtue and Peace
7. Da Xi Lou Grand Opera Tower 8. Le Shou Tang Hall of Happiness and Longevity
9. Yang Ren Feng Garden of Extolling Benevolence 10. Shui Mu Zi Qin Stream and Wood
Naturally in Touch 11. Yang Yun Xuan Gallery of Breeding Clouds 12. Wu Jin Yi Xuan Gallery of
Endless Charm 13. Xie Qiu Xuan Gallery of Composing on Autumn 14. Wan Shou Shan Mt.
Longevity 15. Pai Yun Dian Hall of Dispersing Clouds 16. Jie Shou Tang Hall of Lengthening Life
17. Qing Hua Xuan Gallery of Clear Brightness 18. Yun Hui Yu Yu Gateway of Cloudy Glow and
Jade Eaves 19. Fo Xiang Ge Tower of Buddhist Fragrance 20. Bao Yun Ge Tower of Precious
Clouds 21. Yun Song Chao Nest for Pine trees in Clouds 22. Shan Se Hu Guang Gong Yi Lou
Tower of Hill and Lake at One Sight 23. Ting Li Guan Lodging for Listening to Orioles
24. Yu Zao Xuan Fish Alga Gallery 25. Hua Zhong You House of Travelling in Pictorial World
26. Hu Shan Zhen Yi Gallery of True Sense of Lake and Mountain 27. Yu Quan Shan Yuquan
Mountain 28. Shi Zhang Ting Pavilion of Rocky Senior 29. Qing Yan Fang Stone Boat of National
Peace 30. Xiao Xi Ling Small West Cool Brook 31. Yan Qing Shang Tower of Extensive Elegant
Vision 32. Bei Que Shell Watch Tower 33. Da Chuan Wu Great Dock 34. Xi Bei Men
Northwest Gate 35. Xu Mi Ling Jing Nimbus Land on Sumeru Mountain 36. Su Zhou Jie Suzhou
Market Street 37. Bei Gong Men North Palace Gate 38. Hua Cheng Ge Tower Supported by
Blossom 39. Jing Fu Ge Tower of Great Fortune 40. Yi Shou Tang Hall of Benefiting Health
41. Xie Qu Yuan Garden of Harmonious Interest 42. Chi Cheng Xia Qi Rosy Glow in Red City
43. Dong Ba Suo Eight East Houses 44. Zhi Chun Ting Pavilion of Heralding Spring
45. Wen Chang Ge Tower of Prosperous Civilization 46. Xin Gong Men New Palace Gate
47. Tong Niu Copper Ox 48. Kuo Ru Ting Pavilion of Spacious Views 49. Shi Qi Kong
Qiao Seventeen Arches Bridge 50. Han Xu Tang Hall of Modesty 51. Jian Yuan Tang Hall of
Distinguishing Remote Views 52. Feng Huang Dun Phoenix Mound 53. Xiu Qi Qiao Bridge
of Embroidery 54. Chang Guan Tang Hall of Spacious Observation 55. Yu Dai Qiao Jade Belt
Bridge 56. Xi Gong Men West Palace Gate 57. Dong Di East Causeway 58. Xi Di West
Causeway 59. Kun Ming Hu Kunming Lake 60. Zhi Jing Ge Tower of Making Mirror

Summer Palace
颐和园
Best Preserved Imperial Garden in China

Location: Beijing
Floor Space: 290 hectares
Construction Year: 1115 – 1234
(Jin Dynasty)
Genre of Garden: imperial garden

Located in the western suburb of Beijing, more than 10 kilometers away from the city wall, the Summer Palace is the largest and best preserved imperial garden in China. The previous Summer Palace was pitifully burnt in 1860 by the Eight Allied Invasive Troops. And later, in 1888 Empress Dowager Cixi misappropriated the navy funds to reconstruct a new garden on its original spot and named it Yi He Yuan (Summer Palace). The existing Summer Palace is the product after this reconstruction.

The Summer Palace is composed of three sections: Mt. Longevity, Kunming Lake, and the palace area. It has long been renowned for its gardening technique of combining man-made architectures with natural landscapes. Kunming Lake was once the most spacious water surface among the great number of imperial gardens in Beijing. Several islands stand out of the water, and was connected by a long causeway and stone bridge. Mt. Longevity was located on the north bank of Kunming Lake. Ancient garden design artists and craftsmen arranged the appropriate garden architectures and scenic spots according to the landscape, taking full advantage of the superior natural conditions where a mountain was neighboring to a lake while they designed and constructed this garden (Fig. 108).

The palace area was built interior to the main entrance to the Summer Palace—the Eastern Palace Gate. Qinzheng Hall, the main building in this architectural complex, has nine spans on its eastern side. Renshou Gate (Gate of Benevolence and Longevity) was built in front of it, and two side halls stand to its north and south. The rooms outside Renshou Gate were called Jiuqing Offices (Offices for Nine Ministers) on both north and south sides. All these architectures constituted the major area for all political activities in the Summer Palace of the time. The emperors would spend almost more than two thirds of a year in this garden.

"View borrowing" technique was heavily applied while this garden was designed. In addition to taking into account how to coordinate garden architectures with their neighboring scenic spots, they had given attention to the surrounding natural environment, neighboring gardens, and buildings as well. Such a "view borrowing" technique, borrowing views from interior and exterior sceneries, expands the scale of this garden and enriches the sceneries as well.

The technique of "minor gardens inside a bigger garden" is an eloquent representation of how the Summer Palace took after Chinese traditions and utilized the local geographic features while designing and laying out scenic spots. There was a low-lying place at the eastern foothill of Mt. Longevity, where water accumulated into a pond. Designers used of this geographic feature and made it an independent minor garden, Xiequ Garden (Garden of Harmonious Interest). Such technique supplied the general arrangement with more varieties.

The Summer Palace is a miracle among all Chinese imperial gardens, where unusual natural landscapes integrates with man-made views, and enjoys supreme reputation at home and abroad for its mature art of garden construction and diversified architectural forms.

Kunming Lake

Kunming Lake, the major lake in the Summer Palace, occupies three quarters of its entire floor space, approximately 220 hectares. Located at the south section, the vast front lake with blue waves and misty ripples is facing the rolling mountain ranges to its west and architectural complexes to its north. The West Causeway divides Kunming Lake into three sections—West Lake, Yangshui Lake, and Great Lake.

The northern half of the water surface to the west of this causeway is called West Lake, with a tiny Yezhong Belvedere (Ye Zhong Ge, Belvedere of Casting Bell) in the middle of it; and its southern neighbor is called Yangshui Lake (Lake for Nurturing Water), with an isle called Zaojian Hall; the water surface to the east of the causeway is called Great Lake, with three islands, namely Zhichun Pavilion (Pavilion of Heralding Spring), Dragon King Temple, and Phoenix Mound, standing in a line from south to north. Extending your view westward from Kunming Lake or the lakeside, you will see that the landscapes exterior to the garden have melted into the mountain views and lake scenery interior to the garden. This is an outstanding example of the view borrowing technique typical of Chinese garden (Fig. 109).

FIG. 109 The spacious water surface of Kunming Lake

FIG. 110 A bird's eye view of Mt. Longevity and Foxiang Tower

Seventeen Arches Bridge

Seventeen Arches Bridge, the largest-scaled stone bridge in the garden, stretches across Kunming Lake, linking the East Causeway and South Lake Island together (Fig. 2). More than 500 stone lion statues of various postures and sizes are sitting on the top of railing on both sides.

Wanshou Mountain (Mt. Longevity)

Wanshou Mountain, originally named as Wengshan Hill (Jar Hill), 58.59 meters high, is the offshoot of the Western Mountains in Beijing and the last branch which extends from the main body of the Western Mountains to the Beijing plain area. To celebrate his Queen Mother's birthday—whose respected title was Empress Xiao Sheng Xian, Emperor Qianlong in the Qing Dynasty renamed this hill as Mt. Longevity (Fig. 110). On the front

hill area, the three-storey Foxiang Tower with eight sides and four eaves became the major building in a huge architectural complex. A slant central axis was created by Yun Hui Yu Yu Gateway (Gateway of Cloudy Glow and Jade Eaves) at the foot of the hill, Paiyun Gate, Secondary Palace Gate, Paiyun Hall, Dehui Hall (De Hui Dian, Hall of Virtue and Brilliance), Foxiang Tower, and Zhihuihai Hall on the hill top. A great multitude of foil buildings were arranged at either side of this axis. At the foot of the front hill, Long Corridor with 276 spans winds its way from east to west along the lakeside and the foot of the mountain. Its entire length is 755 meters. The twists and turns of the hill road in the posterior hill area are popular for its tranquility and winding features. Ancient pine trees lean against the road, adding more beauty to this picturesque landscape. At the foot of this

posterior hill is a winding stream called Suzhou River, along which visitors will sometimes find "the hill bend, the stream wind, and the pathway seems to end," and all of a sudden "past willows and flowers

FIG. 111 Indoor scene of Foxiang Tower

in bloom lies another village." It is tinted with the special flavor of the Yangtze River Delta landscapes. On the hillside of the posterior hill lies a group of Tibetan-temple-styled architectural complex, named Xu Mi Ling Jing (Nimbus Land on Sumeru Mountain). And the Glazed Pagoda with Treasures built with bricks and glazed tiles projects on the eastern hillside, where luxuriant woods enjoy their vitality.

Foxiang Tower

Foxiang Tower, a 41-meter-high architecture with eight sides, three storeys, four eaves, and with eight sky-scraper pillars inside it made from lignum vitae, was constructed on a square platform 21 meters in height at the front hill side of Mt. Longevity (Fig. 110). This building has a very complex structure, deserving to be a masterpiece among all classical architectures. It is the central building and the symbol of the whole garden, possessing supreme artistic value (Fig. 111).

Zhuanlun Zang (Revolving Archives)

Zhuanlun Zang was located to the west of Middle Hill Road on the front hillside of Mt. Longevity. The three-room-wide main hall has two storeys and three eaves, decorated with green glazed tiles on its roof. At either side of this front hall is a two-storey rotunda pavilion sheltering a wooden pagoda. This eight-side-and-six-floor pagoda served as storage for Buddhist scriptures and statues. This pagoda could be rotated if forcefully pushed, because an axle was fixed in its middle with a gear underground (Fig. 112).

FIG. 112 Zhuanlun Zang

FIG. 113 Panorama of Paiyun Hall

Paiyun Hall (Pai Yun Dian, Hall of Dispersing Clouds)

Paiyun Hall was situated in the center of the architectural complex in the front hill of Mt. Longevity. The literal meaning of "Pai Yun" indicates that the architectures seem to be located in celestial palaces on a mountain where celestial beings are bound to show up. Observed from afar, Paiyun Hall, its decorative archway, Paiyun Gate, Jinshui Bridge (Golden Water Bridge), and the Secondary Palace Gates were constructed along a straight line along the mountain slope, allowing it the most spectacular architectural complex in the Summer Palace (Fig. 113).

Qingyan Stone Boat (Stone Boat of National Peace)

Qingyan Stone Boat, more popularly known as Stone Boat, is perching at the western end of Long Corridor by the lakeside. Its name indicates that "the Huanghe River becomes clear, the seas calm down, and as a whole the country is peaceful." As the only European style construction, the 36-meter-long boat was built with marble pieces decorated with carvings (Fig. 114).

The boat was composed of two floors. Its deck was covered with floor tiles, its windows inlaid with color glasses, and its roof decorated with brick carvings. Raindrops on the roof would be drained into the lake through four hollow pillars which stand at the four corners, and then out of the four dragon mouth sculptures, truly making it an amazing design.

Baoyun Tower (Bao Yun Ge, Tower of Precious Clouds)

Baoyun Tower, a tower with double eaves and a gable and hip roof, was constructed on a Sumeru platform carved out of white marble stone, which stands in the very center of a courtyard. Four corner booths were built at the four corners of the winding corridor. And four three-span side-halls stand at four sides of this main building.

The northern half of the main building rises up with the mountain slope, and thus, was shaped into a staircase-shaped corridor and connected to its northern side-hall, Wufang Tower (Wu Fang Ge, Tower of Five Directions). The mountain gate of Fu Lan Nuan Cui

FIG. 114 Qingyan Stone Boat

(Vernal Green on Floating Mountain Ranges) was attached to the architectural complex to its south, functioning as the front gate from which a pair of splayed stone stair road lead you to the main courtyard.

Grand Opera Tower

This opera stage is currently the best preserved and the largest-scaled theater in China. Four years spent on the construction of this tower witnessed how it became a grandiose and majestic architecture 21 meters in height and 17 meters wide, with double eaves, upright rake angles, vermilion railings, and emerald pillars. The tower has three floors; the upper floor Fu Platform (Blessing Stage), the middle floor Lu Platform

FIG. 115 Grand Opera Tower

(Nobility Stage), and the lower floor Shou Platform (Longevity Stage). Grand Opera Tower was ingenuously designed (Fig. 115). The seven "sky wells" and mobile wooden stage boards on the floor allow the actors who played the roles of celestials to fall from heaven and permit the actors who played the roles of monsters to suddenly sneak underground. Thus, the stage could provide endless possibilities. A well and five square pools had been excavated beneath this Grand Opera Tower, which could spray water to display surging waves in accordance with plots like "Flooding over Mt. Jinshan."

Huacheng Tower (Hua Cheng Ge, Tower Supported by Blossom)

Hua Cheng Ge, located on the eastern slopes of the posterior hill in Mt. Longevity, is an exquisite and unique architectural complex composed of temples, halls, towers, corridors, rockeries, and a garden. The major buildings include Huacheng Tower, Liujian Zhai (Studio of Six Functions), Duobao Liuli Pagoda (Glazed Pagoda with Treasures) (Fig. 116), and a Buddhist temple called Lian Zuo Pan Yun (Lotus Platform and Crouching Clouds). Thus, this holistic architectural complex with diverse building genres like tower, hall, pagoda, and corridor became the finishing touch to the entire picturesque landscape on the posterior hill area of Mt. Longevity.

Qingzhixiu Rock

Qingzhixiu Rock, the largest ornamental stone in Chinese gardens, was placed in the courtyard of Leshou Hall in the Summer Palace. Lying on a stone

FIG. 116 Duobao Liuli Pagoda in Huacheng Tower

FIG. 117 Renshou Gate

base carved with sea tide patterns, this huge rock, eight meters long, two meters wide, and four meters high, looks more like an extensive screen. Its name was derived from its appearance, azure and smooth, like a piece of glossy ganoderma (Fig. 25).

Renshou Gate

Renshou Gate is the second palace gate to the palace area. Subtly combining diverse features of a decorative archway, secondary front gate to government offices, and Lingxing Gate (literally Star of Literature Gate, a popular architecture built in ancestral temples, palaces, and imperial mausoleums as the gate to paradise) together, it is a gate with distinctive features (Fig. 117).

FIG. 118 The Complex of Xu Mi Ling Jing

Complex of Xu Mi Ling Jing (Nimbus Land on Sumeru Mountain)

The Complex of Xu Mi Ling Jing, a group of more than twenty Buddhist temples varying in scale, and featuring both Tibetan and Han construction styles, stands on the hillside of the posterior hill of the Summer Palace. They scatter from north to south, interlacing each other on the mountain slope (Fig. 118). Thanks to its relatively higher altitude, it is a wonderful site for visitors to appreciate the views of the Western Mountains in the distance. And unlike typical Chinese tradition, the entire architectural complex is facing to the north, on account of its particular location.

Leshou Hall

Leshou Hall, a large four-sided courtyard house with two chain-courtyards standing in line from

FIG. 119 Indoor scenery of Leshou Hall   FIG. 120 Yang Ren Feng Garden

FIG. 121 Extending view from Hu Shan Zhen Yi Gallery to Yuquan Mountain

south to north and two wing courtyards at their sides, is the major building in the residence area of the Summer Palace. Facing Kunming Lake, leaning against Mt. Longevity, connecting with Renshou Hall to its east and Long Corridor to its west, this hall takes up the best position for residence and entertainment in the entire garden. Inside this hall are a throne, an imperial table, palm-shaped fans, and a glass screen. Next to the throne are two porcelain plates decorated with blue dragon figures that were supposed to contain fragrant fruits for people to enjoy the sweetness and four large copper sandalwood incense burners ornamented with nine peaches (Fig. 119). The west wing room served as a bedroom, while the east one a locker room.

Yang Ren Feng Garden (Garden of Extolling Benevolence)

Yang Ren Feng is a small garden to the west of Leshou Hall. The name of its main hall indicates that the emperors would implement a benevolent government in order to pacify the people. Physically, it is a fan-shaped building—block stones were arranged into the framework of a fan at the door steps, and white marble stones were carved into a roller, thus the entire architecture looks like a folding fan that you can seemingly fold and unfold at will (Fig. 120). That is why it is usually known as "Folding Fan Hall."

Extending View from Hu Shan Zhen Yi Gallery to Yuquan Mountain
Hu Shan Zhen Yi Gallery

(Gallery of True Sense of Lake and Mountain) is an open gallery with a wooden partition screen. Facing south, this gallery is three spans in width and has a gable and hip roof. It was located at the geographic turning point where the western front hill ridge of Mt. Longevity turns elsewhere. Its beams at the west side, exquisitely forming a picture frame, collecting the charming sceneries of the Western Mountains and Yuquan Mountain in the distance into a fantastic landscape picture (Fig. 121).

Yuzao Gallery (Fish Alga Gallery)

Its name oriented from the *Book of Songs*. Later generations made it a metaphor indicating the relationship between emperors and the people. That is to say, alga is to fish as common people is to emperors. Meanwhile, the name also suggests that each creature can get its due (Fig. 122).

FIG. 122 Yuzao Gallery

Six Bridges on West Causeway

West Causeway was built after a model of Sudi Causeway in the middle of West Lake in Hangzhou. The six bridge pavilions on this causeway are, from north to south, Jiehu Bridge (Lake Boundary Bridge), Wind Bridge, Jade Belt Bridge, Mirror Bridge, Ribbon Bridge (Fig. 123), and Willow Bridge.

Yudai Bridge (Jade Belt Bridge)

Jade Belt Bridge was located on Long Causeway in the middle of Kunming Lake. This bridge has only one arch, 11.38 meters wide and about 7.5 meters high, completely made from marble stones. The deck presents a double reverse curve and thus, has a wave-shaped profile. The exquisite breast board made of white marble stones set off its extraordinary magnificence. And

FIG. 123 Ribbon Bridge among the six bridges on West Causeway

the arch looks like the narrow point of an egg, rather lofty like a jade belt (Fig. 124).

Zhichun Pavilion

Zhichun Pavilion, a pavilion with double supporting pillars (with the interior pillars supporting the upper eaves and the exterior pillars the lower eaves), double eaves, and four angles, rests on an artificial island only slightly above the water surface by the side of the eastern bank of Kunming Lake (Fig. 106).

If you stay in the pavilion, your vision can be extended up to 2000 meters away. All scenic spots from the front hill area of Mt. Longevity, West Causeway, Yuquan Mountain, and the Western Mountains up to

FIG. 124 Jade Belt Bridge on West Causeway

FIG. 125 Suzhou Market Street

a mountainous garden in an urban region. All the architectures along Suzhou Market Street, either above water or by the side of water, echo with the scenic spots on Mt. Longevity. They were holistically arranged and orderly designed.

Xiequ Garden

Xiequ Garden, covering a sheer 0.8 hectares of land, is a typical minor garden inside a bigger garden—the Summer Palace (Fig. 126). It was located on the plain region at eastern foothill of Mt. Longevity, imitating the design of Jichang Garden, a prestigious garden constructed on Huishan Mountain in the Yangtze River Delta. And

Dragon King Temple, Seventeen Arches Bridge, and Kuoru Pavilion (Pavilion of Spacious Views) will thoroughly be within your sight. Either as a place for sightseeing or as an essential scenic spot, Zhichun Pavilion has taken up the supreme location.

Suzhou Market Street

Suzhou Market Street, located at the back lake in the Summer Palace, is an imitation of the market streets in the riverside cities of southern China. Hidden inside an imperial garden, tiny but exquisite, leaning against the mountain slope and facing a stream, this market seems like a tender picture of the Yangtze River Delta, ornamenting the construction axis from the posterior hill to the back lake (Fig. 125). Thus, Suzhou Market Street,

both a historical and cultural scenic spot and a unique natural landscape, sets off the tranquility and elegance in the back lake area and vividly presents the charm of

FIG. 126 Ichnography of Xiequ Garden
1. Yuan Men Garden Gate 2. Cheng Shuang Zhai Studio of Clear Refreshment 3. Zhu Xin Lou Fresh View Tower 4. Han Yuan Tang Hall with Far Vista 5. Zhan Qing Xuan Gallery of Clearness 6. Lan Ting Orchid Pavilion 7. Xiao You Tian Corridor Pavilion of Small Heaven 8. Zhi Chun Tang Hall of Heralding Spring 9. Zhi Yu Qiao Bridge of Knowing Fish's Happiness 10. Dan Bi Tranquil Greenery Studio 11. Yin Lü Pavilion of Drinking in Greenery 12. Xi Qiu Gallery of Bathing Autumn 13. Yin Jing Pavilion of Clear Mirror 14. Zhi Chun Ting Pavilion of Heralding Spring

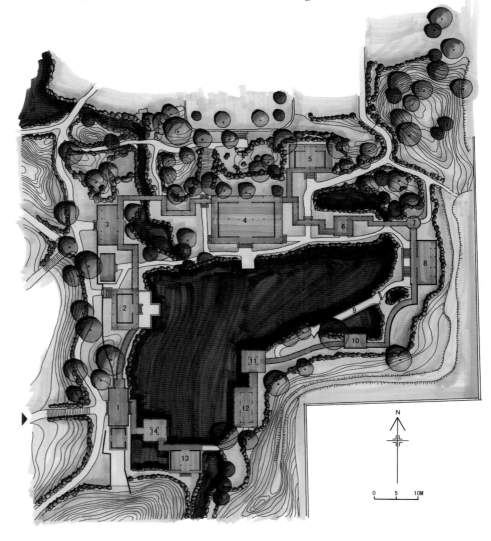

thus, Xiequ Garden became a "minor garden" of the highest reputation in China, thanks to the artistic conceptions typical of northern gardens and southern gardens being combined into one. Among all the gardens with the southern China style that Emperor Qianlong had constructed in northern China, this garden was fortunate enough to be the only one whose prototype still exists today.

Xiequ Garden cleverly enclosed a relatively secluded site at the eastern foothill of Mt. Longevity, making it a geographic component inside the Summer Palace, yet at the same time, a relatively independent entity. The terrain in this region appears higher in the north side and lower in the south. In the northern half, where a five-meter-high bare rock protrudes from the ground, rockeries were piled up, valleys were excavated, and clear water was introduced to create winding brooks within the rockeries. In contrast, in the low-lying southern half, a pond was excavated, an earth mound was piled up, and galleries or waterside pavilions scattered between the pond and the mound. As a whole, such a design basically accomplished a landscape garden with a hill (concrete and solid northern view) and a pond (vacant and low-lying southern view) relying on each other, along with transparent spring water in deep and secluded valleys, and with scattered galleries and open pavilions.

The garden entrance was located at the southwest corner, not only undoubtedly as a way to connect with hill roads and waterway outside the minor garden, but also as a magnifier to take advantage of this oblique perspective so as to expand your depth of focus and enrich the internal spatial level inside this garden. In regard to the entire arrangement, the pond is the very center of this garden around a dozen simple and elegant architectures of diverse scales like a hall, tower, pavilion, and gallery. Each scenic spot was connected to a hugging corridor—which extends like a circle or an embrace. All pavilions and galleries are open to the air, with railing couches named lady stay surrounding them (Fig. 127). A bridge called Zhiyu Bridge (Bridge of Knowing Fish's Happiness) lies above the green ripples, providing the passengers on the bridge with a view of colorful carps entertaining themselves.

The remarkable rockeries perching on the north bank were built after the rockeries in Lion Grove Garden in Suzhou, which was an imperial command issued by Emperor Qianlong. The stone materials chosen for the slope revetment stone and rockeries are precious and expensive Taihu Lake rocks. The architectures and rockery scenic spots like peaks, caves, wood-covered slopes, and lakesides were alternatively laid out. Both architectures and rockeries are few in quantity and small in scale. The majority of rockeries were assembled in the north half, where a huge stone piece projects from an even plain. Its northern slope, so steep and cliffy as if it were cut with a sharp ax, presents an air of rugged steepness. Thus, its eastern front slope is naturally spared for a man-made rockery peak, on the top of which a square pavilion was situated. Sticking out and towering above, the natural huge stone and the artificial rockery hill were intimately integrated into a holistic one, composing a magnificent and living spatial picture. In addition, a stream of spring water winds its way across the courtyard, setting off the cliffs and architectures and vice versa. Thus, these rocky cliffs, deep

FIG. 127 Winding corridor

FIG. 128 Yinlü Pavilion and Xiqiu Gallery

valleys, flowing creeks, and falling springs constitute pairs of contrast: some natural and artificial, some rough and fine, and some static and dynamic. The entire garden overflows with wildness, which is rarely seen in gardens of northern China.

Hanyuan Hall (Han Yuan Tang, Hall with Far Vista) on the north bank of the pond is the main building of Xiequ Garden. It is five span in width and huge in scale, and has surrounding corridors attached to it. It is the major architecture in the garden. And, from Zhuxin Tower (Zhu Xin Lou, Fresh View Tower) on the west bank, you could overlook the scenery of the whole garden. The rest of the buildings are

mainly sitting on the south bank. The overwhelming landscapes on the north bank feature rockeries and brooks in woods, while the dominating views on the south bank are man-made architectures. In that case, they constitute a contrasting pair. Yinlü Pavilion (Pavilion of Drinking in Greenery) is confronting the major scenic spot— the rockeries. And extending your sight from Zhichun Hall (Zhi Chun Tang, Hall of Heralding Spring) on the east bank, you can appreciate the charming views of Mt. Longevity which is borrowed from afar, and which approaches to you through the vista lines constituted by Yinlü Pavilion and the rockeries. In this way, this spot becomes the most extensive perspective line in

this minor garden.

Yinlü Pavilion and Xiqiu Gallery were both built for sightseeing, located at the turning point of a zigzag pond, and exactly the joint point of two axes. The site sticks out into the water of the pond. When bending down to the clear ripples, you will see fish swimming among the algae, and as you look up you can catch sight of the rockeries and pine forest on the north bank. In return, when being watched from the east, north, and west banks, these two buildings are always in a prominent medium-shot position. And you will find that their proportion, shape, and decoration can all stand up to careful observation and appreciation (Fig. 128).

FIG.129 Zhiyu Bridge

Zhiyu Bridge

This bridge lies above the water surface at the southeast corner of the pond, like a slant enclosing a relatively small water surface. Yet the tiny pond is still connected to the bigger part as a holistic whole, only adding one more visual level to the entire scenery (Fig. 129). Likewise, the other three corners of the pond have corridors and bridges above water as well, supplying even more levels to the aquatic sceneries.

"Regular" or "irregular" in structure, "casually scattered" yet "maintaining a sense of orderly arrangement," all the architectures were laid out along two axis lines, a major line, and a minor line. The "major axis" interlinks all architectures from Hanyuan Hall to Yinlü Pavilion, composing a straight line all through the southern end to the northern end. Meanwhile, the "minor axis" starts from the palace gate and ends at Xiqiu Gallery (Gallery of Bathing Autumn). Taking these two axes into consideration, designers arranged the other buildings in line with the local conditions at will, and then connected them with horizontal constructions

like corridors and walls which rolled up and down and winded in zigzag ways. However, such an arrangement does not appear messy or disordered, but adds more vitality, flexibility, and diversity to the well-disciplined regularities.

Xiequ Garden has quite a few valuable aspects, being an imitation of a literati garden in the Yangtze River Delta and a re-creation based on its own natural geographical conditions. It indirectly reflects the high artistic reach and building style of garden construction during the Qing Dynasty.

Baihai Park and the Circular Wall
北海公园及团城
Most Exquisite Imperial Garden in the Capital

Location: Beijing
Floor space: 70.87 hectares
Constructed Year: 907 – 1125 (from the Liao Dynasty)
Genre of Garden: imperial garden

Beihai Park and the Circular Wall, located to the north of Zhongnanhai, Beijing, has 38.87 hectares of water surface and 32 hectares of land, and is currently the most representative imperial garden in China. The construction started from the Liao Dynasty at the northeast suburb of Nanjing of Liao. The dictators of Liao dredged the river system and constructed a temporary palace called Yao Yu (Jade Island) after the model of the celestial wonderland of Penglai. Later, the Yuan Dynasty planned the city of Dadu with Qionghua Island as its center and expanded the territory three times before renaming the island Wanshou Mountain or Wansui Mountain (both meaning Mt. Longevity), and renaming the pond Taiye Pond. Meanwhile, the imperial palace was constructed on the east bank of Taiye Pond. Even later during the Ming and Qing dynasties, this garden was the western palace garden exclusively belonging to the imperial families. And ever since then when the Ming Dynasty set up its political power, Taiye Pond was further divided into three, namely Nanhai, Zhonghai, and Beihai (Fig. 130).

All the architectures that were preserved up to now were built

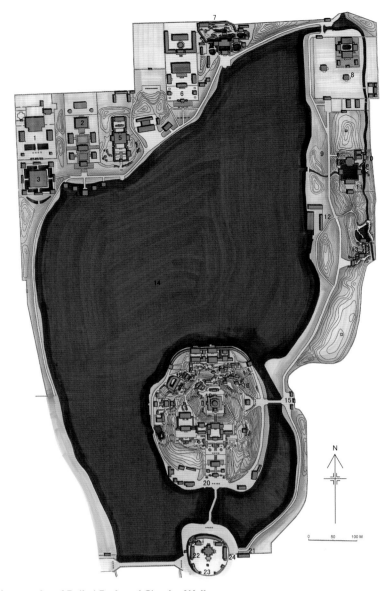

FIG. 130 Ichnography of Beihai Park and Circular Wall
1. Wan Fo Lou Tower of Ten Thousand Buddhas 2. Chan Fu Si Temple of Illustrating Good Fortune 3. Ji Le Shi Jie Complex of West Paradise 4. Wu Long Ting Five-Dragon Pavilions 5. Cheng Guan Tang Hall of Clear View 6. Xi Tian Fan Jing Buddhist Paradise 7. Jing Xin Zhai Studio of Tranquil Heart 8. Xian Can Tang Hall of Ancient Silkworm 9. Long Wang Miao Dragon King Temple 10. Gu Ke Ting Ancient Branches Yard 11. Hua Fang Zhai Painted Boat Studio 12. Chuan Wu Dock 13. Hao Pu Jian Garden Between Hao and Pu Rivers 14. Bei Hai North Sea 15. Dou Shan Men Steep Gate 16. Jian Chun Ting Pavilion of Spring in Sight 17. Xian Ren Cheng Lu Platform of Immortal Receiving Heavenly Dew 18. Mu Jian Shi Room for Appreciating an Acre of Land 19. Bai Ta White Pagoda 20. Qiong Hua Dao Qionghua Island 21. Sang Yuan Men Mulberry Garden Gate 22. Cheng Guang Zuo Men Left Gate of Receiving Sunlight 23. Tuan Cheng Circular Wall 24. Cheng Guang You Men Right Gate of Receiving Sunlight

when Emperor Qianlong was in power. Their layout can be roughly classified into two categories: one is the waterfront constructions and the other is small architectural complexes hidden on the shore. The east bank is typical of hidden architectural complexes, sheltering buildings inside the earth hills or forests. Thus, they become relatively independent, yet they all have accesses to the seaside. Therefore, they are by no means absolutely secluded but correlated with others as a whole.

The Circular Wall was located to the west of the southern gate of Beihai Park, in the central position within the triangle of Beihai, Zhonghai, the Forbidden City,

and Mt. Jing. It echoes with these imperial gardens, and together constitutes the most beautiful scenic area in the Beijing urban area. The Circular Wall is a nearly circular city tower, piled up with bricks. Crenels were built on the top around the edges. Two gates were opened in the east and west walls. The east gate was named Zhaojing Gate (Gate of Clear Landscapes) and the west gate Yanxiang Gate (Gate of Generating Good Luck), both with stairs leading to the top of the city tower. The entire city is more than five meters in height and occupies more than 400 square meters of land.

Both Beihai Park and the Circular Wall have significant value in the art of Chinese classical garden construction and are extremely important entities for historical researches of Beijing development.

Qionghua Island (Jade Sparkle Island)

Qionghua Island was Yao Yu (Jade Island) in the Liao Dynasty, Qionghua Island in the Jin Dynasty, and Wansui Mountain in the Yuan Dynasty (Mt. Longevity). During the Ming and Qing dynasties, this island was known as Qionghua Island or Wansui Mountain, or sometimes both (Fig. 3). It was only after 1651 when the White Pagoda was built that it was named White Pagoda Mountain.

The existing buildings on Qionghua Island can be roughly divided into four areas. The south architectures are a group of Buddhist temples known as Yong'an Temple. After passing through

FIG. 131 Dui Yun Ji Cui Archway

Dui Yun Ji Cui Archway (Piled Clouds and Accumulated Emerald Archway) (Fig. 131), from the mountain foot and then to the peak, visitors will see the main palace halls like Falun Hall (Fa Lun Dian, Hall of Dharma Wheel), Zhengjue Hall (Zheng Jue Dian, Hall of Right Consciousness), and Pu'an Hall (Pu An Dian, Hall of Universal Peace), and their side halls, corridors, a bell tower, and a drum tower. All of them were constructed during the Qing Dynasty. Its ichnography tells us that the temple complex could be grouped into two subsections on account of their specific locations on the terrain. In between, a stone stair road connects these two halves into an organic one (Fig. 132). And caves, tunnels, rockeries, individual rock pieces, stele towers, and stele pavilions were arranged along the rock stair road so that the temple was intimately connected with the garden landscapes. At the south foothill, a Shuanghong Gazebo (Gazebo of Twin Rainbows) and other architectures were built by the pond. Yet from the panorama perspective, the central position on the south slope of Qionghua Island was dominated by Yong'an Temple, which makes it too severe and less flexible.

On the cliffy west slope of Qionghua Island, an architectural complex known as Linguang Hall was constructed in accordance with the mountain range. Hill roads by its side are winding and indirect, occasionally blocked by some fences or moon gates. Thus, the entire atmosphere is rich in diversity and change. Turning right at the back of Linguang Hall, you will find a semi-circular enclosed building—Yuegu Tower along the foothill. The rockeries and winding hill road

FIG. 132 Stone stair road in the rockeries on Qionghua Island

at its back were connected to the north slope, composing a different style of construction.

The lower half of the north slope on Qionghua Island is fairly slow and mild, while in contrast, the higher half is rather steep and quick. Therefore, the architectures built on the north slope are grouped into two complexes according to their locations—the waterfront buildings and those built on cliffs. The major waterfront constructions include an extensive corridor and three projecting towers. This double-layer waterside corridor along the lakeside starts from Yiqing Tower (Yi Qing Lou, Tower of Ripple in Sunshine) in the east and ends its tour at Fenliang Belvedere (Fen Liang Ge, Belvedere of Sharing Coolness) in the west. Halfway on the corridor, three lofty architectures—Yuanfan Belvedere (Yuan Fan Ge, Belvedere of Distant Voyage, later Daoning Studio, Studio of Moral Peace), Bizhao Tower (Bi Zhao Lou, Tower of Green Glow, i.e. Yilan Hall), and the opera tower—introduce more view changes to the corridor. Turning to the cliffs, the main construction is a rockery with a host of decorative building dotting

within it. Fenliang Belvedere is the starting point in the west, and then Yaoshan Pavilion (Pavilion of Inviting Mountain), Hangu Hall, Xie Miao Stone Room (Stone Room of Painting Beauty), Pan Lan Vihara, Yi Hu Tian Di Pavilion (Universe in a Pot Pavilion), and the Fan-Shaped House appear subsequently on your way uphill. Furthermore, the Platform of Immortal Receiving Heavenly Dew stands upright among the rockery peaks. Other architectures built into diverse shapes and styles, like Yanjia Virhara (Virhara of Extending Wonder) and Baochong Room (Room of Maintaining Calm in Heart), are closely integrated with rockery peaks and caves like an organic whole.

The Platform of Immortal Receiving Heavenly Dew, a centralized expression of Chinese garden construction philosophy— "harmony between man and nature," stands on the north slope of Qionghua Island. On the top of a pillar made from white marble, 5.4 meters in height, a copper human statue in ancient costume holds a lotus-shaped copper plate above his head, which is popularly known as "Dew Plate" (Fig. 1). Emperor Qianlong had this statue molded based on the historical account that Emperor Wu of Han prayed to the celestials for immortality. This work of art serves as a theme scenic spot in the garden.

Hangu Hall is an independent courtyard located on the north slope of Qionghua Island. Leaning against the mountain ranges, it has a unique winding corridor and an ornamental gate. The climbing-hill corridor does not perch like a slanted line, but broken into three segments like a folding rule. Such a design is much closer to natural condition and presents a diversified shape.

A group of rockeries—a major rock piece set off by several minor ones—resting at the gate of Hanhu Hall function as the transition from man-made architecture to natural landscape. Though different in scale and scope, in both of the two courtyards, Hangu Hall and Mujian Room, stone stair roads help to link the ornamental gate and the main architectures. Inside the courtyard of Hangu Hall, the stone stair road extends further into the natural hill rocks which organize a flower bed platform, where an ancient Chinese lacebark pine stands upright. Rocks crouching beside the ancient tree constitute an artistic picture (Figs. 133, 134).

Even the east slope on Qionghua Island has its scenic places with pretty views as well, yet it is basically a botanical garden, where man-made architectures occupy the least proportion. The corridor winds its way along the hill slopes, turning and twisting.

The four hillsides of Qionghua Island in Beihai Park present varied views of their specific charms, since they were designed based on their local conditions and geographic features. This planning and design can be ranked as imaginative and original. All architectures on the island are chief scenic spots themselves, yet the vast majority of them are significant places of sightseeing, where you can either overlook the three seas, or extend your view to the remote horizon, covering every corner inside and outside the capital city. In general, the entire island is so gracious, dignified, and well proportioned, ornamented with architectures painted into strongly contradistinctive colors—red, yellow, and all other colors—appearing or disappearing within the greenery. A snow-white pagoda concludes the entire design on the hilltop. When the views are reflected in the seas, the sky and the water melt into each other, and the gleams from the architectures echo each other from the hilltop to foothill.

FIG. 133 Hangu Hall and Mujian Room on Qionghua Island

FIG. 134 The climbing-hill corridor of Hangu Hall

FIG. 135 Circular Wall

FIG. 136 Chengguang Hall

The Circular Wall in Beihai Park

The Circular Wall was located at the west side of the South Gate to Beihai Park. This was a tiny isle in the Yuan Dynasty. During the Ming Dynasty when the isle was reconstructed, city walls were built, the water surfaces to its east and south were filled with earth and leveled, and thereafter, the fundamental scale and surrounding views of the Circular Wall came into being (Fig. 135). The current Circular Wall was basically built during the reign of Emperor Qianlong. Its ichnography appears as a round circle. It was piled up with bricks, up to 4.6 meters above the ground, and 276 meters in perimeter, covering an area of 4,553 square meters. A passenger gate was built in the east and west walls under a gate tower. The east gate was named Zhaojing Gate and the west one Yanxiang Gate. Inside the gate, a stone stair road leads you to the tower platform, which was arranged symmetrically and dealt with according to garden construction techniques. Chengguang Hall (Cheng Guang Dian, Hall of Receiving Sunshine) is the very center of the entire the Circular Wall, with Yuweng Pavilion (Pavilion of Jade Jar) standing to the south and Jingji Hall (Jing Ji Tang, Hall of Promotion with Respect) to the north. These three architectures constitute the axis above the city tower. The entire city tower was built with red bricks and covered with yellow tiles. And among the brilliant and grandiose architectural complex are scores of luxuriant pines and cypresses.

Chengguang Hall, typical of the Qing style and the major

FIG. 137 Chinese lacebark pine

architecture of the Circular Wall, was constructed in 1743 on the original site of Yitian Palace, which was built during the Yuan Dynasty. Its centre is square, three rooms in width and deep. Four side halls were attached to the central hall at each side, to make the entire ichnography a huge cross (Fig. 136).

In addition, a platform was built on the south side. The central hall has a gable and hip roof with double eaves, while the side halls have a round ridge roof with a single eave. The roofs were covered with yellow glazed tiles and green linear glazed decoration. The tile top has upturned eaves (Fig. 107).

An ancient Guasong pine

tree (a kind of Chinese pine with three needle leaves in each bunch) standing at the east side of Chengguang Hall was known to have been planted during the Jin Dynasty, the oldest tree in Beijing recorded in history. The tree top looks like a huge round umbrella and the posture is powerful and vigorous. Two Chinese lacebark pines (Fig. 137) and a Chinese pine had also celebrated several centuries of age. The several dozens of ancient cypress trees in front of Chengguang Hall are still verdant and lively after several hundreds of years. They were planted in proper intervals in between, setting off the tranquil landscapes of the Circular Wall and Chengguang Hall.

FIG. 138 Wulong Pavilion

Wulong Pavilion

Wulong Pavilion standing on the north bank of Beihai was first constructed in 1602 and had been reconstructed several times during the Qing Dynasty. Their roles as protagonist architecture and foils are pretty obvious: the middle one named Longze Pavilion has the largest building scale while its foils (Fig. 138), Chengxiang Pavilion and Zixiang Pavilion, escort it at its left hand side, and Yongrui Pavilion and Fuxui Pavilion at its right hand side. All the five buildings were linked into an architectural complex with marble stone fences. Thus, they seem as though they are floating above the water and swimming, just like a dragon enjoying its aquatic games. That is why this architectural complex was named Five-Dragon Pavilions (Fig. 23).

Xi Tian Fan Jing Buddhist Complex (Buddhist Paradise)

Buddhist Paradise, also known as Hall of Heavenly King, a Buddhist architecture complex completed in 1759, faces to Beihai and right in front of Qionghua Island. The prestigious Nine Dragon Wall, 25.5 meters in length and 6.65 meters in height, lies west. On either side of the screen wall, there are nine crouching dragons patched with

FIG. 139 Nine-Dragon Wall in Xi Tian Fan Jing Buddhist Complex

FIG. 140 Details of Nine-Dragon Wall

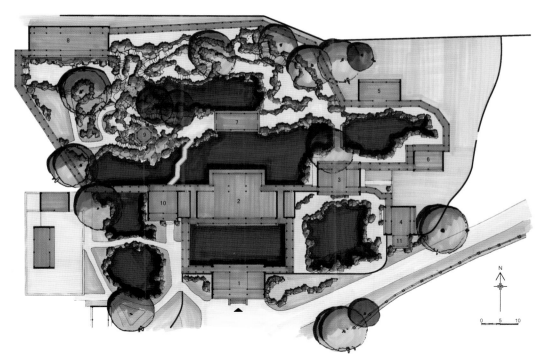

FIG. 142 Courtyard of Baosu Study in Jingxin Studio

colorful glazed tiles with very nice and sophisticated techniques (Figs. 139, 140).

Jingxin Studio

Jingxin Studio located in the far north end in Beihai Park was a unique "minor garden interior to a bigger garden" among all the gardens in Xi Palace Garden area constructed during the Qing Dynasty. Built during the period of 1756 to 1759, it was initially the Crown Prince's reading room. The front gate is just opposite to the center of Qionghua Island. And it is fenced with walls (Fig. 141).

Jingxin Studio can be divided into four independent scenic spots. On entering the main gate, you are inside one of the four spots— a neatly square water-centered courtyard. An artificially carved rockery stands inside the square courtyard around a pond. The main hall in the courtyard, Jingxin Studio, also serves as the major architecture in the entire garden. It is five rooms in width and has a three side halls.

Striding across the main hall, you will enter the north backyard, the principle garden area where natural landscapes dominate the entire garden. A winding corridor and a climbing-hill corridor embrace the pond inside, and rockeries were piled up on its north bank. To enrich the view layers in such a narrow and extensive land, a waterside gazebo, Qinquan Corridor (Corridor of Oozing Springs) was built above the pond, and separates the pond into two scenic layers. Together with the main hall and the entrance, the gazebo constitutes a north-south axis. As to the eastern side courtyard, the major architecture is Baosu Study (Study of Maintaining Simple Life). A natural pond, round in shape, is surrounded by natural-styled revetment in the courtyard (Fig. 142). Gurgling and giggling, the outlet of the pond produces continuous melodies, since water-falling technique had been adopted here. To fully enjoy the pure music of this spring, Emperor Qianlong built Yunqin Studio (Studio of String Music) at its east bank, outside which a tiny Bixian Pavilion

FIG. 143 Zhenluan Pavilion in Jingxin Studio from nearby

FIG. 144 Yanhua Gallery in Jingxin Studio

FIG. 145 Qinquan Corridor Bridge in Jingxin Studio

(Pavilion of Green Freshness) perches.

The minor scenic spot composed by this tiny pavilion and its surrounding rockeries and woods breaks the tedious image of a gable wall with flush gable roof, and provides the visitors with a panoramic view of waves, island, and the refreshing greenery of nature. In the west side courtyard, a pond lined with rock pieces, luxuriant trees and a stone flat bridge above the pond that was completely piled up with natural rock pieces give rise to a natural atmosphere of wild flavor.

The Zhenluan Pavilion (Pavilion Resting on Hill Ranges), a tiny and exquisite building built in 1756, stands upright on the hilltop of Taihu Lake rockeries inside Jingxin Studio. The brick-carving octagonal pavilion roof, with single eaves, looks like a lotus in its full blossom from a distance (Fig. 143). Visitors could enjoy diverse sceneries in Zhenluan Pavilion, since the rolling terrains, the different heights, interleaving planar, and spatial locations of the buildings had all been taken into consideration.

Yanhua Gallery (Gallery of Bright Colorful Pictures) stands on the lofty rockeries at the northeast corner of Jingxin Studio (Fig. 144). The character of "Yan" means "capturing." As the best viewpoint in the entire garden, this pavilion captures the picturesque views in its environment.

Qinquan Corridor Bridge, built in 1887, sits in the central position in Jingxin Studio. It is 12.1 meters long and 2.3 meters wide, with three arches and square granite piers. Above the piers, eight scarlet pillars support a caesious pantile round ridge roof with color painted eaves. Both sides of the corridor bridge were fenced with red wooden railings. And both ends connect with narrow pathways in the rockeries. The entire corridor bridge with caesious tiles and scarlet pillars echoes with the green ripples and lotus leaves, in the embrace of Taihu Lake rockeries (Fig. 145).

Huafang Studio in Beihai Park

Huafang Studio was located on the east coast of Beihai. It was originally built in 1757 for emperors to read books (Fig. 146).

On entering the gate, you are already in a natural-styled courtyard fenced with earth mound. On the slope, bamboo rods and pine forest present a luxuriant vitality. A hall with a horizontal board which was inscribed with "Chun Yu Lin Tang" (literally "Pond in forest in a Spring Drizzle") stands at the south side, and the one with a board reading "Kong Shui Cheng Xian" (literally "Clear and Fresh Water in Sky") sits at the north side. In between is a regular square pond. On its north shore is Huafang Studio, the major hall of the courtyard with a front gallery and a back side-hall (Fig. 147).

In the northeast corner, an exquisitely tiny wing courtyard, Guke Yard (Ancient Branches Yard) is in the embrace of a winding corridor. With the help of painted walls and carved windows, it presents a condensed poetic ambience of the small courtyards of southern China.

Hao Pu Jian Garden in Beihai Park

Hao Pu Jian Garden was built on the east bank in Beihai Park in 1757. As an exquisite and gracious

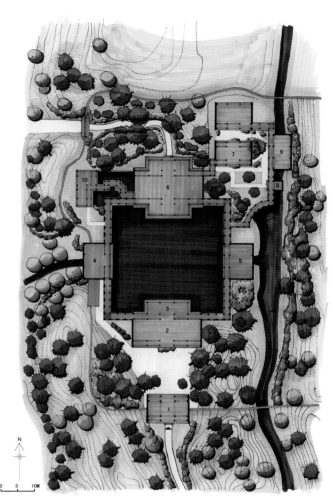

FIG. 146
Ichnography of Huafang Studio in Beihai Park
1. Gong Men Palace Gate 2. Chun Yu Lin Tang Hall of Forest and Pond in Spring Rain 3. Kong Shui Cheng Xian Hall of Clear Sky Reflected in Stream 4. Guan Miao Pavilion of Beauty in Sight 5. Jing Xiang Room of Mirror Fragrance 6. Hua Fang Zhai Painted Boat Studio 7. Gu Ke Ting Ancient Branches Yard 8. Lü Yi Lang Green Tinted Corridor 9. De Xing Xuan Self-Content Gallery 10. Xiao Ling Long Small Exquisite Rock

FIG. 147 Huafang Studio (taken from Chinese Imperial Gardens by Luo Zhewen)

"minor garden interior to a bigger garden," it sets off and makes a contrast to the open and spacious North Sea and the grandiose White Pagoda Mountain. The dominant sceneries inside the garden are natural views, tranquil and solitary, and full of natural vitality (Fig. 148).

The major scenic spot in this small garden is the pond, by the side of which an architecture named Scene along the Hao and Pu Rivers was constructed. The edge of this pond was built with green stone pieces, and a flat stone bridge with nine turns passes through the entire pond (Fig. 149).

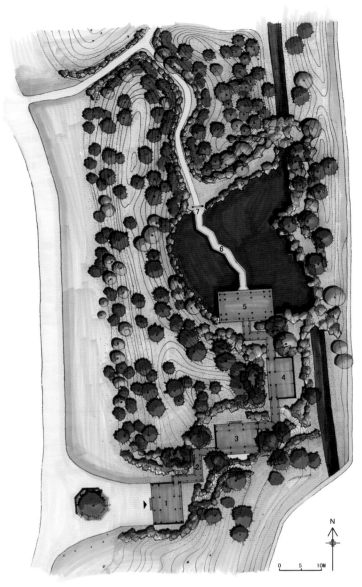

FIG. 148 Ichnography of Hao Pu Jian Garden in Beihai Park
1. Da Men Garden Gate   2. Pa Shan Lang Climbing-Hill Corridor   3. Yun
Xiu Chang Cloud Cave   4. Chong Jiao Shi Room on Lofty Mountain
5. Hao Pu Jian Garden between Hao and Pu Rivers   6. Qu Qiao Zigzag
bridge   7. Shi Pai Fang Rocky Decorative Archway

FIG. 149 Scene along the Hao and Pu Rivers and Jiuqu Bridge

FIG. 150 Climbing-hill corridor

This rockery was piled up with soil and decorated with rock pieces on the top. The major peak entrenches at the southern end of the hill, descends gradually from south to north, and rise up again at the north of the pond. Along the north, east, and west banks, rockeries were piled up to make an "S" shaped valley, reducing the severe invasion of northwest wind in winters and constituting a view barrier with a strong flavor of the natural wilderness. A climbing-hill corridor connects two rooms constructed on the rockeries, namely Yunxiu Room (Room of Cloud) and Chongjiao Room (Room on Lofty Mountain). You can reach Yun Xiu Chang (Cloud Cave) through the winding corridor and then pace down after twists and turns to the waterside gazebo. And even farther, you will step through the Bridge with Nine Turns before entering the zigzag valley.

This is an elaborately planned sightseeing route, shifting your viewpoint both horizontally and vertically (Fig. 150). Distorted peaks, unusual rock pieces, gleaming ripples, and obscure clouds form a dynamic and continuous scroll describing the natural landscapes. Sitting at the Cloud Cave, visitors could see the gracious posture of the White Pagoda to the south and can even borrow the views of Mt. Jing into the garden.

Jianxin Studio on Fragrant Hill 香山见心斋
Circular Courtyard Architecture Complex

Location: Beijing
Floor space: 1.20 hectares
Construction Year: 1522 – 1563
(during the Jiajing Period of Ming Dynasty)
Genre of Garden: imperial garden

Fragrant Hill, a forest park, was located at the east foothill on the Western Mountains in the western suburb of Beijing, over 20 kilometers away from the city center, occupying over 2300 *mu* (153.33 hectares, 378.90 acres) of land. In 1745, Emperor Qianlong organized a large-scaled construction activity, accomplishing 28 scenic spots and fencing the sceneries with "Tiger Skin Wall" (Irregular Stone Wall), and named it Jingyi Garden.

Jianxin Studio (Studio of Witnessing Heart) is a minor garden inside Jingyi Garden (now the Xiangshan Park) on Fragrant Hill. It was reconstructed in 1796. Unlike other imitated literati gardens, this garden was laid out according to the natural geographic features on Fragrant Hill (Fig. 151). Just as what was illustrated in the *Craft of Gardens*: "Among all the possible sites for garden construction, mountain forests are the best choices, since the geographic features there vary a lot, with both towering peaks and sunken valleys, both winding streams and profound pools, both high cliffs and suspending escarpment, and even plain as well. The wildness is naturally created with no need of any human

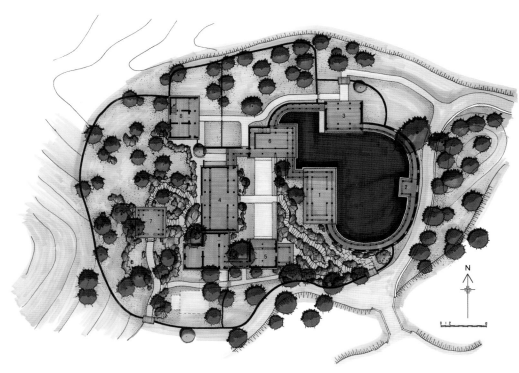

FIG. 151 Ichnography of Jianxin Studio in Fragrant Hill
1. Jian Xin Zhai Studio of Witnessing Heart   2. Zhi Yu Ting Pavilion of Knowing Fish   3. Bei Chang Ting North Open Hall   4. Zheng Ning Tang Hall of Condensing Healthy Atmosphere   5. Nan Pei Fang Southern Side-House   6. Bei Pei Fang Northern Side-House   7. Fang Ting Square Pavilion   8. Chang Feng Lou Tower of Smooth Wind

touch."

The garden was located at a triangular site inside a "Y" shaped valley, where the hill ranges rise and fall naturally. The major architecture inside the garden is facing an open and spacious field in the east. The foreground view is the rolling ranges on Yuquan Mountain and Mt. Longevity, while its distant view is Beijing. This building leans against Fragrant Hill in the west, from which you can catch sight of Xianglu Peak (Incense Burner Peak). Zhao Temple (Luminous Temple) stands to the south, and winding hill ranges where layer after layer of hillocks and greeneries to the north. This garden has very few rockeries, but is divided into a terrace with three steps according to its original geographic features.

Based on the gardening principle that "a water source should be situated in a secluded place and a pond or stream should be excavated in a low-lying place," a half-moon pond was made on the first step and fenced with a circular corridor. And a tiny pavilion named Zhiyu Pavilion (Pavilion of Knowing Fish) is erected in the middle of this corridor. Zhengning Hall (Zheng Ning Tang, Hall of Condensing Healthy Atmosphere), a bilateral symmetrically arranged three-sided courtyard was constructed on the second step. And a square pavilion and a two-storey tower named Changfeng Tower (Chang Feng Lou, Tower of Smooth Wind) occupy the third step, presenting a tranquil and secluded view of a mountainous residence.

Southern Side of Jianxin Studio

Once stepping inside Jianxin Studio from the south gate, you will catch sight of an elegant small-scaled landscape picture composed of a few rocks and several bamboo rods. And as you pace further, the road branches off into two, one being a road of stone stairs leading to the secondary courtyard and the other turning right into a water-centered courtyard through a small door on the circular corridor (Fig. 152).

Jianxin Studio and the Northern Side-House

Jianxin Studio, the major architecture of the entire garden, faces to the east, opposite to Zhiyu Pavilion. And the north open hall sits to the north. To the northwest of Jianxin Studio is the northern side-house, which connects both the first courtyard and the secondary courtyard. This house has three rooms, among which the western one has only

FIG. 152 Scenery at the southern side of Jianxin Studio

FIG. 153 Jianxin Studio and the northern side-house

FIG. 154 Square pavilion

one storey. The western wall has a flush gable roof. The eastern room, a two-storey waterfront tower with a gable and hip roof, is in the territory of the first water-centered courtyard. This architecture, asymmetrically laid out, is a persuasive example of integrating man-made architecture into natural landscapes (Fig. 153).

Zhiyu Pavilion

The pavilion was located in the middle section of the half-circular corridor around Jianxin Studio. Three sides of it face the pond. And railings were set up below. At one side, an ancient pine tree outside the garden extends its branches into the garden, bending down and

touching the water surface like a twisting dragon.

Square Pavilion

The square pavilion is the main architecture in the backyard, located a little southward away from the center (Fig. 154). It was situated here since Changfeng Tower—a large-scaled two-storey building—was placed to the northwest of Zhengning Hall. Thus, the square pavilion had to be located southward to construct a balanced layout, in opposition to Changfeng Tower. From the backyard of the square pavilion, you can watch the views of the Zhao Temple (Luminous Temple) and Glazed Pagoda.

Imperial Garden in the Forbidden City
故宫御花园
Largest Existing and Best Preserved Classical Wooden Architectural Complex

Location: Beijing
Floor space: 1.170 hectares
Construction Year: 1420 (the 18th year during the Yongle Period in the Ming Dynasty)
Genre of Garden: imperial garden

The Imperial Garden was located to the north of Kunning Palace (Palace of Earthly Tranquility) and at the northern end of the architectural axis in the Forbidden City in Beijing. Man-made architectures are the dominant elements in this palace garden, where the foil buildings set off the protagonists symmetrically. Rockeries and woods are only decorative elements setting off the architectures and

courtyards. This garden is most brilliant in its compact arrangement and grandiose buildings, which strive for diversities in the general stately dignity and neat formation, releasing a condensed atmosphere of a palace garden. This garden is 130 meters long from east to west and 90 meters in width from north to south, covering about 11,700 square meters of land, which is about 1.7% of the total area of the palace city (Fig. 155).

Just like the entire Forbidden City, the scenic spots in the Imperial Garden can be divided into three sections. Qin'an Hall, the largest scaled architecture, was located in the central position by north in the middle section. The low walls surrounding the hall are only slightly higher than the foundation of this hall, setting off the towering palace hall as a sharp contrast. While architectures in the eastern and western sections are relatively smaller in scale and scope, and symmetrically scattered

FIG. 156 Decorative paving in the Imperial Garden

with Qin'an Hall as their center.

All pavements in the Imperial Garden are elaborately designed figure cobble roads with appealing patterns, instead of sheer passageways covered with blue rock pieces or bricks, and thus, could be considered as one of the miracles of the garden. Continuous figure cobble roads integrate with their neighboring gorgeous architectures and luxuriant flowers and woods, composing special artistic effects (Fig. 156).

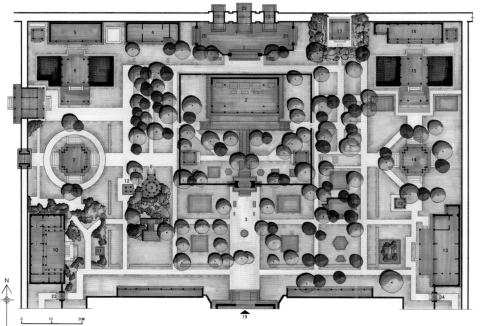

FIG. 155 Ichnography of Imperial Garden in Forbidden City
1. Cheng Guang Men Gate of Duplicate Lights
2. Qin An Dian Imperial Peace Hall
3. Tian Yi Men Only Gate in Universe
4. Yan Hui Ge Tower of Extending Brightness
5. Wei Yu Zhai Studio for Natural Cultivation
6. Cheng Rui Ting Pavilion with Pure Auspice
7. Qian Qiu Ting Pavilion of a Thousand Autumns 8. Si Shen Ci Temple of Four Celestials 9. Lu You Deer Garden
10. Yang Xing Zhai Studio of Cultivating Temperament 11. Ji Tai Altar 12. Jing Ting Well Pavilion 13. Jiang Xue Xuan Gallery of Rosy Snow 14. Wan Chun Ting Pavilion of Ten Thousand Spring Seasons 15. Fu Bi Ting Pavilion of Floating Greenery 16. Chi Zao Tang Hall of Flourishing Civilization
17. Yu Jing Ting Imperial View Pavilion 18. Dui Xiu Shan Piled Elegance Hill 19. Kun Ning Men Gate of Earthly Tranquility 20. Ji Fu Men Gate of Collecting Good Fortune 21. Yan He Men Gate of Extending Harmony 22. Shun Zhen Men Gate of Obedience and Virginity
23. Qiong Yuan Xi Men Western Gate of Jade Palace Garden 24. Qiong Yuan Dong Men Eastern Gate of Jade Palace Garden

FIG. 157 Wanchun Pavilion and the Camel Hump Cypress beside it

Wanchun Pavilion

Wanchun Pavilion is a square pavilion with four side halls attached to its sides. All these side halls have their own stairs and breast boards made from white marble stones. The green glazed ventilation walls were decorated with yellow turtle shell patterns, and the ventilation windows and partition boards of doors all have three-battened lozenge patterns (a typical pattern on the royal architectures constructed during the Qing Dynasty, composed of three pieces of batten resembling a snowflake). All its wooden frameworks were ornamented with dragon brocaded pattern color painting.

The round pavilion roof was called "umbrella" style during the Ming Dynasty and was covered with yellow glazed bamboo-joint tiles (Fig. 157). The round upper roof and square lower roof present the concept of "round heaven and square earth," as imitation of the traditional model for a "Ming Tang (an ancient imperial architecture of palace halls with a round top roof and square main body, indicating the ancient philosophy that human beings were obeying the laws of heaven and earth)."

Two phoenix patterns were painted on the internal ceiling, and a gilded relief of a curling dragon holding a precious pearl in its mouth decorated the caisson (Fig. 158). The entire pavilion is so colorful and exquisite that it could be ranked as the champion among all pavilions constructed in royal palaces.

FIG. 158 Caisson of Wanchun Pavilion

FIG. 159 Qin'an Hall

FIG. 160 Detailed decoration on chest boards of Qin'an Hall

Qin'an Hall

Qin'an Hall, the major architecture in this garden, was located in the middle of the northern end of the Imperial Garden. Built in 1420 and rebuilt in 1535, it is currently the only intact architecture made during the Ming Dynasty. This five-room-wide building has five side halls and double eaves covered with a yellow glazed flat-topped roof (Fig. 159).

Qin'an Hall separates the garden into two halves: eastern section and western section. Over 20 diverse architectures in the entire garden—palace halls, pavilions, and studios of various styles—were basically symmetrically arranged beside this hall. Only some small-scaled but exquisite pavilions could be exceptions. Consequently, the symmetrically arranged buildings could not be seen at the same time. Such a design seems to visually expand the garden.

Qin'an Hall was built on the base of a Sumeru platform made from white marble stone. All the elegant dragon and phoenix relieves on the railing pillars and chest boards were carved during the Ming Dynasty (Fig. 160). The roof is flat,

surrounded by four ridges. This hall was dedicated to the True Warrior Grand Emperor, a Taoist deity, and is the only Taoist architecture existing in the Forbidden City at present.

Duixiu Hill (Piled Elegance Hill) and Yujing Pavilion

Resting in the northeast of the Imperial Garden, Duixiu Hill was piled up with Taihu Lake rocks of diverse shapes. It stands as high as 14 meters leaning against the garden wall. An artificial fountain was built at the foot of this hill. Ancient people brought water up with barrels and sprayed it down. Currently, tap water system takes its place. This hill was manually piled up in a "Dui Xiu" style—a term hill piling artisans coined—and was thus named Duixiu Hill.

In front of the hill sits a pair of stone lion sculptures. And a couple of dragon head sculptures rest on the two lion-sculpture-supported stone beds, spraying water up to 10 meters high. A square pavilion with four-angle pavilion roof was constructed on the hilltop, named Yujing Pavilion (Fig. 161). On every Double Nines Day (the ninth day in the ninth month in

the Chinese lunar calendar), the emperors would climb up this rockery and enjoy the autumn sights in this pavilion together with his queen and imperial concubines.

FIG. 161 Duixiu Hill and Yujing Pavilion

FIG. 162 The carved window in a pattern of "wan shou wu jiang" in Jiangxue Gallery

FIG. 163 Jiangxue Gallery

Jiangxue Gallery (Gallery of Rosy Snow)

Jiangxue Gallery perches at the southeast corner of the Imperial Garden. All the gates and windows were made from nanmu timber and carved into patterns. All the lattice windows were carved in a pattern of *"wan shou wu jiang* (literally immortal life)" (Fig. 162). Emperor Qianlong had paid regular visits to this gallery, composing poetry and rhymed articles here (Fig. 163). In the glazed flower bed in front of the house lives a rare flower called Peace Flower, which was moved from Henan province during the late Qing Dynasty on the Empress Dowager Cixi's command.

Yangxing Studio

Yangxing Studio, a tower located on the hilltop of a rockery resting in the western section of the Imperial Garden, has rockery embellishing the front gate and is embraced in rockeries just like in a rocky courtyard. It echoes with Jiangxue Gallery in the east section of the Imperial Garden from afar, being a tiny study for emperors in the Qing Dynasty (Fig. 164).

Famous Ancient Woods

As many as 160 pieces of prestigious ancient trees are still alive in the Imperial Garden at present, among which the ancient catalpa, cypresses, pines, Chinese pagoda tree, and cloves are the most popular. Camel Hump Cypress at the north side of Wanchun Pavilion (Fig. 157), Phoenix Cypress at the west side, Big Belly Arhat Cypress by the side of Yanhui Tower, and the 18 upright Arhats Cypresses standing in a line from south to north in the western section of the Imperial Garden were all planted during the Ming Dynasty. All of them look magnificent and grandiose with extraordinary disposition. Even the Chinese pagoda tree in its vigorous senility has luxuriant branches and leaves.

FIG. 164 Yangxing Studio

Back Garden of Prince Gong's Mansion 恭王府
Garden of Ten Thousand Happiness

Location: Beijing
Floor space: 2.70 hectares
Construction Year: 1754 (the 19th year of Emperor Qianlong's reign)
Genre of Garden: resident garden

Prince Gong's Mansion located on Liuyin Street in the Shichahai area is currently the best preserved royal mansion of the Qing Dynasty in Beijing. It was initially possessed by He Shen, a Grant Secretary during the Qianlong period and had been rebuilt twice when Emperor Xianfeng and Emperor Tongzhi were in power during its history of over 200 years. In the course of reconstruction, a garden was built at the back of this mansion, and the general layout was maintained, sticking to the original scale and system of the late Qianlong period.

The front section of Prince Gong's Mansion is dominated by majestic and magnificent mansion houses and the back section is an exquisite and elegant garden. Occupying as much as 60,000 square meters of land, the mansion area could be divided into three sections—middle, east, and west sections, or multi-layer four-sided courtyard houses with their specific axes (Fig. 165).

The front part of the middle section is composed of a three-room-wide front gate and a five-room-wide secondary gate. The east section has three four-sided courtyard houses. The front hall in the west section was called Cijin Studio (Studio of Granting Promotion). Behind these three sections of courtyards is a two-

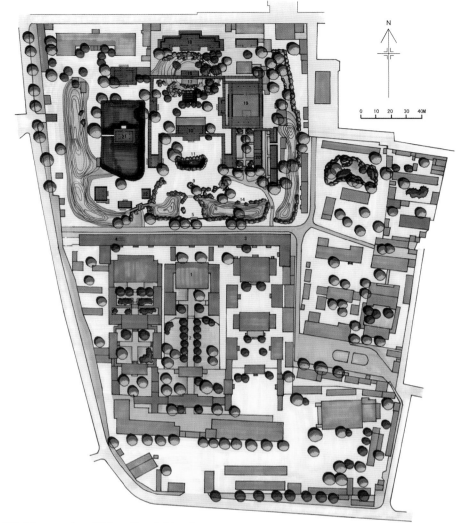

FIG. 165 Ichnography of Prince Gong's Mansion
1. Jia Le Tang Hall of Joyful Happiness   2. Tian Xiang Ting Yuan Courtyard of Heavenly Fragrance
3. Yan Ji Lou Tower of Sunny Eaves   4. Bao Yue Lou Tower of Precious Agreement   5. Yuan Men
Garden Gate   6. Chui Qing Yue Suspending Green Shades   7. Cui Yun Ling   Green Cloud Range
8. Qu Jing Tong You Winding Path Leading to Secluded Wonderful Views   9. Fei Lai Shi Flying Stone
10. An Shan Tang Hall of Peace and Kindness   11. Fu He Bat River   12. Yu Guan Elm Pass
13. Qin Qiu Ting Pavilion with Oozing Autumn Taste   14. Yi Shu Pu Vegetable Garden   15. Di Cui
Yan Green Drops Rockery   16. Lü Tian Xiao Yin Hall for Slightly Hiding in Green Paradise
17. Yao Yue Tai Platform of Inviting Moon   18. Fu Ting Hall of Auspicious Bats   19. Da Xi
Lou Great Opera Tower   20. Yin Xiang Zui Yue House for Chanting Fragrance and Drinking to
Moon   21. Guan Yu Tai Platform for Watching Fishes   22. Miao Xiang Ting Pavilion of Remarkable
Sweetness

storey backyard tower, 160 meters in length from the east end to the west end, and with more than 40 rooms. The east side of the tower is named Yanji Tower (Yan Ji Lou, Tower of Sunny Eaves), while the western part is Baoyue Tower (Bao Yue Lou, Tower of Precious Agreement). And Cuijin Garden (Garden of Accumulating Brocade-like Scenery) is located behind the tower, publicly known as the Back Garden of Prince Gong's Mansion.

There is only a narrow lane between the garden and the mansion.

7,586 square meters of land within the entire garden, which occupies nearly 2.7 hectares, was taken up by 31 ancient architectures. This garden was also known as the Garden of Ten Thousand Happiness because, as it was said, ten thousand bat images were hidden in Prince Gong's Mansion. In Chinese, the name for "bat (fu, 蝠)" and "happiness (fu, 福)" are homophones,

FIG. 166 Garden gate

FIG. 167 Indoor scene of Great Opera Tower in the garden

elements in the entire garden. A white marble stone archway blocks the garden gate from the mansion houses (Fig. 166). The garden entrance opens to the south, with two rockeries piled up with Cloud Rubbles on the east and west sides. Right at the entrance, a piece of "Flying Stone" occupies the small introductive space, behind which is the first courtyard, a three-sided courtyard house. The front lofty hall is Anshan Hall (An Shan Tang, Hall of Peace and Kindness). Behind it is the secondary courtyard, a typical four-sided courtyard house with a central pond. Dicui Rockery, the main hill in the entire garden, was piled up with lake rocks above the water surface. An open hall Lü Tian Xiao Yin (Hall for Slightly Hiding in Green Paradise) and the platform in front of the hall named Yaoyue Platform (Platform of Inviting Moon) were constructed at the top. Behind this rockery is the

so this garden was named Wan Fu Yuan. Among all such "*fu*," the "*fu*" character appearing in "Stele of Happiness" written by Emperor Kangxi is the only Chinese character of "happiness," though secluded in Miyun Cave (Cave of Mysterious Clouds) on Dicui Rockery (Green

Drops Rockery); while the rest 9,999 "happiness" were embedded in the bat images. It is safe to say that the "happiness" culture in Prince Gong's Mansion is in reality the "happiness hiding" culture.

The architectures built in the middle section are the dominant tertiary courtyard where Fu Hall (Fu Ting, Hall of Auspicious Bats) was constructed.

The main building in the east section is the Great Opera Tower, an architecture with three interconnected rolling-hill roofs, occupying 685 square meters of land. The south side interior to the tower is a stage, about one meter high. Palace lamps were hung on the ceilings and the ground was covered with square bricks. This opera tower served both as a theatre and a ceremonial site for weddings or funerals previously (Fig. 167). To the south of Great Opera Tower is Yi Shen Suo (Refreshment Place), where people admired flowers and played waging games in the old days.

A castle-styled city wall with battlements and archways, around 50 meters long, stands on the west section of the hill. The stone board on the gate was inscribed with two Chinese characters "Yu Guan" (Elm Pass) (Fig. 168), and the megalith

FIG. 168 Yu Guan (Elm Pass) in the garden

on the hill road was inscribed with three characters "Cui Yun Ling" (Green Cloud Range). In the northeast of Yu Guan Pass stands a Miaoxiang Pavilion (Pavilion of Remarkable Sweetness).

Prince Gong's mansion and its magnificent garden were said to be the prototype of Ronggguo House and the Grand View Garden described in *A Dream of Red Mansions* (红楼梦, *Hong Lou Meng*), a masterpiece in Chinese literature,

in that their design presents a majestic and brilliant style, all architectures twist and turn and are full of diversity and the landscapes are profound, tranquil, and elegant.

Fu Hall

Fu Hall was located in the third section of this multi-layer courtyard house in the middle section of Prince Gong's Mansion. The hall in the north end sits exactly on the central axis. Its main hall has five rooms with a flush gable roof with round edges, and three side halls with a gable and hip roof were attached to the front and back. Three zigzag penthouses with flush gable roofs were attached to either side of the main hall. Resembling the shape of a bat, this architectural complex was consequently named "Bat Hall" (Fig. 169).

Guanyu Platform (Platform for Watching Fishes)

Guanyu Platform, located in the center of a lake to the north of Elm Pass, is an open and spacious hall confronting the vast water surface, where visitors could enjoy glittering ripples.

FIG. 169 Fu Hall

Ornamental Gate to Lotus Courtyard

This is the secondary gate in the eastern section of the garden, named on account of the two short suspending pillars under the door eaves, which look like a pair of buds hanging upside down. The gate takes the style of a Buddhist monk's hat typically used in a royal palace (Fig. 170). The bat pattern (indicating bliss or happiness) and "卐" pattern (homophone of "ten thousand," indicating endless) paintings on the counter forts symbolizing endless bliss.

Dicui Rockery

Dicui Rockery, the protagonist scene located exactly on the axis in the garden, was piled up with North Taihu Lake rocks (a kind of rock material produced in Zhoukoudian in Fangshan Mountain, a Beijing suburban area). The rocks had been stuck with sticky rice soup, which made it pretty solid and firm. A typical

FIG. 171 Dicui Rockery in the garden

Ming style construction, the hill top looks like two dragons playing with a pearl. A holey water jar had been hidden under either dragon head, so that the water inside would drop into and moisten the rockery during summer and fall, when green mosses creep all over the rockery like dropping green dews, appealing to visitors. In front of the rockery is a pond enclosed with engraved railings. A cave named Miyun Cave is sheltered by the rockery, inside of which "Stele of Happiness" written by Emperor Kangxi stands (Fig. 171).

Miaoxiang Pavilion

Miaoxiang Pavilion, a wooden two-storey pavilion with a round roof and square fundament, reflects the traditional cosmologic viewpoint held of the ancient sages—"round heaven and square earth." The tiny pavilion sheltered in luxuriant woods is a wonderful choice for visitors to relax and enjoy the cool air (Fig. 172).

FIG. 170 Ornamental gate to Lotus Courtyard in the garden

FIG. 172 Miaoxiang Pavilion in the garden

Tanzhe Temple 潭柘寺
Earliest Buddhist Temple in Beijing

Location: Beijing
Floor space: 2.50 hectares
Construction Year: 307 (during the Yongjia Period of the Western Han Dynasty)
Genre of Garden: temple garden

Tanzhe Temple, was located on Tanzhe Mountain in Mentougou District, Beijing. This temple was popularly known as Temple of Pool and Zhe Tree (Cudrainia Triloba), since a dragon pool lies at the back of this temple and Zhe trees stand on the hillside. Celebrating a history of more than 1,700 years, it is the oldest Buddhist temple in Beijing, which enjoys a saying that "Tanzhe Temple was constructed earlier than Beijing." Hence, it is a vital historical exhibit in the researches of Buddhist development in Beijing. And all present architectures were built in the Ming and Qing dynasties.

Tanzhe Temple occupies a tremendous floor space, with 2.5 hectares inside the temple and 11.2 hectares outside the temple. In addition to the forests and hill area around it, the temple takes charge of a total area of over 121 hectares. Confronting to the south and leaning against Baozhu Peak (Precious Pearl Peak), it is embraced by nine towering peaks, which form a horse-shoe-shaped circle, as if it were supported by nine gigantic dragons. The lofty hills shelter the temple from cold currents from the northwest, leaving the local circumstances in a warm and moist climate. Subsequently, the surroundings are very charming, with sky-scraping ancient trees

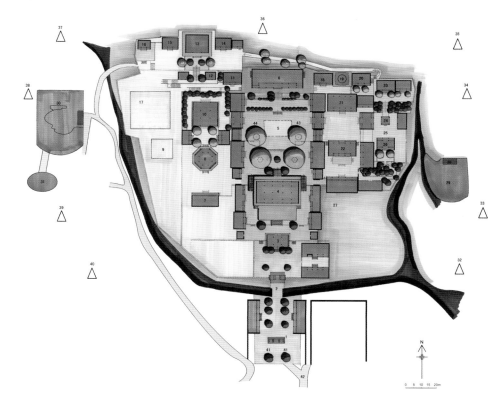

FIG. 173 Ichnography of Tanzhe Temple
1. Pai Lou Decorative Archway   2. Shan Men Front Gate of the Temple   3. Tian Wang Dian Hall of Heavenly King   4. Da Xiong Bao Dian Jeweled Hall of Great Hero   5. San Sheng Dian Hall of Three Wise Emperors 6. Pi Lu Ge Mahavairocana Tower   7. Li Shu Yuan Pear Tree Courtyard   8. Leng Yan Tan Altar of the Suramgama-Samadhi   9. Xie Jing Shi Room for Copying Sutra   10. Jie Tai Ordination Platform   11. Yao Shi Dian Hall of Medicine Budda   12. Kong Que Dian Peacock Hall   13. Guan Yin Dian Bodhisattva of Compassion Hall   14. Wen Shu Dian Manjusri Hall   15. Shi Yu Stone Fish   16. Long Wang Dian Dragon King Hall   17. Da Bei Tan Altar of Universal Benevolence   18. Yuan Tong Dian Perfect Penetration Hall   19. She Li Ta Buddhist Relics Pagoda   20. Di Zang Dian Ksitigarbha Hall   21. Fang Zhang Yuan Abbot House   22. Qing Shan Ju Lodging in Green Hill   23. Qian Long Bao Dian Precious Hall of Emperor Qianlong   24. Liu Bei Ting Floating Cup Pavilion   25. Xing Gong Yuan Temporary Palace   26. Yu Cha Fang Imperial Tea House   27. Zhu Lin Yuan Bamboo Courtyard   28. Cai Shen Dian Hall for God of Wealth   29. Xi Guan Yin Dong West Avalokiteśvara Cave   30. Dong Guan Yin Dong East Avalokiteśvara Cave   31. Lao Hu Ting Jing Dong Cave Where Tiger Listened to Sutra Teaching   32. Hui Long Feng Coiled Dragon Peak   33. Hu Ju Feng Tiger Peak   34. Zi Cui Feng Green Peak in Violet Mist   35. Ji Yun Feng Cloud Gathering Peak   36. Bao Zhu Feng Precious Pearl Peak   37. Ying Luo Feng Pearl Necklace Peak   38. Jia Yue Feng Peak of Bridging the Moon   39. Xiang Wang Feng Peak of Elephant King   40. Lian Hua Feng Lotus Peak   41. Zhe Shu Three-Bristle Cudrania   42. Gu Xiang Dao Ancient Fragrant Path   43. Di Wang Shu Emperor Tree   44. Pei Wang Shu Empress Tree

and one-after-another Buddhist pagodas (Fig. 173).

The scenes in the temple could be divided into three sections. The middle section is the major architecture area, appearing so solemn and tranquil with lofty and magnificent halls set off by vigorous pines, verdant cypresses, and towering ginkgos in the spacious courtyard. The western section is a minor architecture area, with a smaller courtyard where ancient pine trees and slender bamboos were planted everywhere and a brook babbling from outside. The

eastern section is basically a garden where a running rill winds its way among the prosperous woods, bamboo forest, and famous flowers. In addition, rockeries were piled up, waterfall dashes down, fleet creeks run across shallows, and a floating cup pavilion was constructed. Such a brocade-like pleasurable garden atmosphere serves as a sharp contrast to the middle section.

Several scenic spots, including An Le Yan Shou Hall (An Le Yan Shou Tang, Hall of Extending Life in Peace and Happiness), Mingwang Hall (Ming Wang

FIG. 174 Jeweled Hall of Great Hero

Dian, Deity Hall), a pavilion, Dragon Pool, Cave of Bodhisattva of Compassion, and two pagoda courtyards—either on the upper or lower side of the hill—distribute in the periphery of the temple like stars escorting a moon.

Jeweled Hall of Great Hero (Mahavira Hall)

The Jeweled Hall of Great Hero was located at the back of the Hall of Heavenly King (Deveraja Hall). The Bell Tower and Drum Tower standing in the middle of the courtyard in front of this hall have the same construction style, both occupying a land 6 meters in length and width. The Hall rests on a platform about 2.33 meters high, surrounded with exquisite white marble railings with nice relieves (Fig. 174). And Guardian Hall (Sangharama Hall) and the Hall of Patriarch, another pair of same-structured buildings, sit on both sides in front of it.

Hall of Heavenly King

The Hall of Heavenly King is the first hall inside the temple gate, it is a wooden structure with a gable and hip roof and single eave, three-room-wide, 37 *chi* high (12.33 m, 40.46 feet), 34 *chi* in depth (11.33 m, 37.18 feet), and 50 *chi* in width (16.67 m, 54.68 feet). The roof was covered with green glazed tiles and the dragon-head ridge ornaments were covered with yellow glazed tiles. Four round aeolian bells jingle at the four corners of the hall, whose forehead hangs a gilded inscribed board with calligraphy written by Emperor Kangxi, "Hall of Heavenly King." Inside the hall, a gilded wooden sculpture of a sitting Maitreya Buddha is worshiped (Fig. 175).

FIG. 175 Hall of Heavenly King

FIG. 176 The main hall of Mahavairocana Tower

Mahavairocana Tower

Mahavairocana Tower
(Mahavairocana, the name of a
Buddha in Sanskrit, indicating
Buddhist lights and bless given to
all creatures) behind Sansheng Hall
(Hall of Three Wise Emperors,
namely Yao, Shun and Yu) was
originally a storage keeping
Buddhist sutras granted by
emperors from different dynasties,
and therefore, was publicly known
as the Tower of Buddhist Sutras.
This tower, the last architecture on
the axis and the largest-scaled one
in this temple, is a seven-room-
wide two-storey building with a
flush gable roof. It is 47 *chi* (15.67
m, 51.39 feet) high, 38 *chi* (12.67
m, 41.55 feet) in depth, and 100
chi (33.33 m, 109.35 feet) in width.
The brick carvings on the top of
the roof are the most characteristic
of all (Fig. 176).

Shiyu Hall (Shi Yu Dian, Stone Fish Hall)

Shiyu Hall, a 22 *chi* high (7.33 m,
24.06 feet), 21 *chi* in depth (7 m,
22.96 feet), and 25 *chi* in width
(8.33 m, 27.34 feet) architecture
with a flush gable roof, is also
known as Dragon King Hall.

Below the left front eave hangs a
dark-green stone fish sculpture, 5 *chi*
in length (1.67 m, 5.47 feet), which
looks like a copper sculpture from
afar and stone carving from nearby.
In reality, it was engraved out of
a coppery stone material. When
knocked, it sounds like metal and
stone percussion instrument. What
is most striking is that it produces
different tunes when varied places
are knocked just like a musical
instrument is playing music. This
stone fish is the only treasure among
"the four precious items in Tanzhe
Temple" that still exists (Fig. 177).

FIG. 177 Stone fish

FIG. 178 Jin Gang Yan Shou Pagoda

Jin Gang Yan Shou Pagoda (Pagoda of Buddha's Warrior Extending Longevity)

The lofty Jin Gang Yan Shou Pagoda sits at the east of Mahavairocana Tower. This Tibetan-style pagoda looks like a huge white-washed up-side-down alms bowl, supported by a square Sumeru platform 5 *zhang* long (16.67 m, 54.68 feet) and 5 *zhang* wide. A lofty and sharp cone decoration stands on the top of the main body, and ornaments in the shape of the sun, the moon, and the stars are even higher. In all, the entire pagoda is over 5 *zhang* (16.67 m, 54.68 feet) in height (Fig. 178).

Floating Cup Pavilion

The pavilion, located in the temporary palace courtyard, was constructed for Emperor Qianlong to enjoy the delight of "floating a wine-up in a winding stream." Escorted by the bamboo forest and ancient pine trees, the sceneries surrounding the pavilion look so tranquil and secluded, and serve as a fantastic place to cool yourself in summer. The ground was covered with huge white marble stone slabs, on which a winding channel was carved into a combinative pattern with a dragon crouching in the south section and a tiger stretching in the north section. Spring water is sprayed out of a stone dragon's mouth in the northeast corner of the pavilion, introduced along the channel, winding forward at one moment and backward at another, and slowly turning left and right.

Bodhisattva of Compassion Hall (Avalokiteśvara Hall)

Avalokiteśvara Hall stands at the highest altitude in this temple, located at the north end in the western section of the temple. The hall, 3 rooms wide, 41 *chi* in height (13.67 m, 44.83 feet), 49 *chi* in depth (16.33 m, 53.58 feet), and 6 *zhang* in width (20 m, 65.62 feet), has a roof covered with yellow glazed tile. A platform extends in front of the Hall (Fig. 179). In the center, a standard statue of Avalokiteśvara Buddha is worshiped.

Guangshan Ordination Platform (Universal Benevolence Ordination Platform)

The main hall of the ordination platform is a square architecture with a flush gable roof, 37 *chi* in height (12.33 m, 40.46 feet), 55 *chi* (18.33 m, 60.14 feet) both in length and width, and covered with caesious wavy tiles. The

yellow glazed tiles set in the roof were organized into diamond patterns that indicate this hall was built according to an "imperial order."

In the center sits the ordination platform, built with white marble stones. It was composed of three storey of square grounds, the lowest being the largest (16 *chi* both in length and width, 5.33 m, 17.5 feet) and the top being the smallest. Therefore, the three storeys pile up a pyramid, with each one constructed into a Sumeru platform. The entire platform is as high as 10 *chi* (3.33 m, 10.94 feet).

The Forest of Stupas

This ancient temple has witnessed the alternation of more than ten dynasties. In such a large-scaled

and grandiose temple, countless monks had been devoting their lives to Buddha and stayed perpetually here. Hence, numerous stupas rest in the neighborhood. To be specific, over 70 Buddhist stupas are still well-preserved in front of the temple, which are diverse in construction styles and were built during different dynasties.

The most towering stupa was honorifically entitled Guang Hui Tong Li Stupa (Stupa of Extensive Wisdom and Profound Understanding) in the Jin Dynasty (1115 – 1234). This nine-floor pagoda has intense eaves, built with solid bricks in 1614. It was also known as the "Pagoda of Ten Thousand Monks" since an immense number of monks was settled here over the course of several hundred years.

FIG. 179 Bodhisattva of Compassion Hall

Emperor Tree and Empress Tree

The two most prestigious ancient trees in Tanzhe Temple are two lofty gingko trees. The "Emperor Tree," standing in the east side (Fig. 180), was honorably entitled by Emperor Qianlong when he visited Tanzhe Temple to pay respect to Buddha. West of it was the wife called "Empress Tree". Unfortunately, these two ginkgo trees were mistaken as a perfect match to each other since both are male, and consequently had never born any fruit.

Three-Bristle Cudrania

Three-Bristle Cudrania is a species of tree growing in southern China but rarely seen in northern China, so the one in Tanzhe Temple is extremely rare and precious. The tree, roughly 5 meters high, stands in front of the temple gate and at the west side of the archway, fenced by white marble stone railings. It was in reality transplanted from the back hill in 1978 when the temple was reconstructed.

The Sal Tree

The Sal tree is also named seven-leaf tree since every leaf cluster has seven leaves. This species of tree was originally planted in India and respected as the Buddhist Devine Tree on account of some religious legends that said that Sakyamuni (the Buddha) was born, passed away, and missionized his teachings under this tree. The two in the picture enjoy more than 600 years of age (Fig. 181).

FIG. 180 Emperor Tree

FIG. 181 The Sal tree

Mountain Resort 避暑山庄
Largest-Scaled Imperial Garden in China

Location: Chengde, Hebei province
Floor space: 564 hectares
Construction Year: 1703 (the 42nd year of Emperor Kangxi's reign in the Qing Dynasty)
Genre of Garden: imperial garden

The Mountain Resort at Chengde, also known as the Hot River Temporary Palace or the Detached Palace in Chengde, was the place where emperors in the Qing Dynasty stayed during summers and conducted various political activities. The construction started in 1703 and was roughly finished after five years. When Emperor Qianlong was in power, he had it reconstructed and expanded in a large scale. The major construction work was eventually accomplished only in 1790, more than 80 years later. Therefore, it has enjoyed more than 290 years of history. This spacious mountain resort was the largest existing ancient garden. In 1994, it was listed as a world cultural heritage site by UNESCO.

In 1711, Emperor Kangxi named 36 scenic spots with four character phrases, for example Yan Bo Zhi Shuang (Refreshing Mists and Ripples). The *Picture of Mountain Resort* painted by Leng Mei was a fundamental reflection of the garden views in this period. Later in 1754, Emperor Qianlong recognized another 36 scenic spots and granted three Chinese character names to them, in which "Li Zheng Men (Beautiful Front Gate)" was included. Thus, together with the 36 scenic spots confirmed in Emperor Kangxi's period, they were collectively known as

"72 scenic spots." The *Picture of Mountain Resort* painted by Qian Weicheng described the peak time of this resort when all the principal constructions were finished.

The Mountain Resort can be roughly divided into two sections: the palace area and the landscape area (Fig. 182).

The palace area located at the southern section of the resort is constituted of four architectural complexes, namely Major Palace, Songhe Studio (Studio of Pine and Crane), Wan He Song Feng Complex (Complex of Wind through the Pine Valley), and East Palace, where the emperors in the Qing Dynasty dealt with their administrative business and resided.

The landscape area could be separated into three sections: lake area, plain area, and mountainous area. To be specific, the lake area spreads to the north of the palace area, serving as the central scenic area in the resort where glittering ripples flicker, isles and islands dot irregularly on the water surface, and pavilions and belvederes are hidden in luxuriant flowers and woods, presenting a typical landscape of the Yangtze River Delta.

The plain area is a narrow triangle embraced by a lake to the south, a garden wall to the east, and a mountain to the northeast. The plain covers roughly the same floor space as the lake area. The two dominate the land from south to north. There are very few architectures on the plain area so as to expose the open and spacious plain views. The mountainous area occupies two thirds of the entire garden, where the architectures founded on a plump hill terrain look more secluded than distinctive, more loosely laid out than densely

arranged, so as to set off the natural theme of a mountainous resort.

The Mountain Resort copies and represents all natural geographic features in all of China, accumulating construction features in the gardens of both southern and northern China with unique construction techniques. It is safe to say this resort is a reservoir of all the artistic achievements in Chinese ancient gardens.

Wan He Song Feng Complex

The Wan He Song Feng Complex, the earliest architectural complex in the territory of the palace area, was built in 1708. This group of buildings was named so because it was surrounded by thousands of ancient pines (Fig. 183). Emperor Kangxi granted the side hall in this resort, "Wan He Song Feng" to Hongli (1711 – 1799, later the Emperor Qianlong), as his residence. Whenever he had dinner or read reports from his officials, he would have Hongli stay with him, in order to give administrative instruction to him day and night. After Hongli took the throne, he renamed the hall Ji'en Hall (Ji En Tang, Hall for Memorizing Grandpa's Love).

Yan Bo Zhi Shuang Hall

Constructed in 1710, this hall is the first one among the 36 scenic spots in Emperor Kangxi's period, serving as the major imperial bedroom. This hall with a gable and hip roof and a round edge covered with tiles is 7 rooms wide and has short corridors attached to the front gate and back (Fig. 184). The hall presents simple elegance on the outside, but magnificently furnished inside (Fig. 185). Every spring and summer, every moment

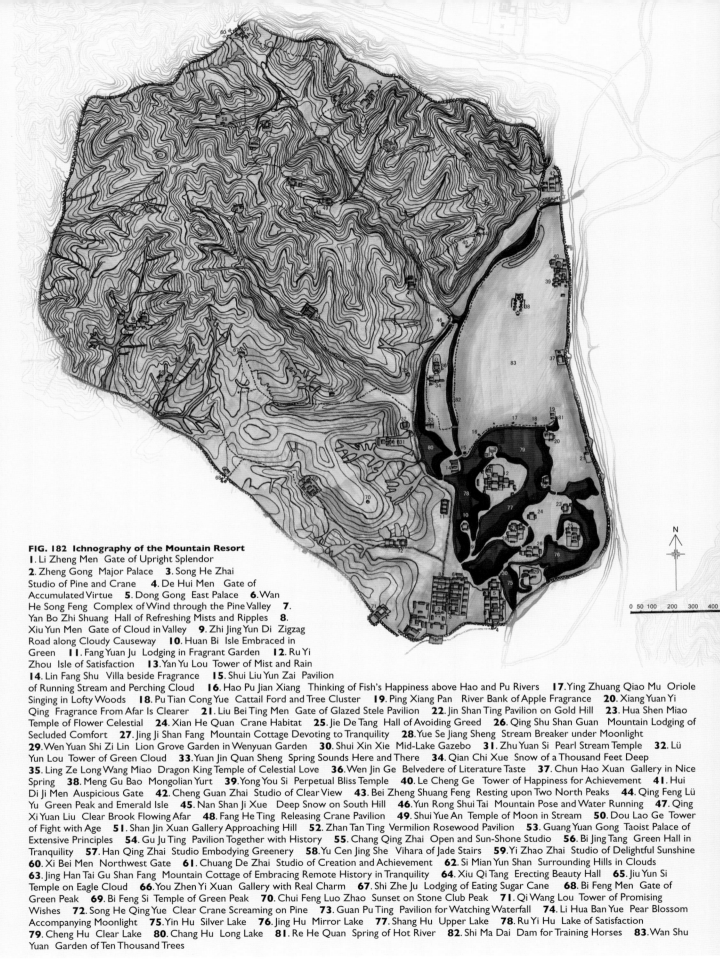

FIG. 182 Ichnography of the Mountain Resort

1. Li Zheng Men Gate of Upright Splendor
2. Zheng Gong Major Palace   3. Song He Zhai
Studio of Pine and Crane   4. De Hui Men Gate of
Accumulated Virtue   5. Dong Gong East Palace   6. Wan
He Song Feng Complex of Wind through the Pine Valley   7.
Yan Bo Zhi Shuang Hall of Refreshing Mists and Ripples   8.
Xiu Yun Men Gate of Cloud in Valley   9. Zhi Jing Yun Di Zigzag
Road along Cloudy Causeway   10. Huan Bi Isle Embraced in
Green   11. Fang Yuan Ju Lodging in Fragrant Garden   12. Ru Yi
Zhou Isle of Satisfaction   13. Yan Yu Lou Tower of Mist and Rain
14. Lin Fang Shu Villa beside Fragrance   15. Shui Liu Yun Zai Pavilion
of Running Stream and Perching Cloud   16. Hao Pu Jian Xiang Thinking of Fish's Happiness above Hao and Pu Rivers   17. Ying Zhuang Qiao Mu Oriole
Singing in Lofty Woods   18. Pu Tian Cong Yue Cattail Ford and Tree Cluster   19. Ping Xiang Pan River Bank of Apple Fragrance   20. Xiang Yuan Yi
Qing Fragrance From Afar Is Clearer   21. Liu Bei Ting Men Gate of Glazed Stele Pavilion   22. Jin Shan Ting Pavilion on Gold Hill   23. Hua Shen Miao
Temple of Flower Celestial   24. Xian He Quan Crane Habitat   25. Jie De Tang Hall of Avoiding Greed   26. Qing Shu Shan Guan Mountain Lodging of
Secluded Comfort   27. Jing Ji Shan Fang Mountain Cottage Devoting to Tranquility   28. Yue Se Jiang Sheng Stream Breaker under Moonlight
29. Wen Yuan Shi Zi Lin Lion Grove Garden in Wenyuan Garden   30. Shui Xin Xie Mid-Lake Gazebo   31. Zhu Yuan Si Pearl Stream Temple   32. Lü
Yun Lou Tower of Green Cloud   33. Yuan Jin Quan Sheng Spring Sounds Here and There   34. Qian Chi Xue Snow of a Thousand Feet Deep
35. Ling Ze Long Wang Miao Dragon King Temple of Celestial Love   36. Wen Jin Ge Belvedere of Literature Taste   37. Chun Hao Xuan Gallery in Nice
Spring   38. Meng Gu Bao Mongolian Yurt   39. Yong You Si Perpetual Bliss Temple   40. Le Cheng Ge Tower of Happiness for Achievement   41. Hui
Di Ji Men Auspicious Gate   42. Cheng Guan Zhai Studio of Clear View   43. Bei Zheng Shuang Feng Resting upon Two North Peaks   44. Qing Feng Lü
Yu Green Peak and Emerald Isle   45. Nan Shan Ji Xue Deep Snow on South Hill   46. Yun Rong Shui Tai Mountain Pose and Water Running   47. Qing
Xi Yuan Liu Clear Brook Flowing Afar   48. Fang He Ting Releasing Crane Pavilion   49. Shui Yue An Temple of Moon in Stream   50. Dou Lao Ge Tower
of Fight with Age   51. Shan Jin Xuan Gallery Approaching Hill   52. Zhan Tan Ting Vermilion Rosewood Pavilion   53. Guang Yuan Gong Taoist Palace of
Extensive Principles   54. Gu Ju Ting Pavilion Together with History   55. Chang Qing Zhai Open and Sun-Shone Studio   56. Bi Jing Tang Green Hall in
Tranquility   57. Han Qing Zhai Studio Embodying Greenery   58. Yu Cen Jing She Vihara of Jade Stairs   59. Yi Zhao Zhai Studio of Delightful Sunshine
60. Xi Bei Men Northwest Gate   61. Chuang De Zhai Studio of Creation and Achievement   62. Si Mian Yun Shan Surrounding Hills in Clouds
63. Jing Han Tai Gu Shan Fang Mountain Cottage of Embracing Remote History in Tranquility   64. Xiu Qi Tang Erecting Beauty Hall   65. Jiu Yun Si
Temple on Eagle Cloud   66. You Zhen Yi Xuan Gallery with Real Charm   67. Shi Zhe Ju Lodging of Eating Sugar Cane   68. Bi Feng Men Gate of
Green Peak   69. Bi Feng Si Temple of Green Peak   70. Chui Feng Luo Zhao Sunset on Stone Club Peak   71. Qi Wang Lou Tower of Promising
Wishes   72. Song He Qing Yue Clear Crane Screaming on Pine   73. Guan Pu Ting Pavilion for Watching Waterfall   74. Li Hua Ban Yue Pear Blossom
Accompanying Moonlight   75. Yin Hu Silver Lake   76. Jing Hu Mirror Lake   77. Shang Hu Upper Lake   78. Ru Yi Hu Lake of Satisfaction
79. Cheng Hu Clear Lake   80. Chang Hu Long Lake   81. Re He Quan Spring of Hot River   82. Shi Ma Dai Dam for Training Horses   83. Wan Shu
Yuan Garden of Ten Thousand Trees

FIG. 183 Wan He Song Feng Complex

FIG. 184 Yan Bo Zhi Shuang Hall

FIG. 185 Indoor scene of Yan Bo Zhi Shuang Hall

FIG. 186 Jinshan Pavilion in the Tian Yu Xian Chang Complex

FIG. 187 The courtyard of Dan Bo Jing Cheng Hall

FIG. 189 The pavilion on Huanbi Isle

after the rain, the endless ripples in the mist refresh the viewers' mind.

Tian Yu Xian Chang Complex

Tian Yu Xian Chang Complex, a small isle built in 1703, rests off the eastern bank of Ruyi Lake. Standing at the highest place in this isle is a three-floor octagonal pavilion, Jinshan Pavilion (Pavilion on Gold Hill) (Fig. 186). Piled up with hill rocks, this isle is in the huge of lake water at three sides, and the last one side was left for steep precipice, where winding brooks creep through. The entire isle embraced by the lake water looks so grandiose. This scenic spot serves both as a critical place for sightseeing and as an essential scenic spot in itself, and thus one of the major view-making components in this area. A host of regional landscapes adopt this isle as part of their composition center.

Dan Bo Jing Cheng Hall (Hall of Pure Respect and Sincerity)

This hall, built in 1711, was the major hall in the Major Palace, occupying a land of 583 square meters. It was also called Nanmu

Hall since it was reconstructed with nanmu timber in 1754. The hall is 7 rooms in width and 3 rooms in depth (Fig. 187). All door planks and window frames were constructed with nanmu timber and no paint was applied, presenting an elegant and bright style. Once the rain falls, the entire hall will be infused with the timber fragrance (Fig. 188). This was where emperors in the Qing Dynasty held official ceremonies and received his officials and officers, minority noblemen, and foreign ambassadors when they settled temporarily in this resort.

Huanbi Isle (Isle Embraced in Green)

Huanbi Isle is the smallest-scaled island in the resort among all the "three celestial islands in one pond" that is connected by Zhijingyun Causeway (Zigzag Road along Cloudy Causeway). The construction started in 1708 at the west side of this causeway. It sticks out of Ruyi Lake (Lake of Satisfaction) as a peninsula, surrounded by green waves, which is why Emperor Kangxi named it "Huan Bi," indicating that it was

FIG. 188 Long windows in Dan Bo Jing Cheng Hall

embraced by a green mountain and water (Fig. 189). This isle used to be a reading room for princes and was later a relaxation site for the emperor and his imperial wives after A Ge Suo (Princes' Dormitory) was constructed.

FIG. 190 Shuixin Gazebo

FIG. 191 The rockery at the south side of Yanyu Tower

FIG. 192 Shui Liu Yun Zai Pavilion

Shuixin Gazebo (Mid-Lake Gazebo)

This gazebo, constructed in 1709, is composed of three component gazebos standing in a line. These exquisite gazebos were built here lest the original sluice in the spot should degrade the holistic charm of the garden, and became one of the renowned scenic spots ever since then. They were built into different styles. The one standing in the middle is a double-eave, three-span rectangular gazebo with eight supporting pillars and a gable and hip roof with a round edge. The side buildings are both three-span square gazebos with 16 pillars, pyramid roof, and double eaves (Fig. 190).

Yun Shan Sheng Di Tower (Tower of Viewing Cloudy Mountains)

This tower, built in 1710, was located behind Yan Bo Zhi Shuang Hall. This two-storey building, 5 rooms in width and 1 room in depth, has no staircase for passage. Instead, the natural stone stair road in the rockery is available for visitors to climb up to the second floor. Looking down upon the lake area from the backside hall on the second floor, all man-made architectures—towers, platforms, pavilions, and gazebos—and the natural landscapes of the woods in the mist above the water will all dash into your eyes. This was how the tower was named. The north gate, Xiuyun Gate (Gate of Cloud in Valley), leads to the lake area.

Yanyu Tower (Yan Yu Lou, Tower of Mist and Rain)

Yanyu Tower, constructed in 1780, was located on Qinglian Island (Island of Blue Lotus) in Chenghu Lake (Clear Lake). This two-storey tower embraced by a circular winding corridor, five rooms in width and three rooms in depth, is a complete imitative work after the model of Yanyu Tower in South Lake of Jiaxing, Zhejiang province.

Three gate halls are attached to the tower in the front, and stone railings and baluster shafts stand in lines along the lakeside in the back. This was where the emperors of the Qing Dynasty and their empresses and concubines spent their summer enjoying the landscapes (Figs. 37, 191).

Shui Liu Yun Zai Pavilion (Pavilion of Running Stream and Perching Cloud)

Shui Liu Yun Zai Pavilion built in 1708 is the last one among the 36 scenic spots entitled by Emperor Kangxi," located at the west end along the north bank of Chenghu Lake. The principal pavilion is a three-room-wide square pavilion with double eaves. Each of the four sides extends farther into a side room. Therefore, there are 12 angles on the first eave, four on the top eave, and they add up to altogether 16 angles, for which this pavilion is popularly known as Sixteen Angles Pavilion (Fig. 192).

FIG. 193 The rockery and pond in the center of Lingering Garden, Suzhou
The central scenic area of Lingering Garden is known for rockery and water scenery. The majority of
its southeast subsection is excavated into a pond, while the northwest part is occupied by a rockery.
Thus, a landscape layout made up of a mountain in the north (which represents solid view) and water
in the south (which symbolizes void scenery) forms a positive pair of contrasts.

2. Gardens in Southern China

Existing private gardens in southern China are located mainly in the Yangtze River Delta and areas in and around Guangdong province. Each represents their specific garden construction styles, thus forming the Yangtze River Delta private gardens and the Lingnan (the area to the south of the Five Ridges, namely Yuecheng, Dupang, Mengzhu, Qitian, and Dayu, present day Guangdong, Guangxi, and parts of Hunan and

Jiangxi provinces) private gardens. All of them are relatively small in scale and were closely attached to private mansions where their original owner resided. So they are primarily resident gardens in nature.

Gardens in the Yangtze River Delta, though small and exquisite, stresses poetic and picturesque tastes and artistic conceptions hidden within. And they present diverse and very sophisticated construction techniques. Those in Lingnan are located at the southern end of China, where the climate

is even more scorching than that in the Yangtze River Delta, and consequently, the Lingnan private gardens are more open and airy than the former. And they appear lighter and livelier in their profiles. Furthermore, these gardens were heavily influenced by western garden styles, inclining to adopt regular and geometric shapes. The chosen examples are mainly those located in Suzhou, Hangzhou, and Yangzhou as far as the former is concerned, and those situated in Guangzhou as far as the Lingnan private garden is concerned.

Individual Garden 个园
Example of Borrowing Seasonal Views

Location: Yangzhou, Jiangsu province
Floor Space: 2.30 hectares
Construction Year: 1818
Genre of Garden: residence garden

The Individual Garden, located along Dongguan Street in Yangzhou, was originally the residence garden which belonged to Huang Zhijun (1770 – 1838, the leader of the salt guild in the extensive Huaihe River drainage area in the Qing Dynasty). Since a character in the owner's name, 筠 (*jun*), indicates bamboo and he had been enamored with it, more than ten thousand rods were planted in the garden and was organized into a sea of bamboo. Moreover, the Chinese written form of the character 个 (*ge*, individual) is half that of 竹 (*zhu*, bamboo), and symbolizes the shape of a bamboo leaf. Accordingly, this garden was named Ge Yuan (Individual Garden), indirectly referring to the precious characteristics of bamboo; they never bend to power, maintain humility, and always strive for self-improvement.

The Individual Garden is dominated by four rockeries which distinguish themselves as hills in different seasons, therefore are known as "four seasons rockeries." Their design theme and material rocks are both unique and original, reproducing poetic and picturesque scenes for visitors. "The Spring Hill is as bewitching as a smile on beautiful cheeks, the Summer Hill is soaked in emerald green as if verdant dews are bound to drop, the Autumn Hill is clear and clean like a charming lady with exquisite make-up, and the Winter Hill appears dismal as if it were asleep." In addition, "the Spring Hill is a wonderful choice for a tour, the Summer Hill for watching, the Autumn Hill for mountaineering, and the Winter Hill for a residence." They were piled with different rock materials; stalagmite, lake rocks, yellow stones, and Xuancheng stones, respectively. These four rockeries were arranged clockwise from west to east. To be specific, the Spring Hill stands in a cluster of green bamboos, declaring the garden owners' virtues with the landscapes; Summer Hill is in front of a stream, accompanied by clouds and water; Autumn Hill perches against the Zhuqiu Belvedere (Zhu Qiu Ge, Belvedere of Autumn Habitat), presenting its multitude of unusual peaks; and the Winter Hill is neighboring to the wind holes on the southern garden wall, indicating wind and snowstorms. Such a "four seasons rockeries" is the only case in Chinese gardens, and doubtlessly one of the most reputable garden views in Yangzhou.

The main architectures in the Individual Garden include Yiyu Gallery, Hu Tian Zi Chun Tower (Tower of Charming Spring in a

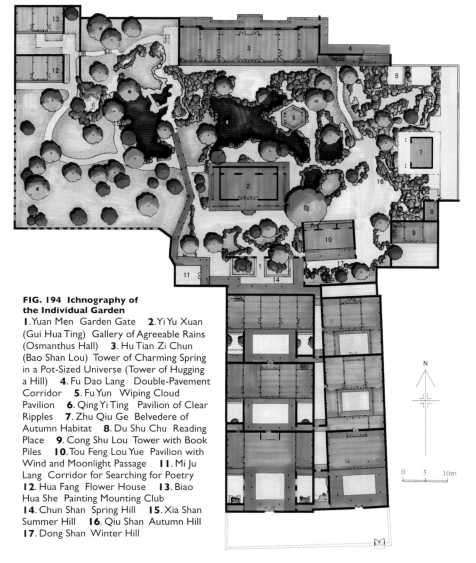

FIG. 194 Ichnography of the Individual Garden
1. Yuan Men Garden Gate   2. Yi Yu Xuan (Gui Hua Ting) Gallery of Agreeable Rains (Osmanthus Hall)   3. Hu Tian Zi Chun (Bao Shan Lou) Tower of Charming Spring in a Pot-Sized Universe (Tower of Hugging a Hill)   4. Fu Dao Lang Double-Pavement Corridor   5. Fu Yun Wiping Cloud Pavilion   6. Qing Yi Ting Pavilion of Clear Ripples   7. Zhu Qiu Ge Belvedere of Autumn Habitat   8. Du Shu Chu Reading Place   9. Cong Shu Lou Tower with Book Piles   10. Tou Feng Lou Yue Pavilion with Wind and Moonlight Passage   11. Mi Ju Lang Corridor for Searching for Poetry   12. Hua Fang Flower House   13. Biao Hua She Painting Mounting Club   14. Chun Shan Spring Hill   15. Xia Shan Summer Hill   16. Qiu Shan Autumn Hill   17. Dong Shan Winter Hill

FIG. 195 Garden gate

Pot-Sized Universe), Tou Feng Lou Yue Gallery (Gallery with Breeze and Moonlight Passage), Congshu Tower (Cong Shu Lou, Tower with Book Piles), Zhuqiu Belvedere, and Qingyi Pavilion (Pavilion of Clear Ripples). Among all these building, Hu Tian Zi Chun Tower, a two-storey building with 11 rooms, is the largest-scaled architecture in all of the Yangtze River Delta gardens. Two ponds stretch either in the eastern or the western sections, embraced by rockeries and pavilions (Fig. 194).

Garden Gate

The front gate is a moon gate, with an inscribed board hung over it which reads "Ge Yuan." A variety of bamboos with luxurious branches and leaves were planted on both sides of the front gate, appealing to views. "With moonlight peeping at the bamboo leaves, they produce thousands of the Chinese character 'bamboo' on the gate" is the vivid description of this view on the forehead of this gate. Stalagmite rocks dot among the bamboo rods, just like pieces of vigorous bamboo shoots in early spring. The gate wall was piled up with bath bricks and decorated with geometric window openings on both sides that are neatly designed and exquisitely and elegantly shaped (Fig. 195). Inside the front gate is a flower bed piled up with Taihu Lake rocks, in which golden sweet osmanthus trees dominate the entire flower parterre and winter jasmines, yellow jasmines, miniature crabapples, and other minor flowers only serve to escort them at the edge area. These flowery trees echo with the emerald bamboo outside the wall, together presenting all natural sceneries in four seasons, which is utmost appealing to visitors.

Spring Hill

This rockery is one of the "four seasons rockeries," leaning by the side of the front gate. Spring Hill is a collective scenic spot constituted of stalagmite rocks, Taihu Lake rocks, bamboo rods, and sweet osmanthus. Such a view-making technique, with bamboo and rocks as the dominant elements, is novel and ingenious. The waving bamboos in tender breeze stand for the mountainous woods in spring, and the stalagmite rocks symbolize the new shoots after a spring rain. Spring Hill seems to be an introduction to a piece of travel note, inviting a nice feeling that everything is fresh again with the advent of a new spring.

FIG. 196 Summer Hill

Summer Hill

Summer Hill stands beside the Lotus Pond, like a tiny isle on the water surface. A slab stone bridge connects it with the bank (Fig. 196). This hill was piled up with natural Taihu Lake rocks, among which the Fish-Bone Stone is its icon. This piece of rock was named after its appearance. With branches of a winter jasmine hanging down from above, the rockery appears vigorous and lively. The front aspect of Summer Hill facing to the south has very thickly dotted crumples on the grey rock surface, which produce various shadows under the sun, appearing like floating clouds in summer. And this is why this rockery was named Summer Hill. It is sheltered by gracious and luxurious pine trees that extend like umbrellas. And a narrow stream from the pond winds its way into a cave. The refreshing and tender curves of Taihu Lake rocks grant Summer Hill an elegant and tranquil atmosphere.

Autumn Hill

Most picturesque among all the four, Autumn Hill was piled up with yellow stones produced in Anhui province, which feature steep cliffs. Such rocks, either brownish yellow or rouge vermilion, patch up a precipice as sharp as one produced by a divine knife or ax, whose bold and carefree straight lines transplant the grandiose and spectacular landscape in nature right here (Fig. 197). Autumn Hill faces to the west, so when the sun sets, a pink evening glow tints the hill red, and produces very eye-catching colors. On the top of this rockery rests a small pavilion for visitors to extend their views to the distance. You will see range after range, peak after peak under

FIG. 197 Autumn Hill

FIG. 198 Winter Hill

your feet, which create a majestic landscape of hundreds or thousands of miles wide, though in reality this is but a miniature.

Winter Hill

Winter Hill was piled up with Xuancheng stone, on the surface of which the white crystals look just like frozen snow. Furthermore, this rockery was piled up under the south garden wall, perpetually within its shadow. A series of small holes were excavated on this wall for breezes to blow through and produce whistles, provoking a sound of north gales roaring in winter, and therefore, glamorizing a severe winter image (Fig. 198). Many hill-piling techniques had been applied to this rockery. The design is pretty original and ingenious, taking advantage of the shape, color, and sound to describe the thrilling and dreary winter.

FIG. 199　Crane Pavilion

He Pavilion (Crane Pavilion)

This pavilion built on the top of Summer Hill was said to have been where the former owner reared cranes. An old winding pine tree looks like a dragon, twisting and turning in front of the pavilion and bound to soar up into the style. The pine and crane indicate that "it is a promised celestial land where cranes dance above the clouds." The most characteristic feature of this pavilion lies in the image of a section of hill range winding its way through the Crane Pavilion, exactly like a crane just landing on the hill for a rest (Fig. 199).

Qingyi Pavilion

Qingyi Pavilion has six angles and appears charmingly tall and straight. A multitude of Taihu Lake rocks surrounding this building are further surrounded by a winding green stream. Thus, the layout of a pavilion in the center of rocks, rocks inside a stream, and a stream inside a garden interest the visitors (Fig. 200). Furthermore, the two characters *qing yi* expose how the water surface remains calm when a slight breeze tenderly touches the pond.

Tou Feng Lou Yue Gallery (Gallery with Breeze and Moonlight Passage)

Tou Feng Lou Yue Gallery, with a flush gable roof and single eave, 11.6 meters in width and 7.15 meters in depth, was located to the north of Winter Hill. Air and wind could enter and depart through the north and south walls. From the perspective of the structure, the hall is a square hall, with square rafters, pillars, drums in front of the gate and even square wooden carved window grills (the pattern within the window frame which settles the shape of a window), covered with square bricks. The eastern and western walls are vermilion wooden partition, while its southern and northern walls are sheer engraved window grills (Fig. 201). On entering the hall, you are thrilled by the sense of coldness inside it. The character *lou* (literally leaking) in the name vividly describes how moonlight spontaneously beams into the hall through the dense leaves and window grills. It was said that Huang Zhijun was particularly in favor of appreciating the snowy sceneries with a heater by his side.

FIG. 200 Qingyi Pavilion

FIG. 201 Tou Feng Lou Yue Gallery

He Garden 何园
The Supreme Garden Constructed in the Late Qing Dynasty

Location: Yangzhou, Jiangsu province
Floor Space: 1.40 hectares
Construction Year: 1883
Genre of Garden: residence garden

He Garden or Resort for Ease of Singing was located in Diaojia Street, Xuningmen, southeast of Yangzhou. As the largest-scaled classical garden in Yangzhou, the original Rockery Built with Pieces of Stones possessed by the Wu family was bought and later reconstructed and expanded into the present huge garden of today by He Zhidao—a regional official in charge of Hanyang, Huangzhou and De'an areas, three cities in Hubei province, during the Emperor Guangxu's reign (1871 – 1908) of the Qing Dynasty. This garden was publicly known as He Garden. In spite of the fact that it was in reality built on a plain ground, this garden still gives a sense of staying in a secluded and dangerous mountainous world where hill, stream, and distorted rocks echo each other thanks to the rugged rocks, winding stair roads, and the architectural complex purposefully laid out at the foothill or beside a lake.

He Garden can be divided into two sections: east and west. The west section is dominated by a pond, in the middle of which Shuixin Pavilion (Mid-Lake Pavilion) had been constructed for opera playing. Guihua Hall (Gui Hua Ting, Osmanthus Hall), Hudie Hall (Hu Die Ting, Butterfly Hall), and Shangyue Tower (Shang

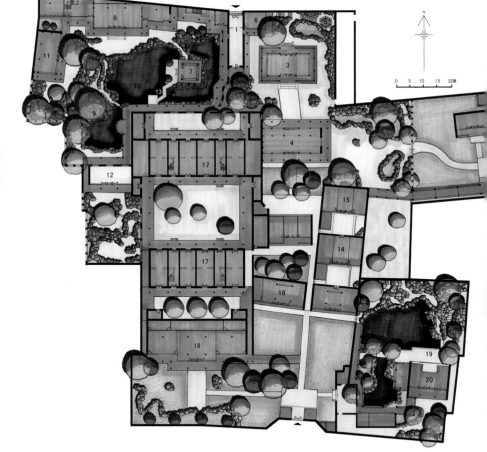

FIG. 202 Ichnography of He Garden
1. Dong Kou Garden Gate   2. Fu Lang Double-Pavement Corridor   3. Chuan Ting Boat-Wise Hall   4. Mu Dan Ting Peony Hall   5. Yue Ting Moon Pavilion   6. Ban Yue Tai Half Moon Platform   7. Shui Xin Ting Mid-Lake Pavilion   8. Hu Die Ting Butterfly Hall   9. Jia Shan Rockery   10. Shui Chi Pond   11. Gui Hua Ting Osmanthus Hall   12. Shang Yue Lou Tower for Appreciating Moonlight   13. Xiao Qiao Mini Bridge   14. Dong Er Lou Second Eastern Tower   15. Dong San Lou Third Eastern Tower   16. Zou Ma Lou Tower for Horse Riding   17. Yu Xiu Lou Tower of Embroider Charms   18. Xi Chun Lou Tower of Vernal Spring   19. Pian Shi Shan Fang Rockery Built with Pieces of Stones   20. Ming Nan Mu Ting Nanmu Hall Built in the Ming Dynasty

Yue Lou, Tower for Appreciating Moonlight)—all are two-storey towers—were constructed nearby. A grandiose rockery perches at the southwest bank of this pond. Visitors can take steps through a stair road in the rockery and reach Osmanthus Hall. The east section is dominated by architectures and plants on a zigzag terrain, such as Nanmu Hall, Mudan Hall (Mu Dan Ting, Peony Hall), Yuxiu Tower (Yu Xiu Lou, Tower of Embroider Charms), and Boat Hall. Nanmu Hall was very nicely and finely decorated though grandiose in scale. While Boat-wise Hall is in reality a metaphor, where the

hall is compared to a boat and the cobbles on the paving are compared to waves, indicating navigating on a stream. What an ingenious composition! All four sides of the hall have French windows, through which you can enjoy all the sceneries in the garden (Fig. 202).

The sightseeing route and spatial arrangement of He Garden are unique and ingenious. Different elements in different locations interconnect with others, views inside and outside are not blocked, they even echo each other vertically. Therefore, visitors may find countless charming sceneries and delights.

FIG. 203 Shuixin Pavilion and Butterfly Hall

Shuixin Pavilion

Shuixin Pavilion, with a square planar graph, stands in the center of the pond in the western section, known as "the number one pavilion in the universe" since it is the only aquatic theatre above water surface. The pavilion is surrounded by water, and a zigzag bridge at the northern side leads to Ming Tower (Ming Lou, Luminous Tower) and another one at the southern side connects with the double-pavement corridor (Fig. 203). The towers surrounding the pond could serve as balconies when an opera was playing. And exquisitely, the music played in this pavilion would be strengthened by the physical resonance on the water surface and in the corridor.

Butterfly Hall

Butterfly Hall located to the north of Shuixin Pavilion is the dominant architecture in the western section of this vial, and was where the garden owner received his guests and held banquets. The two-storey tower has three rooms in the center and two wing rooms at either side, therefore, it is known as Butterfly Hall. Lofty palm trees were planted at the corner where the major tower and the eastern wing tower joined into each other. These trees were so well positioned that they create a very striking visual effect together (Fig. 203).

Decorative Paving

All the roads and ground in He Garden had been patched into

FIG. 204 Decorative paving

various patterns with cobble stones and broken tiles and bricks. The paving technique is consummate and unsurpassable. The patterns include "five bats circulating a peach", "enjoying longevity with pine and deer" (Fig. 204), natural landscapes, human figures, fairy tales, and historical events. And all of them are tinted with the typical local cultural features of Yangzhou.

FIG. 205 Double-pavement corridor

Double-Pavement Corridor

This two-storey covered corridor goes straight and turns from time to time throughout the entire garden, and connects the two sections with the mansion into one. It single-handedly offers convenient passage from one architecture to another and visual diversity in the garden. The extensive length (1500 meters), the complicated three-dimensional mode of transportation, and the magnificent artistic language of the architectural construction enable this corridor to become the most characteristic building among all in He Garden. The design is a miraculous one in the Yangtze River Delta gardens, and had won quite a few reputations as "number one pavilion in the universe," "rudiment for Chinese flyovers," and "only wonder of this kind in the Yangtze

FIG. 206 Scenery on the second floor of double-pavement corridor

FIG. 207 A corner in Rockery Built with Pieces of Stones

River Delta gardens" (Figs. 205, 206).

Rockery Built with Pieces of Stones

Rockery Built with Pieces of Stones located in the east side of He Garden is in reality a minor garden inside this bigger garden. A winding pond extends from the north end to the south end. Along the north bank is a rockery leaning against the garden wall, which is said to be the only design work by Monk Shi Tao (1634 – 1724, monk and great painter in the early Qing Dynasty whose original name was Zhu Ruoji). This rockery is an exceptional masterpiece, which was admired as the "number one hill in the universe." It was named for the two rooms hidden under the hill (Figs. 207, 208).

FIG. 208 Rockery Built with Pieces of Stones

Outlook Garden 瞻园
Best Garden in Jinling (Nanjing)

Location: Nanjing, Jiangsu province
Floor Space: 0.55 hectares
Construction Year: 1368 – 1644 (early Ming Dynasty)
Genre of Garden: imperial garden

Outlook Garden, the oldest garden in existence in Nanjing, was located on Zhanyuan Road in the western part of the Confucius Temple in Nanjing, and has a history of over 600 years. This garden is especially renowned for its exquisite gardening art and ingenious construction style, and is therefore one of the reputable gardens in the Yangtze River Delta.

Outlook Garden took on a new look after several reconstruction and maintenance activities, absorbing garden styles typical of the gardens in Suzhou and Yangzhou and constructing rockeries, pavilions and corridors, and planting woods. This garden is more famous for its rockeries, which scatter in the north, west and south part of the garden.

In regard to its general layout, the garden is composed of three sections: Jingmiao Hall (Jing Miao Tang, Hall of Wonder of Tranquility), a tiny pond and a rockery in the south; the northern rockery and the big pond in the north; and another rockery in the west. The water in the lake circulates and links the three sections, creating a landscape of hill and water embracing each other (Fig. 209).

Rockeries

Hills are the dominators in Outlook Garden, while water only serves as foils. The protagonist views include three diverse rockeries: the northern one steep and upright, the western one twists and turns like a dragon, and the southern one majestic and masculine. Before such views, visitors would forget going back home, for they are totally amazed.

Piled up with Taihu Lake rocks which feature changeable shapes, the northern rockery presents some of the piling techniques typical of the Ming Dynasty, which is "the free-hand landscape painting technique—adopting part of the landscape to symbolize all of nature." In front of the pond stands a rock cliff, and at the foot of it a rock road winds away. A double-curved bridge is hardly above the water surface. Inside the main body of the rockery there are caves named Pan Shi (Surrounding Rock Cave), Fu Hu (Defeating Tiger Cave), and San Yuan (Three Apes Cave). Below the rock cliff two huge stone jetties, high or low, bulging or sunken. A suspending cave opens in the middle of this cliff just like a natural cave. And the coastline below it varies frequently.

The western rockery is basically an earth hill with Taihu Lake rocks

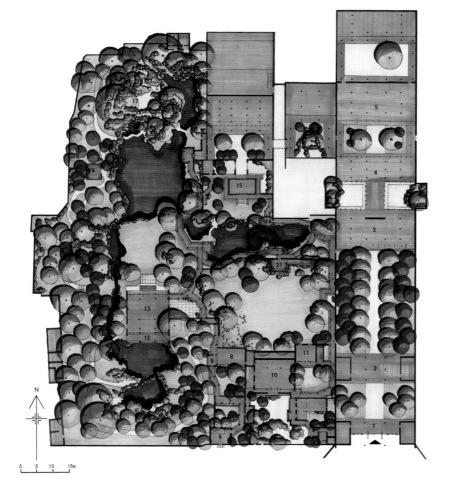

FIG. 209 Ichnography of Outlook Garden
1. Da Meng Front Gate   2. Yi Men Secondary Gate   3. Da Tang Main Hall   4. Er Tang Secondary Hall   5. San Tang Third Hall   6. Men Lang Covered Corridor   7. Zhi Shuang Xuan Refreshing Gallery   8. Hua Zhu Ting Hall of Flower and Bamboo   9. Ban Ting Half Pavilion   10. Jie Dai Shi Reception Room   11. Ban Gong Office   12. Shui Xie Gazebo   13. Jing Miao Tang Hall of Wonder of Tranquility   14. Yan Hui Ting Pavilion of Ushering in Light   15. Yi Lan Ge Belvedere of All Views at One Glance   16. Shui Lang Waterside Corridor   17. Ping Tai Platform   18. Bei Jia Shan Northern Rockery   19. Sui Han Ting Pavilion of Cold Year   20. Shan Ting Fan-Shaped Pavilion   21. Yi Ran Ting Pavilion of Flapping Wings   22. Nan Jia Shan Southern Rockery

FIG. 210 Southern rockery

lining up the edge. The rocks seem to have sprouted from the earth, creating an enormous natural wild atmosphere. A cave intentionally opens at the side for visitors to seek secluded miracles. Two sightseeing pavilions—Suihan Pavilion (Pavilion of Cold Year) and Fan-Shaped Pavilion were situated on the top. Around the fan-shape pavilion are evergreen arbors the color of emerald dew drops. Such a tranquil and gracious mountainous forest is no less than a celestial wonderland.

In the 1960s, Liu Dunzhen (1897 – 1968, a prestigious Chinese architect, educator, and expert of architectural history) designed the southern rockery and directed the construction activity. He selected rock materials from over a thousand tons of Taihu Lake rocks, patched their textures into coherent slants, stuck them by pouring cement mortar into the gaps between every two pieces at their back, and all gaps were vertically overlapping

each other. To support this gigantic hill, pegs were set up on the ground in a quincunxial style, and rocks were stuffed into the gaps among the pegs so that the fundament could endure the climbing activities and violent storms (Fig. 210).

The rockery can be divided into two layers, applying "earth in stones" and "stones in earth" techniques alternatively. Watched from outside, a low hill escorts a

lofty mountain, making the entire southern rockery a splendor with diversified postures, rugged shapes, rolling peaks with many ups and downs, and distinctive layers. In addition, the manmade waterfall, artificial water caves, wisteria, red maple trees, and Black Pines that scatter everywhere on the rockery together dress the southern rockery up into a picturesque scroll of green pines accompanying cliffs, full of vigor and luxuriance. Therefore, this rockery becomes a classic model in the Chinese art of rockery and garden construction.

Jingmiao Hall

Jingmiao Hall, lying in the center of the garden, is the major architecture and the best sightseeing spot in Outlook Garden, which helps to divide the entire garden into two sections, the south and north scenic areas. This hall is in reality a waterside lovebirds hall, whose southern hall was adopted to receive female guests since it appears small yet exquisite, refreshing and elegant, while the northern hall, unlike its neighbor, full of antique flavor, bold, and carefree, was used to receive male guests (Fig. 211).

FIG. 211 Jingmiao Hall

FIG. 212 Zigzag corridor stretching to the east part of the garden

FIG. 213 Zigzag bridge

Eastern Zigzag Corridor

The space between this corridor and the eastern wall is occupied by several tiny courtyards of different shapes. This layout is very convenient for drainage. Bamboos, rocks, and plants scatter around the space in the courtyards, which produce small-scaled sketches with white-washed walls like painting scrolls (Fig. 212). A zigzag corridor helps to add scenic depth and layers to the scenic area, and bring more pairs of spatial contrasts, so that visitors could enjoy different views as they move forward.

Zigzag Bridge above Pusheng Spring

Pusheng Spring (Spring of Universal Love) rests below the zigzag bridge at the northwest corner of the northern rockery. It was excavated during the 12th century and enjoys a history of

FIG. 214 Stele corridor

FIG. 215 Yiran Pavilion

FIG. 216 Suihan Pavilion

over 800 years. Even in the year of 1778 when Qinhuai River ran out of water, this spring didn't dry up, which amazed the public at the time. Pusheng Spring is the water source of the pond water in Outlook Garden. Ancient spring waters gurgling in a secluded valley and a zigzag bridge above the ripples integrate with the northern rockery which has diverse poses and varied appearances, setting off each other's charm (Fig. 213).

Yanhui Pavilion (Pavilion of Ushering in Light)

Yanhui Pavilion, in reality Guanyu Pavilion (Pavilion for Watching Fish), is a tranquil and elegant waterside architecture with flying eaves and curled-up angles, full of antique flavor.

Yilan Tower (Yi Lan Ge, Tower of All Views at One Glance)

Yilan Tower, a two-floor building, is the highest architecture in the garden. When visitors look down the garden views from this building, the panoramic view with water glitters and mountainous verve will be all within their sight.

Stele Corridor

The stele corridor winds through

the garden from the north to south end. The five ancient and fifteen new steles not only record the history and evolution of this garden and its reconstruction details, but also present poetic works composed by the literati of different dynasties and written by contemporary calligraphers. They record historical events or extol garden views, inscribed in all varieties of writing styles like running script (*xingshu*), cursive script (*caoshu*), official script (*lishu*), regular script (*kaishu*), and seal character (*zhuanshu*), producing profound meanings (Fig. 214).

Yiran Pavilion (Pavilion of Flapping Wings)

Yiran Pavilion is one of the previous 18 scenic spots in Outlook Garden. The roof rises up like a pair of wings extending out, ready to take off, so this pavilion was named "Yi Ran" (flapping wings) (Fig. 215).

Suihan Pavilion

Located on the top of the western rockery, Suihan Pavilion (a square pavilion with four angles and a pyramid roof) serves as the opposite scene to the waterside gazebo on the east bank of the pond. Beside the pavilion, pine trees, bamboos, and plum trees were planted, and

FIG. 217 Snow Wave Stone

as a result the pavilion was also known as "Pavilion of Three Friends in Winter" (Fig. 216).

Snow Wave Stone

Outlook Garden is reputable for rockeries, among which the Snow Wave Stone is most well known. It looks like spoondrifts after a rock was thrown into a stream and also like a snow ball bound to melt, full of dynamic vigor and transparent senses (Fig. 217).

Jichang Garden 寄畅园
An Unfolded Landscape Painting

Location: Wuxi, Jiangsu province
Floor Space: 1 hectare
Construction Year: around 1527
Genre of Garden: literati garden

The Garden for Lodging One's Expansive Feelings or Jichang Garden was located at the east foothill of Huishan Mountain in Wuxi, the northeast corner of Xihui Park. This garden was constructed by Qin Jin (1467 – 1534), one of the ministers in the Ming Dynasty, and reconstructed by his descendant, Qin Yao (1544 – 1604).

The landscape making techniques applied to this garden are not sheer abstraction or generalization, presenting the entire universe in a limited space or creating a miniature mountainous wood, but fully adopting the natural conditions so that "the natural flavor arises spontaneously in no need of manual construction." In accordance with Ji Cheng's hill-piling theory that "a rockery should not look artificial," the designer did not pile up an entire mountain in this garden, but instead, reproduced a section of a brook in a fragmentary valley and part of the foothill. The rockery was laid out in line with Huishan Mountain's rolling tendency, seemingly a branch of the mountain extending into the garden, integrating the artificial rockery inside and the real mountain outside as one. In addition, ancient trees on the hilltop shelter the entire rockery to constitute an intensified mountainous forest atmosphere, giving a sense of an artificial work

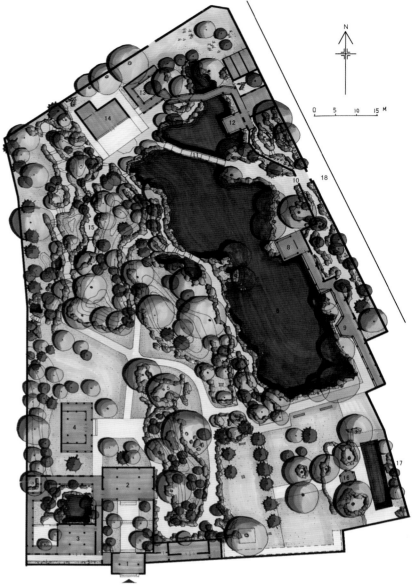

FIG. 218 Ichnography of Garden for Lodging One's Expansive Feelings
1. Da Men Front Gate   2. Shuang Xiao Ci Ancestral Temple for Two   3. Bing Li Tang Courtesy Abidance Hall   4. Han Zhen Zhai Studio of Insisting on Virginity   5. Jiu Shi Tai Nine Lions Platform   6. Jin Hui Yi Pond of Accumulating Brocade-Like Ripples   7. He Bu Tan Rocky Beach for Cranes' Walking   8. Zhi Yu Jian Pavilion of Knowing Fish's Happiness   9. Yu Pan Ting Pavilion with Insoluble Gloom   10. Qing Xiang Yue Dong Clear Music in Moon Cave   11. Qi Xing Qiao Seven Stars Bridge   12. Han Bi Ting Pavilion of Embracing Greenery   13. Da Shi Shan Fang Megalith House   14. Jia Shu Tang Hall of Auspicious Tree   15. Ba Yin Jian Eight Tones Ravine   16. Yu Bei Ting Imperial Stele Pavilion   17. Jie Ru Feng Peak of Uprightness   18. Qin Yuan Lu Qin's Garden Road

that seems to have been made by nature.

In regard to the general arrangement, a pond lies slightly to the east side, whose west band is dominated by a rockery piled up with earth and stones. The pond and rockery organize the basic hill-lake framework of the garden. The rockery occupies roughly 23% of the entire floor space, while the water surface 17%, and they together take up over one

third of the land in this garden. Architectures were loosely laid out, relatively fewer in number than the rockeries. The garden is well-proportioned and present natural wild atmosphere and tranquil and antique garden features with ingenious artistic approaches. From the lofty place in the garden, visitors could extend their views to Huishan Mountain and Xishan Mountain (Fig. 218). Xiequ Garden (Garden of Harmonious

Interests) in the Summer Palace in Beijing was a copy of Jichang Garden in Wuxi.

Hebu Rockery Beach (Rocky Beach for Cranes' Walking)

Hebu Rockery Beach, laid out with lake rocks, is the view opposite to Zhiyujian Pavilion. "Cranes' Walking" indicates longevity. The entire beach was patched up with huge yellow stones, which extends further into the water. This is a natural landscape where rockeries and water join together.

Stone Beauty

This rock piece stands at the southeast corner of the garden. To the east of Linfan Belvedere (Lin Fan Ge, Belvedere beside Buddhist Songs) is a small pavilion, which sits in front of Mirror Pond. The rectangular pond is so calm that the surface looks just like a mirror. A piece of lake rock stands on the east bank, against a wall, like a graceful beauty making herself up in front of a mirror. The rock is so charming

FIG. 220 Qixing Bridge

and well-postured that it was named Stone Beauty (Fig. 219).

Jinhuiyi Pond (Pond of Accumulating Brocade-Like Ripples)

Jinhuiyi Pond is a long narrow pond in the east of the garden, pointing to the south and north directions. It is a central part of the garden, accumulating numerous scenic spots as beautiful as brocade patterns, which was how it was named. Reflections of hills, pagoda, pavilions, trees, flowers, and birds are all within the same pond (Fig. 8). The earth mound at the north bank, covered with arbors and shrubs, is connected with the mountain peaks of Huishan Mountain into an undistinguishable whole. And extending your views eastward from Jiashu Hall (Jia Shu Tang, Hall of Auspicious Tree), you will find "reflection of a pagoda on the water surface of this mountainous pond," evidence that Longguang Pagoda is had been successfully integrated into the garden views, making it a model work of view borrowing.

Yupan Pavilion (Pavilion with Insoluble Gloom)

Yupan Pavilion was located at the southeast corner of Jinhuiyi Pond.

This tiny hexagonal pavilion shelters an ancient and simple round table made from grey stone and four stone drum-like stools. It was said, according to historical research, to be the original items possessed by the Qin Family in the Ming Dynasty. Legend says that Emperor Qianlong sent for a monk from Huishan Temple to play chess with him. Yet, the monk was outstanding in the game and Emperor Qianlong was frantic all the time until this monk made a feint strike and lost the game. Even though he had defeated the monk, Emperor Qianlong was quite aware that he could never outmatch this opponent. He was so gloomy that he issued an imperial decree and renamed the pavilion as Yupan Pavilion.

Qixing Bridge (Seven Stars Bridge)

Seven Stars Bridge, a flat bridge patched up with seven stone slabs, extends low above the water surface of Jinhuiyi Pond, dividing the extensive water into two sections. Thus, this bridge adds more spatial layers to the waterscape and creates lingering verve above the water surface. The deck of the bridge is 4.5 meters wide at its widest point, and a sheer 0.6 meters wide at its narrowest point (Fig. 220).

FIG. 219 Stone Beauty

FIG. 221 Zhiyujian Pavilion

name from a saying in *Zhuangzi* (庄子, *Zhuang Zi*), "How do you know that I don't know fishes' happiness?" This scenic spot is a charming view-borrowing site in the garden.

Bingli Hall

Bingli Hall, the protagonist architecture, was located in the northwest corner of the garden. Simple yet elegant in style, Bingli Hall has 18 French windows down to the ground, which are decorated with wooden grids (Fig. 222). This hall was where the previous owner worshiped their ancestors and held ritual activities.

Gateway with Tile Carving

This gateway, located to the northwest of Zhiyujian Pavilion, simulates the construction style typical of the Ming Dynasty. A rockery stretches in front of it like a screen wall (Fig. 223). Meanwhile, visitors could watch the real mountain through the holes on the artificial hill, making the real mountain a part of the garden views.

Bayin Ravine (Eight Tones Ravine)

The ravine was piled up with yellow stones at the back of the main hall in Jichang Garden. The range gradually rises up higher from east to west, extending 36 meters long. A bridge is merely above the water surface, inviting visitors to stay closer to water. The rocky road in the middle of the valley twists and turns from time to time. Lush woods shelter the rockery high above, meanwhile two clear brooks are introduced into the garden, making appealing sounds when the water pours swiftly into the winding pond (Fig. 224).

Zhiyujian Pavilion (Pavilion of Knowing Fish's Happiness)

It is a tiny square pavilion with nine ridges and flying-up eaves in the middle section of Jinhuiyi Pond. It sticks out from the land into the pond, embraced by the water at three sides. Visitors could either lean against the railings and enjoy swimming fishes and flickering algae, or watch Huishan Mountain in the distance (Fig. 221). The

FIG. 222 Bingli Hall

FIG. 223 Gateway with tile carving

FIG. 224 Bayin Ravine

Humble Administrator's Garden
拙政园
Largest Ancient Garden in the Yangtze River Delta

Location: Suzhou, Jiangsu province
Floor Space: 4.80 hectares
Construction Year: 1506 – 1521
(during Zhengde period of the Ming Dynasty)
Genre of Garden: literati garden

The Humble Administrator's Garden was located at the northeast corner in Suzhou. The previous owner was Wang Xianchen, an administrative censor in the Ming Dynasty. The two Chinese characters *zhuo zheng* (literally humble administrator) indicate the owner's expectation for retirement and settling into pastoral life. Over 400 years, this garden had been divided and shifted from one person to another for several times. The present architectures and scenic spots are mostly typical of the later Qing style. It is the largest scaled classical garden in Suzhou so far.

The Humble Administrator's Garden could be divided into four sections: east, middle, west, and residential sections. The east section is dominated by remote mountain ranges, even hummocks, pine forest, lawn, bamboo dock, and winding stream. The middle section occupies roughly 1.23 hectares of land, within which a pond takes up one third of it. So the pond is the central element in the general layout, with architectures like hall, pavilion, gallery, and belvedere standing around it. The west section is relatively loosely laid out and feels leisurely, whose rockery and waterscape construction is similar to that in the middle section. The residential section is a typical folk residence in Suzhou and serves as the exhibition room of Garden Museum now (Fig. 225).

The essence of the entire garden lies in the middle section, where the water surface serves as the center of general arrangement in an open and extensive space. Layer after layer of scenes extend to the profound distance, with nice and exquisite architectures dotting everywhere. Yuanxiang Hall is the major architecture there. To the southeast is a peaceful and simple loquat garden tinted with

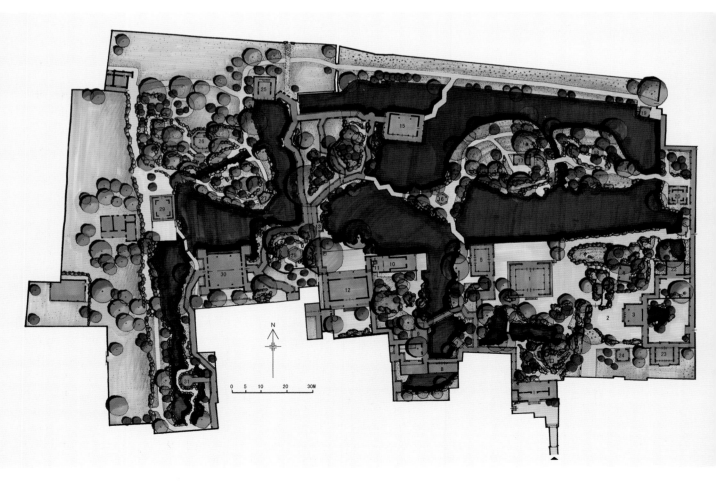

luscious pastoral atmosphere on account of the loquats, bamboo, and banana trees planted within it and the exquisite furnishings in this nicely-arranged courtyard. This garden also connects other courtyards like Tingyu Gallery (Gallery for Listening to Raindrops) and Courtyard of Hai Tang Chun Wu (Col in a Spring with Begonia Flowers). These profound courtyards create gracious sceneries.

Adjacent to this loquat garden in the north side is a small hill with Xiuqi Pavilion, from which you can catch sight of the entire garden views in the middle section. To the north of Yuanxiang Hall and opposite to Lotus Pond lies an earth mound dotted with some unknown rocks and covered with green trees and rare flowers, among

FIG. 226 Wu Zhu You Ju Pavilion

which Xue Xiang Yun Wei Pavilion stands. Jianshan Tower located at the northwest of the middle section and surrounded by water is a wonderful place for visitors either to enjoy the charming views on Tiger Hill or to turn southeast to appreciate the panoramic scenery inside the garden. To the southwest of Yuanxiang Hall lies the Xiaocanglang Waterside Courtyard (Little Waterside Courtyard of Great Wave), where Xiaofeihong Bridge strides above the pond to divide the water surface into two halves. The waterside architectures here, originally where the garden owners enjoyed reading, are appealingly exquisite and small. A two-floored stone boat perches to the south of Jianshan Tower, embraced by water from three sides. An inscribed board with two Chinese characters *xiang zhou* (literally fragrant isle) written by Wen Zhengming was hung in

the middle front. To the west is a refreshing and tranquil courtyard named Yulan Hall (Yu Lan Tang, Magnolia Hall). To the north, He Feng Si Mian Pavilion echoes with it from the opposite side of the pond. This pavilion is the traffic hub in the garden and also a nice place to enjoy lotus blossoms.

The west section had once been bought by a wealthy merchant in Wuxian county, Zhang Lüxiu, who named his garden Bu Garden (Revamped Garden) after it was completed. This section occupies 12 *mu* (0.80 hectare, 1.98 acres) of land. A small rockery rises up in the middle of a pond, above which Fucui Belvedere (Fu Cui Ge, Belvedere of Floating Greenery) stands upright as the highest point in the west section. 36 Yuanyang Lodging, the major architecture in this area, can be divided into two halves, the south half suitable for winter stay and the north half as a summer resort. In the west of this area, Liuting Belvedere (Liu Ting Ge, Belvedere of Staying to Appreciate Sound Images) faces south. Through the glass doors and windows set in all four sides, you can enjoy the entire garden views in the west section. And Yiliang Pavilion (Pavilion Suitable for Both Views) was constructed above the earth mound leaning against the east wall. Visitors could either watch eastward for the miraculous waterscape in the middle section or northwestward for sceneries in the west section. This is an effective view-borrowing example.

The majority of the original architectures and rockeries in the east section vanished into history, and the existing works were mainly constructed after 1949. Lawns stretching on mild hummocks dominate this section; while pond, rockery, and pavilions were constructed as their ornaments. This general layout maintains its original tradition but creates new elements at the same time, refreshing visitors and leaving them with a sense of delightfulness.

Courtyard of Hai Tang Chun Wu

An independent courtyard fenced by a tracery wall to the east of Linglong Lodging (Exquisite Lodging) is named Hai Tang Chun Wu. An intricate scroll-shaped name board engraved with a brick was set in the south wall. Inside the courtyard are two Begonia trees and the courtyard ground was patched into the same pattern with blue, red, and white cobblestones. Even the decorative patterns on the table echo the Begonia trees. In the early spring, hundreds and thousands of flowers blush at the same time, as if a gorgeous smile bursting from a shy girl, presenting an extraordinary charm.

Wu Zhu You Ju Pavilion

Wu Zhu You Ju, an exquisitely designed pavilion, is the protagonist scenic spot on the east bank in the middle section. The pavilion with red pillars and white walls, flying eaves, and rake angles leans against a long corridor in the back, confronts a spacious pond, and is

sheltered by a phoenix tree by the side. The masterstroke in the design lies in the four moon-shaped door openings on the four white-washed walls, which overlap and correlate each other (Fig. 226). Observed from different perspectives, you can figure out very unusual images of staggered segmental circles, smaller circle in a bigger one, or two closely connected circles. The four moon gates, transparent and elegant in of themselves, form four lattice window frames, presenting different charming pictures— a small bridge above a running stream, water ripples echoing with mountainous scenery, and an elegant phoenix tree answering to bamboo clusters (Fig. 227).

Xiaofeihong Bridge

Xiaofeihong Bridge is the only gallery bridge in the gardens constructed in Suzhou. The vermilion railings reflect on the glittering ripples just like a rainbow, and this is how it was named. Besides functioning as a connector between water surface and land, it constitutes a unique scenic spot with a bridge as the central element. The main body is a splay stone bridge composed of three spans, with Swastika-shaped (卍) guard rails standing at both sides. Eight pillars support the corridor roof, under whose eaves wooden hollow decorations are hung. Two winding corridors are connected with the bridge at both sides. It is indeed an ingenious bridge (Fig. 59).

Yu Shui Tong Zuo Gallery

Yu Shui Tong Zuo Gallery is a pretty interesting gallery in the west section of the Humble Administrator's Garden. In

FIG. 227 Looking outward from Wu Zhu You Ju Pavilion

FIG. 228 Xiaocanglang Waterside Courtyard

accordance with the original geographic features on the bank of the pond, the designer cleverly planned a small-scaled waterside architecture whose planar graph looks like a folding fan. The roof surfaces, door opening, window opening, stone table, stone stools, lampshade, and inscribed board hung on the wall are all fan-shaped (Fig. 99). Therefore, it is also called "Fan-Shaped Pavilion." A line in Su Dongpo's (1037 – 1101) poetic work says, "With whom shall I sit? Bright moon and clear breeze." Therefore, the architecture was named "With Whom Shall I Sit Gallery."

Yuanxiang Hall

Yuanxiang Hall, in reality a four-sided hall, is the major building in the middle section of the Humble Administrator's Garden (Figs. 4, 75). This three-room-wide hall with a gable and hip roof and single eave, facing the pond, was a dining hall where the host treated his guest. From the hall, visitors could fully appreciate the neighboring sceneries—the spacious platform in the north, the open and clear water in the pond. The name of the hall originated from a lotus whose leaves flourish in summer and the

pleasurable sweet sent drifted to the distance. It is indeed a wonderful place to enjoy the beauty of the lotus. All four walls were furnished with orderly French windows, transparent and exquisite, through which all the surrounding sceneries will be within sight.

Xiaocanglang Waterside Courtyard

Xiaocanglang Waterside Courtyard occupies a sheer one twentieth of the entire floor space of the middle section of the Humble Administrator's Garden. It is a three-room-wide waterside

belvedere located to the west of a waist-high gate in the garden, to be specific, at the end of the sightseeing route of the Jianshan Tower scenic area. Two sides of the tower face a pond (Fig. 228). This tranquil courtyard is small in scale, but charming with many twists and turns and plentiful spatial changes.

Xiangzhou Stone Boat

Xiangzhou Stone Boat, one of the symbol of the Humble Administrator's Garden, is a typical "stone boat" architecture (Fig. 229). It is embraced by water from three sides and has two floors.

FIG. 229 Xiangzhou Stone Boat

FIG. 230 Waterside Corridor

The entire building is composed of five construction forms, namely platform, pavilion, gazebo, belvedere, and tower.

The sightseeing platform in the front, like a boat deck fenced with stone railings on three sides, is a good place for appreciating the swimming fishes and enjoying the neighboring views. A small square pavilion stands behind the platform, a waterside gazebo serves

FIG. 231 Inside the 36 Yuanyang Lodging

as the middle cabin on a boat, and Chengguan Tower (Cheng Guan Lou, Tower of Clear View) sits at the rear. Chengguan Tower, a two-floored building, has white-washed walls and vermilion partition boards, appearing gracious and decent. The gang board is composed of three slab stones. Once on board, you can look forward to Yiyu Gallery, turn left and see Jianshan Tower, or turn right and peep at Xiaocanglang Waterside Courtyard. Even in days under scorching sun, this place is cool in every corner, chilled down by breezes from the lotus pond. While in cold days, birds still hover around and fishes still swim in the pond, presenting a view even nicer than in the spring. This dry boat not only attracts visitors with its elegant and exquisite construction techniques, but also provokes a spiritual pursuit for noble characteristics.

Waterside Corridor

The waterside corridor hall in the Humble Administrator's Garden winds along the east wall, rolls up and down along with the geographic features. When it ends be the waterside, it becomes a wave-like corridor, in the middle of which a small pavilion named "Fishing Platform" sticks out. When strolling on the corridor bridge, visitors would feel that they are walking above ripples. This corridor invites you through a winding yet smooth and sprightly territory, so it is superior to other views for its zigzags and grace (Fig. 230).

36 Yuanyang Lodging

This building is the major architecture in the western section. The southern half is called "18 Mandragora Lodging" and the northern half is 36 Yuanyang Lodging. The roof appears like an arch, which helps sounds to reverberate, therefore, the sound effects in this house are incredibly nice. Furnished with antique and simple furniture and ornaments, this lodging was where the host met his guest, took a rest, or hosts dinner parties (Fig. 231).

Lingering Garden 留园
Garden with the Richest Elements

Location: Suzhou, Jiangsu province
Floor Space: 2.30 hectares
Construction Year: 1522 – 1565
(during the Jiajing Period of Ming
Dynasty)
Genre of Garden: literati garden

Lingering Garden, located outside
Changmen Gate in Suzhou, is one
of the large-scaled classical gardens
in the city. Lingering Garden is
divided into four sections—central,
east, north, and west sections (Fig.
232). The scenic area from Hanbi
Mountain Hall to Wufengxian
Lodging is the central section which
is advantageous in natural landscape,
and where the essential charm of
this garden rests. This section could
be further divided into east and west
subsections, two minor gardens.

Waterscape is the dominant
element in the west subsection,
where rockeries and architectures
were built around water and a
dozen of ancient trees of more
than a hundred years of age create
a wild mountainous atmosphere.
In contrast, the east subsection
is composed of buildings in the
southeast, a pond in the center, and
a rockery in the northwest. Such a
spatial layout places the protagonist
scene—the pond beside a hill—
in the sun drenched site, a regular
arrangement in large-scaled classical
gardens in Suzhou. Guanyunfeng
Courtyard (Courtyard of Cloud-
Capped Peak), renowned for its
rockery and architectures, occupy
the eastern section. In addition,
buildings like Lin Quan Qi Shuo
Lodging (Old Hermit Scholars'
Lodging) and Yifeng Gallery

FIG. 232 Ichnography of Lingering Garden
1. Tian Jing Courtyard   2. Qu Lang Zigzag corridor   3. Ci Tang Ancestral shrine   4. Men Ting
Gate Hall   5. Da Ting Main Hall   6. Gu Mu Jiao Ke Ancient Interlocking Branches   7. Lü Yin Xuan
Gallery in Green Shade   8. Ming Se Lou Brilliant and Refreshing Tower   9. Han Bi Shan Fang Hall
of Green Water   10. Yuan Xi Xing Walking along Brook   11. Huo Po Po Di Gazebo of Lively Place
12. Bie You Dong Tian A Different World   13. Shu Xiao Ting Pavilion of Releasing Roar   14. Zhi
Le Ting Pavilion of Super Happiness   15. Hua Fang Flower House   16. Wen Mu Xi Xiang Xuan
Osmanthus Fragrance Gallery   17. Ke Ting Pavilion of Contentment   18. Yuan Cui Ge Belvedere
for a Far View of Green Wood   19. You Yi Cun Another Village   20. Xing Li Yuan Garden of
Apricot and Plum   21. Ji Gu De Geng Chu Where I Benefit from Ancient Learning   22. Qing Feng
Chi Guan Lodging for Breezes and Pond   23. Xi Lou West Tower   24. Qu Xi Lou Tower beside
Winding Brook   25. Hao Pu Ting Pavilion upon Hao and Pu Rivers   26. Zi Teng Jia Wisteria Frame
Bridge   27. Xiao Peng Lai Minor Penglai   28. Wu Feng Xian Guan Celestial Lodging of Five Peaks
29. He Suo Crane Habitat   30. Shi Lin Xiao Wu Small House in Rock Woods   31. Jing Zhong
Guan Observatory of Watching in Tranquility   32. Yi Feng Xuan Gallery of Greeting Mountain
Peak   33. Huan Wo Du Shu Chu Tower of Returning to Reading   34. Jia Qing Xi Yu Kuai Xue Ting
Pavilion of Charming Sunshine, Promising Rain and Pleasant Snow   35. Xiu Yun Feng Cloud Peak
36. Guan Yun Feng Cloud-Capped Peak   37. Rui Yun Feng Auspicious Cloud Peak   38. Guan Yun
Lou Tower Above Cloud   39. Huan Yun Zhao Pond of Washing Cloud   40. Zhu Yun Ge Cloud
Staying Tower   41. Lin Quan Qi Shuo Zhi Guan Old Hermit Scholars' Lodging   42. Yi Bu Er Ting
Pavilion of Only Approach To Buddha   43. Jiu Sheng Zhai Old Residence of Sheng's Family
44. Liu Yuan Lu Lingering Garden Road   45. Ru Kou Garden Gate

(Gallery of Greeting Mountain
Peak) are also here, connected with
each other by a winding corridor.

The northern section is a
fruit forest and bamboo forest
featuring the natural flavors of a
mountainous village. The west
section has Zhile Pavilion (Pavilion
of Super Happiness) and Huo Po
Po Di Gazebo, where maple trees
and gingko trees shelter the hill,
constituting a wildly abundant
atmosphere. And the ups and
downs produced by the wavy walls
complements this mountainous

scenery. Between these four scenic
areas, some are linked by a zigzag
corridor; some are segregated by a
wall. Yet even the divisive walls have
window openings, carved windows,
and door openings. Therefore,
different spatial sections are relatively
independent, and meanwhile,
integrated into each other.

Lingering Garden can be ranked
as the champion among all of the
Yangtze River Delta gardens and a
rare case among all private gardens
constructed at the same time in
China, as far as spatial diversity is

FIG. 233 Guanyunfeng Rock

concerned. It is a complex of diverse spaces, accumulating all wonders in garden spatial arrangement and fully representing the supreme garden construction techniques and wisdom of the ancient architects and artisans.

Guanyunfeng Rock (Cloud-Capped Peak)

Guanyunfeng Rock is a nonesuch among all Taihu Lake rocks, which exposes all four charming points of Taihu Lake rocks—thin, crumpled, leak, and holey. The rock is as high as 6.5 meters, so lofty that it seems to be penetrating the clouds. It was said that this piece was originally one of the relics within Bureau of Strange Flowers and Marble Shippment (*hua shi gang*) in the Northern Song Dynasty (Fig. 233).

Mingse Tower

Mingse Tower is a light and exquisite building with 2.5 floors, and only one side has a gable and hip roof and round edge. Three sides of the upper floor are furnished with shell-tiles and prop-up windows (windows whose upper part can be propped and lower part can be dismantled). The stair road was piled up with Taihu Lake rocks outside the tower. Beside the stair road stands a peak inscribed with three Chinese characters "Yi Ti Yun" (literally Cloud Ladder).

Hanbi Mountain Hall

Hanbi Mountain Hall, the major architecture in the central section, is a three-room-wide building with a flush gable roof and round edges. Perching in front of a lotus pond with transparent blue water, the house appeals to anyone expecting a cool breeze in the summer. This house, opposite to the protagonist scenes—hill and pond—in the west subsection of the central section, and thus, becomes the most important sightseeing spot in the entire west subsection (Fig. 234).

18 French windows extend down to the ground at the south and north walls, together with round beams on the frame of the hall, appearing graceful and open, setting off the landscape outside with ease. A stone platform is

attached to the building on the north side, confronting the water; a small courtyard supports it on the south side; and Mingse Tower (Ming Se Lou, Brilliant and Refreshing Tower) connects with it on the east side. Look from Ke Pavilion (Pavilion of Contentment) in the opposite, Hanbi Mountain Hall and Mingse Tower seem to be a boat mooring at waterside. It is indeed an ingenious arrangement.

Lüyin Gallery (Gallery in Green Shade)

There used to be an ancient maple tree on the west side, which sheltered the little gallery under its shadow. The gallery was named on account of this image. This building with a flush gable roof looks much like a pavilion confronting water. Lady stay is settled on the north side in front of the pond (Fig. 235). The small Penglai Island, Wisteria Frame Bridge, and Hao Pu Pavilion in the middle of the pond is a prelude for the entire sightseeing

FIG. 234 Hanbi Mountain Hall

tour. The window openings on both of the gable walls offer an opportunity to enjoy the lake rocks and Mingse Tower (Fig. 236).

Hao Pu Pavilion (Pavilion Upon Hao and Pu Rivers)

Hao Pu Pavilion, a square building with four angles, a gable and hip roof with a single eave, projects out onto the water surface in the north. The rock outside this pavilion looks like a full moon, whose reflection in the water grants its name "Yin Yue (literally Moon Print)."

Quxi Tower (Qu Xi Lou, Tower beside Winding Brook)

Quxi Tower, a narrow and long building of five rooms in

FIG. 235 Lüyin Gallery (Gallery in Green Shade)

FIG. 236 The inside view of Lüying Gallery

FIG. 237 Quxi Tower

width, appears more like a long corridor since its depth is rather shallow. Accordingly, the designer intentionally planned a one-sided gable and hip roof with pattern ridge ornaments to make the profile perfect. On the second floor, you can see three semi-windows and the two

side walls are furnished with lattice windows patched with octagonal bright-finished bricks, whose patterns are beautiful. Downstairs, the whitewashed walls are furnished with window openings lined up with ground bricks, through which visitors could appreciate the framed scenery one after another in the garden (Fig. 237).

Wen Muxixiang Gallery

The square open gallery, with a gable and hip roof and single eave, stands on the rockery at the west bank of the pond. Leaning against a wavy wall, this hall is relatively simply and elegantly furnished. The patterned hanging fascias between each pair of vermilion pillars are pretty characteristic, indicating everlasting happiness and welfare (Fig. 238). Two climbing-hill corridors wind their way on both

sides of the building, connecting the Hanbi Mountain Hall to the south and Yuanxui Belvedere to the north. Clusters of osmanthus and rocks stand within the vicinity.

Qingfengchi Lodging

This building is a waterside lodging open to the west, with a gable and hip roof and single eave. Standing in front of the pond, visitors would feel open and delighted at the views of Hao Pu Pavilion and Minor Penglai Island nearby and Ke Pavilion in the mountainous woods, Wen Muxixiang Gallery and Mingse Tower in the distance (Fig. 239). All the landscapes are definitely clearly in their sight. The ancient trees and rock pieces beside the pavilion set off each other, making this corner beside the pond even more tranquil and elegant.

FIG. 238 Wen Muxixiang Gallery

Huo Po Po Di Gazebo

Ho Po Po Di, located in the west section of the garden, is a waterside gazebo leaning against a hill and half of its body situated on solid land, while the other half suspending above the water of a stream. This belvedere has a gable and hip roof, round edge and rake angles like flapping wings. The building is surrounded by a transparent cloister and three white-washed walls help to enclose a space as an inner chamber (Fig. 240). Fish hawks flap their wings, fishes hop out of water, and every creature is presenting their natural vigor to their fullest. So this place was named "Lively Place."

Minor Penglai Island

Minor Penglai Island is a tiny isle in the central section of the garden, after the model of the Penglai celestial island. This isle, small in scale yet very exquisite, connects to the bank with the help of two bridges. Swimming fishes playing game and wisteria bending down to the water surface together compose a picturesque scene (Fig. 241).

FIG. 239 Qingfengchi Lodging

FIG. 240 Ho Po Po Di Gazebo

FIG. 241 Minor Penglai Island

Master of the Nets Garden 网师园
Model Work among Small-Scaled Gardens

Location: Suzhou, Jiangsu province
Floor Space: 0.40 hectares
Construction Year: 1174 (the first year during the Chunxi period of the Song Dynasty)
Genre of Garden: literati garden

Master of the Nets Garden was initially named Yuyin Garden (literally Hermit Fisherman Garden). After experiencing quite a few vicissitudes of life, this garden was renamed Wang Shi Yuan, since master of nets refers to fishermen, and indicates retreat from social life into the natural world, just echoing the original name "Hermit Fisherman." The landscape layout and titles of all the scenic spots embody an atmosphere of a very luscious hermit life. Later, this garden had been moved from one hand to another several times until Qu Yuancun took this property in the last year during Emperor Qianlong's reign. This new owner reconstructed the garden according to its original scale and added some other architectures, and the garden was publicly known as "Qu Garden" (Garden of Qu Family). It was only around 1765 that this garden was eventually renamed Master of the Nets Garden and settled down to the layout of today. The scale, sceneries, and architectures at present are mostly inherited from Qu Garden. An old residential architecture complex of an aristocratic family and a moderate-scaled classical landscape garden had been basically well preserved up to now. Master of Nets Garden is a cultural legacy for

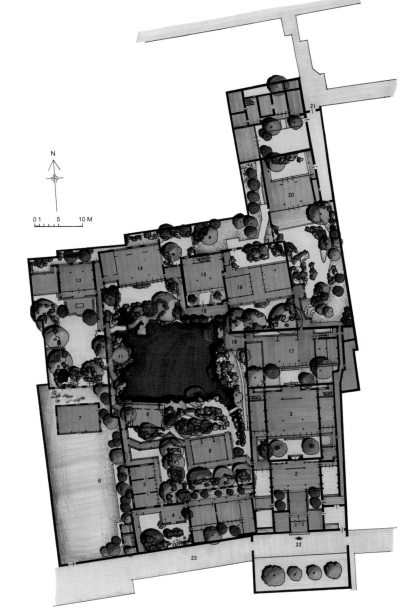

FIG. 242 Ichnography of Master of the Nets Garden
1. Da Men Garden Gate 2. Jiao Ting Palanquin Hall 3. Da Ting Main hall 4. Qin Shi Musical Instrument Room 5. Dao He Guan Peaceful Lodging 6. Miao Pu Nursery Garden 7. Hua Fang Flower House 8. Xiao Shan Cong Gui Xuan Gallery of Osmanthus Clusters on Hill 9. Zhuo Ying Shui Ge Waterside Belvedere for Washing Cap Ribbon 10. Yun Gang Hill Range on Clouds 11. Yue Dao Feng Lai Ting Pavilion of Moon and Wind Visiting 12. Leng Quan Ting Pavilion of Cold Spring 13. Dian Chun Yi Late Spring Study 14. Kan Song Du Hua Xuan Gallery of Watching Pine and Painting 15. Ji Xu Zhai Studio of Upright Self-Cultivation 16. Zhu Wai Yi Zhi Xuan Gallery of a Few Bamboos 17. Xie Xiu Lou Tower of Picking Flowers 18. She Ya Lang Duck Shooting Corridor 19. Du Hua Lou Tower for Reading and Painting (upstairs) Wu Feng Shu Wu Five Peaks Study (downstairs) 20. Ti Yun Shi Room of Cloud Ladder 21. Wang Shi Yuan Hou Men Back Gate to Master of Nets Garden 22. Ru Kou Entrance 23. Kuo Jia Tou Xiang Lane of Kuojiatou

the whole universe.

Master of the Nets Garden, a smaller moderate-sized classical garden in the Yangtze River Delta, is closely adjacent to a private mansion on the east side. Buildings inside the garden are graciously shaped, small yet exquisite.

Pavilions around the pond are especially remarkable, characteristic of small scale, lower structure and interaction between different views. The pond is the center of the entire garden, which can be divided into five sections: residential area in the east, banquet area in the south,

FIG. 243 Zhu Wai Yi Zhi Gallery

area surrounding the pond, internal garden Dian Chun Yi (Late Spring Study) in the west, and a study area in the north. The holistic garden is well-proportioned and orderly and compactly laid out. And the interior space is further divided into different sections in line with their dominant sceneries. All the five sections present diverse and varied views (Fig. 242).

Xiao Shan Cong Gui Gallery (Gallery of Osmanthus Clusters on Hill) is the major architecture in the garden, yet compared with parlors constructed in other gardens in Suzhou, it is relatively small in scale. Rockeries were piled up in the front and back. A flower bed patched with lake rocks lies low by the south side, and sweet-scented osmanthus is the host flower in it. In contrast, the Yungang Rockery (Hill Range on Clouds) piled up with yellow stones on the north side

is steep with maple, osmanthus, and magnolia trees loosely dotting it and thus, creating various images. Walking along the corridor of this pavilion, visitors can reach Daohe Lodging (Peaceful Lodging) and the musical instrument room. This area is rather narrow and secluded, while the corridor winds its way, full of twists and turns, making the surroundings more solitary and tranquil.

Stepping along a low and obscure zigzag corridor starting from Xiao Shan Cong Gui Gallery, visitors will arrive at the central section, where ripples slightly undulate and the view is suddenly enlightened. Because the designer had made use of the darkness in the corridor to set off the well-lit space, and adopted rockery as a contrast to the water in the pond. The central pond takes up a half *mu* of land (0.03 hectare, 0.08

acre), roughly a square with almost no branches except the two at the southeast and northwest corners, so the water surface is pretty integrated. All pavilions, corridors, belvederes, and bridge are close above the water surface. The open and spacious water surface and the low banks which were made into caves with yellow stones inspire a sense of a gigantic endless water source. No algae or lotus had been planted in the pond, leaving room for the sky, hills, architectures, and trees to reflect onto the water surface, and the scenery is, accordingly, enriched.

Extending your sight northward from the south bank, you will see a low Kan Song Du Hua Gallery (Gallery of Watching Pine and Painting) hidden in the bushes; two towers queue in line at the northeast corner; lofty ancient cypresses, a zigzag bridge, and a rock dock just above water lie in sequence in the middle of the pond; and Zhu Wai Yi Zhi Gallery beside the pond is exquisite and transparent. All these buildings constitute an irregular scenic composition.

On the south bank, a light Zhuoying Waterside Belvedere (Zhuo Ying Shui Ge, Waterside Belvedere for Washing Cap Ribbon) and heavy Yungang Rockery make up an appropriate contrasting pair. An extensive high wall lies at the east bank, neighboring to the residential area. The designer adopted vacant pavilion, vacant corridor, added horizontal molding and pseudo carved windows on the wall surface, piled up rockeries in front of the wall and planted liana plants like wisteria and climbing figs in order to break up the tedious stiffness of the wall.

Kan Song Du Hua Gallery, Jixu Studio (Studio of Upright Self-Cultivation), and Dian Chun Yi Study in the north section develop into several independent courtyards, where rocks were piled up to make flower beds, different courtyard views were designed with bamboo clusters, flowery plants, and rock peaks. Behind the main house, there is a small courtyard, ready to offer fresh air and light. Inside the small courtyard, several pieces of lake rocks, a few loosely scattered bamboos, plum flowers, and banana trees fill up the framed scenery through the window openings.

Considered as a whole, this garden with water as its protagonist scene is well-designed. All spatial scales are appropriate. And the designer successfully applied pairs of comparison and contrast, achieving a very nice artistic effect. This garden could be considered as

FIG. 244 Dian Chun Yi Study

a representative of the moderate-scaled classical gardens constructed in Suzhou.

Zhu Wai Yi Zhi Gallery

This narrow gallery is three rooms in width from the east to west end, looking like a tiny boat above water from afar. The pavilion has a flush gable roof and round edge, and at the side facing the water, the lady stay was fixed to the gallery (Fig. 243). To the north rests a courtyard named Jixu Studio (Studio of Upright Self-Cultivation), where a couple of green and stylish bamboo clusters wave in the courtyard. Visitors can peep at it from the lattice windows in Zhu Wai Yi Zhi Gallery and access it through a door opening. To the east of it is Wufeng Study (Five Peaks Study), and on the east wall, there are two pieces of nice tile carving works with garden, flower, and bird patterns on them. The window openings on the west wall frame some Begonia flowers outside the window into a picture. Looking out into the distance at the opposite side of the pond, you will see Yungang Rockery, the best mountainous scenery in the garden.

Dian Chun Yi Study

Dian Chun Yi Study is an independent study courtyard located at the northwest corner, taking up less than one *mu* of land (0.07 hectare, 0.16 acre). In the courtyard, rocky peaks stand like opposing troops, trees loosely scatter, and the furnishings are simple and neat (Fig. 244). The study stays on the north side, and Lengquan Pavilion (Pavilion of Cold Spring) and Hanbi Spring (Spring of Embracing Greenery) rest on the south side, enriching the views in the courtyard. The landscape in the protagonist scenic area infiltrates into the courtyard from the gaps by the side of such architectures. Thus, this courtyard appears not absolutely secluded or segregated from the rest of the garden, truthfully a competitive work among all the small courtyard inside gardens in Suzhou.

In 1979, Astor Court, a Chinese courtyard, was constructed in the Metropolitan Museum of Art in New York, USA, following the prototype of Dian Chun Yi Studio. The next year, Astor Court became a permanent part of the museum.

FIG. 245 A little courtyard of Tiyun Room

Tiyun Room (Room of Cloud Ladder)

Tiyun Room is a three-room-wide open gallery room with a flush gable roof and round edge located at the north end of this garden. French windows down to the ground were set in the south and north walls of the major room, while the side-rooms have only semi-windows on their low walls. An ancient and simple platform fenced with stone railings rests to the south, opposite to a lake rockery. Climbing up the rockery along the stone stair road, you can reach the study on the upper floor. The name of the house originated from "climbing up the ladder of cloud to reach the moon." In the courtyard, pines, hollies, and red maple trees were planted in the lake rock flower-beds. The exquisite rocks and the lush and well-spaced trees compose different sceneries in different seasons (Fig. 245). The courtyard ground in front of Tiyun Room was paved into auspicious patterns—*wu fu peng shou* (five bats surrounding a peach, indicating both welfare and longevity go together).

Wanjuan Hall (Wan Juan Tang, Hall with Ten Thousand Books)

Wanjuan Hall, the major hall in the entire residential area, was where the host met his guests, held dinner parties and grand celebrations, such as birthdays, weddings, and funerals. A screen door was placed at the five seventh spot of the entire depth of the hall. The hall is well illuminated with sunlight and neatly furnished with a natural table, a worshiping table, a flower stool, chairs, and a tea table. All the furniture are made from rosewood in the style typical of the Ming Dynasty—with a noble shape, simple structure, fluent lines, and practical uses. An inscribed board with three Chinese characters "Wan Juan Tang" written in Wen Zhengming's writing style is hung above the head of the hall (Fig. 246).

FIG. 246 Door leaves in Wanjuan Hall

FIG. 247 Yungang Rockery

FIG. 248 Lengquan Pavilion

Wufeng Study

Wufeng Study, located between the residential area and the garden area, is an independent courtyard. This study is a five-room-wide tower with a flush gable roof and "feeding-chicken" decorative ridge. To the north and south of this tower is an enclosed courtyard. In the middle of the southern wall is a French window down to the ground, while the other walls have semi-windows, and consequently, the air inside is fresh and unobstructed. Frame covers were set in walls to protect the books against moisture and to divide the space inside at will according to personal preferences.

Yungang Rockery

Yungang Rockery reproduces the mountainous views on the cliffs or hillocks beside the pond. In the evaporated mist, the rockery strives to present the image of a lofty cliff. It is decorated by osmanthus, cypress, wintersweet, and crape myrtle (Fig. 247). The uniqueness of this rockery lies in the exquisite hill-piling technique and ingenious view-making in response to weather changes. For example, when it rains, the raindrops from the north and south eaves fall down onto the hilltop. The rain water flows down along the hill ranges and goes into a dynamic and spectacular waterscape.

Lengquan Pavilion

Lengquan Pavilion is a semi-

FIG. 249 Sheya Corridor and the pond in front of the corridor

pavilion covered with a delicate tile roof typical of the Ming Dynasty. A gigantic yet exquisite and dainty Lingbi rock is situated under the pavilion (Fig. 248). The dark grey rock looks like a goshawk flapping its wings ready to take off. When knocked slightly, it twangs like metal.

Sheya Corridor

"Duck shooting" was a popular game among the maidens serving in the royal palaces in ancient times. Aquatic birds were reared in the ponds for the maidens to catch with rattan hoops, producing an interesting scene. Therefore, this waterside corridor was named after this traditional game. The north end of this corridor is connected with Zhu Wai Yi Zhi Gallery. And the south end is linked to an open pavilion, whose side confronting the pond is covered with a gable and hip roof with round edge and rake angles (Fig. 249), composing a contrasting pair with Sheya Corridor—a lofty roof vs. a low corridor.

FIG. 250 The little bridge resting at the southeastern corner of a pond in Master of the Nets Garden

Tiny Bridges and Stone Jetties

Two small bridges perch at the southeast and northwest corner of the pond, indicating the inlet and outlet of the stream. The one at the southeast corner is a pretty reputable three-step-wide arch bridge Yinjing Bridge (Bridge Leading to Tranquil Water). The water inlet here is a sheer three *chi* (0.1 m, 3.28 feet) wide so the small arch bridge above it is so nice and exquisite that it is ranked as the champion among all small-scaled bridges in all of the gardens of Suzhou (Fig. 250). A zigzag bridge winds its way across the water surface in the northwest corner of the pond (Fig. 251). Even the neighboring foil scenery, stone jetties on the bank, is full of variations. Some rocks rise out of the water surface to connect with the bank, so it seems that the bank extends into the water gradually like natural stairs, or as if the rocks were floating above the water. Some stick out slightly above as though the water flow just below the rocks. Therefore, the water depth seems unpredictable (Fig. 252).

FIG. 251 The zigzag bridge resting at the northwestern corner of a pond in Master of the Nets Garden

FIG. 252 Stone jetties outside Sheya Corridor

Lion Grove Garden
狮子林
A World of Rockeries

Location: Suzhou, Jiangsu province
Floor Space: 0.88 hectare
Construction Year: 1342 (the second year of the Zhizheng Period of the later Yuan Dynasty)
Genre of Garden: temple garden

Lion Grove Garden was located on the Garden Road in Suzhou. A disciple of a Buddhist monk, Tianru constructed a small temple named Shilin Temple (Temple of Lion Grove) in 1342, which was renamed the Temple of Authentic Bodhi, also known as Lion Grove. Emperor Kangxi and Qianlong had both been here several times. The temple was magnificently furnished and decorated with

FIG. 254 Plants and rockeries

peony patterns, appearing regal and luxurious. It was recorded that this garden appealed particularly to Emperor Qianlong, who left a multitude of inscriptions and imperial-styled poems after his six

visits. Furthermore, he copied three pictures of the *Panorama of Lion Grove Garden* composed by Ni Yunlin. On account of his incomparable passion for this garden, he constructed Lion Grove Gardens in both the Summer Palace and the Mountain Resort at Chengde (Fig. 253).

Lion Grove Garden is most reputable for its lake stone rockeries, which is superior to any other for their unusual ingenuity in creating winding caves in and

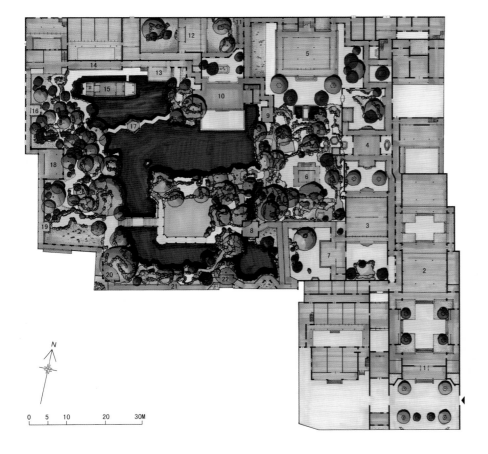

FIG. 253 Ichnography of Lion Grove Garden
1. Men Ting Gate Hall **2**. Ci Tang Ancestral Shrine **3**. Yan Yu Tang Hall of Swallow Fame **4**. Xiao Fang Ting Small Square Hall **5**. Zhi Bai Xuan Gallery of Pointing to Cypress **6**. Wo Yun Shi Room of Resting on Clouds **7**. Li Xue Tang Hall of Standing in Snow **8**. Xiu Zhu Ge Belvedere of Slender Bamboo **9**. Jian Shan Lou Mountain-in-View Tower **10**. He Hua Ting Lotus Hall **11**. Ban Ting Semi-pavilion **12**. Wu Gu Song Ting Five Ancient Pines Pavilion **13**. Zhen Qu Ting Pavilion of Real Charm **14**. An Xiang Shu Ying Lou Tower of Obscure Fragrance and Sparse Branches **15**. Shi Fang Stone Boat **16**. Fei Pu Ting Pavilion of Flying Waterfall **17**. Hu Xin Ting Mid-Lake Pavilion **18**. Wen Mei Ge Belvedere of Questioning Plum Flower **19**. Shuang Xiang Xian Guan Celestial Lodging of Two Fragrances **20**. Shan Mian Ting Fan-Shaped Pavilion **21**. Wen Tian Xiang Bei Ting Stele Pavilion of Wen Tianxiang's Poem **22**. Yu Bei Ting Imperial Stele Pavilion **23**. Xiao Chi Bi Small Red Cliff

0 5 10 20 30M

FIG. 255 Rockery at the southern section in the Lion Grove Garden

out of the rockeries. All the peaks in this garden were piled up with Taihu Lake rocks. The fossil wood and stalagmites are remains dating back to the Yuan Dynasty (Figs. 254, 255).

The architectures surrounding this garden are neat and orderly lofty walls and towering buildings, whose arrangement is not free from the general model in small-scaled gardens where buildings surround hill and pond. They present diverse yet unmatched architectural styles. Though they were built at different altitudes, their scales and scopes were basically in need of further thinking. Some regional layouts present great ingenuity, like Yanyu Hall, Fan-Shaped Pavilion, the ancient Wusong Garden, Small Red Cliff rockery, and Xiuzhu Belvedere, all of which possess some redeeming features.

Yanyu Hall

Yanyu Hall, the main hall in Lion Grove Garden, is spacious and recherché with the construction material and building techniques. This hall has a front courtyard and a back skywell, and was where the owner held dinner parties and hosted his guests (Fig. 256). This elegant architecture is a magnificent and luxurious work among all those built in Suzhou during the late Qing Dynasty. It is one of the relatively renowned lovebirds hall in the city, which is divided into two halves—one in the north and another in the south—with a screen door and hanging fascias.

FIG. 256 Rockery in Yanyu Hall courtyard

FIG. 257 Xiuzhu Belvedere

FIG. 258 The waterfall beside Feipu Pavilion in Lion Grove Garden

Xiuzhu Belvedere

Xiuzhu Belvedere located to the south of the lake stone rockery is an open hall with a gable and hip roof and round edge. This building bestrides above a valley and is based on an arch tunnel piled up with rocks. It receives a brook from north, looks down upon a pond to the south, connects with a double-pavement corridor in the east, and leans against rockery peaks on the west side (Fig. 257). The entire surroundings are pretty elegant, full of wild atmosphere in the mountainous forest. Lady stay seats take the place of the north and south walls for visitors to rest or enjoy the landscapes in peace.

Feipu Pavilion (Pavilion of Flying Waterfall)

Feipu Pavilion, also known as Tingtao Pavilion (Pavilion of Listening to Waves) sits in the west of Lion Grove Garden. This is a semi-pavilion with a gable and hip roof and round edge on the top of a "earth in stones" rockery, connected with a climbing-hill corridor to the south. An inscribed board that reads "Ting Tao" (literally listening to waves) is hung in the pavilion. Beside it, a steam rushes out from a lofty place in the valley into a pond, jumping down three lake rock steps. The visual and sound images of this waterfall—the only man-made waterfall in all the gardens of Suzhou—touch your heart deeply (Fig. 258). The low Mid-Lake Pavilion inside the pond echoes this lofty pavilion, adding more charm to the garden views.

FIG. 259 Huxin Pavilion

Huxin Pavilion (Mid-Lake Pavilion)

The Mid-Lake Pavilion stands inside the lake in Lion Grove Garden. A small hexagonal pavilion with a pyramid roof sits on the lake rock foundation, connected with the banks by a slab stone zigzag bridge. The bridge has nine turns, attached to the pavilion's east and west sides. On the pavilion hangs an inscribed board with two Chinese characters meaning "watching waterfall." Extending your views to the west, you will find an extraordinarily impressive waterfall dashing down from above. Alone in the pavilion, you can enjoy the tender breezes from afar, slight ripples, lotus in full blossom above the water surface, and the abundant lotus fragrance. This is indeed a charming and appealing scenery above the pond (Fig. 259).

Fan-Shaped Pavilion

The Fan-Shaped Pavilion inside Lion Grove Garden sits at the turning point where the climbing-hill corridor turns from west to south. The roof has no angles but a pitch arc. A small space to the east of this pavilion was spared for banana trees and bamboos. In the summer twilight, visitors could feel cool breezes from the east, west, and north, without being interrupted by the warm wind from the south. Lady stay and a stone table inside the building are all fan-shaped. Visitors could fully enjoy the garden views from this site.

Garden of Cultivation
艺圃
Exquisite Mini Garden Sheltered by Whitewashed Wall and Tree Shadow

Location: Suzhou, Jiangsu province
Floor Space: 0.38 hectares
Construction Year: 1541 (the 20th year during the Jiajing Period of the Ming Dynasty)
Genre of Garden: literati garden

The Garden of Cultivation is located on No. 5, Wenya Street in Suzhou. The existing layout of the hill and pond is basically intact, just like how it looked at the end of the Ming and the beginning of the Qing Dynasties. Some of the architectures inside it present the original taste typical of the Ming Dynasty.

Once inside the main gate to the residence, you should go along a winding street until you reach the front hall—Shilun Hall (Shi Lun Tang, Hall of Generation Continuity), and then turn westward into the garden (Fig. 260). To the south of the main hall in the garden—Boya Hall (Bo Ya Tang, Hall of Encyclopedic Knowledge)—is a small courtyard with a lake rock flower-bed and a five-room-wide waterside gazebo suspending above the pond. The two wing-rooms of this waterside gazebo are also constructed beside the pond and linked with the side rooms on the east and west banks. In general, this pond is the dominant element in the overall layout. The north bank is taken up by architectures; and the south bank is occupied by an earth-and-rock hill with lush

and dense woods on its ranges. An independent courtyard fenced by walls stays to the southwest of this pond and can connect with the rock-lined pond in the center through a moon gate. Pavilions, corridors, trees, and rocks loosely scatter on the east and west banks, serving as transitional spaces from the south to north sections, and as a visual contrast to both.

Turning south from the east wing-room of the waterside gazebo and pacing along the narrow path beside the east bank, you can reach Ruyu Pavilion (Pavilion of New-born Fish), whose wooden structure was a relic dated back to the Ming Dynasty. Water accumulates at the southeast side of this pavilion into a small pond, above which a slab stone bridge with a very slight arch bestrides. This was the primary work when the garden was initially constructed. Stepping across the bridge and stopping at the foothill, you will find the road leads to two directions: one enters a rock cave which winds its way uphill to the hexagonal pavilion; while the other turns west along a sharp cliff on the south bank and reaches the zigzag bridge perching at the southwest corner of this pond. This bridge is slightly above the water surface and leads to a winding corridor to the west and a small courtyard through a door opening. A small pond was excavated inside the courtyard to connect with the bigger pond. Several lake rocks and flowery trees scatter inside it to make up the most secluded and tranquil corner in the garden. A library tower no longer exists.

The pond in this garden takes up roughly one *mu* (about 0.07 hectares, 0.16 acres) of land, whose water surface is a lack of branches. The only exceptions include two inlets at the southeast and southwest corners respectively, with a slab stone bridge above each of them. Therefore, the water surface appears open and spacious; meanwhile, the winding inlets constitute a sharp contrast to the major part of the pond. The only deficiency lies in the north bank where a waterside gazebo looks too boring and tedious since it goes too straight ahead. The east and west banks also lack spatial layers. The rockery on the south bank is an earth mound, whose waterfront side was piled up with lake rocks into a steep cliff with dangerous hill roads. Looking from the north bank, these rugged rocks and luxuriant trees are the principal scenes opposite to it. Though rather economical in using rocks, the hill roads and caves inside the rockery twist and turn, full of variation.

Generally speaking, the layout of the garden is simple and spacious, featuring low banks and concentrated water surface, leaving no room for obstructive feelings. The garden is natural and simple, preserving the original style and construction regulations in its earliest period, and thus, this garden is of relatively high historical and artistic value.

Ruyu Pavilion

This small quadrangular square pavilion with a single eave and pyramid roof is typical of the Ming style, simple yet elegant. This pavilion, supported by eight pillars, stands above water. And the lady stay seats between each pair of pillars are a good place to enjoy the delight of watching fishes. The beam timbers were painted with color patterns, a rare artistic

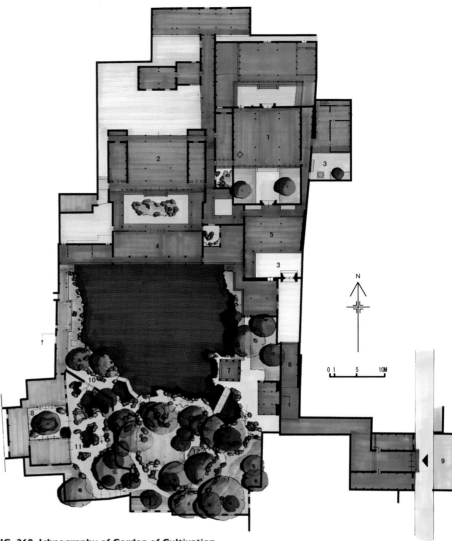

FIG. 260 Ichnography of Garden of Cultivation
1. Da Ting Main Hall   2. Bo Ya Tang Hall of Encyclopedic Knowledge   3. Tian Jing Sky Well
4. Shui Xie Waterside Gazebo   5. Shi Lun Tang Hall of Generation Continuity   6. Yi Pu Garden of Cultivation   7. Ru Yu Ting Pavilion of New-Born Fish   8. Xin Yi Flos Magnoliae   9. Zhao Bi Screen Wall   10. Yu Ou Men Gull Bathing Gate   11. Yu Ou Chi Yuan Luo Gull Bathing Pond
12. Zhao Shuang Ting Pavilion of Morning Refreshment

work in Suzhou gardens. The red carps swim leisurely below the shallow water surface (Fig. 261). In all, this tranquil environment is quite suitable for reading. To the southeast of Ruyu Pavilion, the water produces a small inlet with a slab stone arch bridge named Ruyu Bridge across the water. This bridge is exactly a miniature of the stone bridges in the regions of the Yangtze River Delta.

Courtyard of Yu'ou Pond (Gull Bathing Pond)

As a minor garden inside a bigger

one, this courtyard served as a bathtub for all the aquatic birds reared by the garden owner. Gulls flying above the water surface are a classical metaphor indicating a leisurely and carefree lifestyle. The name suggests that the garden owner enjoyed hermit life, never troubling himself with earthly annoyance. The pond inside and the lake outside this courtyard are interrelated. Several lake rocks scatter beside the pond, and flowers and woods are planted in an irregular way. Vines suspend down from the white-washed walls,

FIG. 261 A bird's eye view of Ruyu Pavilion

FIG. 262 A tiny courtyard around Yu'ou Pond

producing a huge picture of dead sticks and new twigs. In the north wall there is a moon gate, serving to relate it with the outside world and an opening for visitors to peep at the bigger garden views. In addition, the pond and the external lake are linked together, so this garden is a minor garden inside a bigger one, this pond is a secondary pond inside a larger pond. They echo with each other, creating quite a unique charm (Fig. 262).

Rockery on the Southern Bank

The lake stone rockery on the south bank is piled up with rugged stones and sheltered under gigantic woods, full of the wild atmosphere of the mountainous villages. The rockery was built beside the pond, whose two inlets stay at the east and west corners. Two three-fold low bridges twist and turn above the inlets. And stone jetties and stone platforms scatter along the banks, making different scenic spots.

This rockery area on the southern bank is the sightseeing center, observed from different viewpoints. It seems that a landscape scroll is unfolded in front of us, constituting a sharp contrast to the middle waterscape area: a secluded area vs. an open space, a concentrate construction vs. a loosely arranged scene and a lofty work vs. a low water surface (Fig. 263). From either side of the pond, visitors could approach the mountainous wood area through the two slab stone bridges. Then several rock roads twist and turn along the dangerous rocks to the hill top or lead you into a distorted cave to escape reality in secret.

FIG. 263 Rockery on the southern bank

Great Wave Pavilion
沧浪亭
Longest Historical Classical Garden in Suzhou

Location: Suzhou, Jiangsu province
Floor Space: 1.08 hectares
Construction Year: 960 – 1126 (during the Northern Song Dynasty)
Genre of Garden: literati garden

Great Wave Pavilion is roughly in the Sanyuanfang District, to the south of Suzhou. This garden enjoys the longest history among all the classical gardens constructed in Suzhou.

Great Wave Pavilion was reputable for "lofty piers and spacious water surface," which had taken up several dozens of *mu* of land. Boats could even sail through Panmen Gate. Currently, the water surface outside this garden is still broad enough, which is a rare case among all the gardens in Suzhou. The earth hill interior to the garden is a relatively higher place compared with other gardens in the city. In the past, visitors were able to watch the peaks to the southwest of the urban area from this hill. It has favorable geographic condition. The existing architectures were mostly constructed after Emperor Tongzhi in the Qing Dynasty took power (Fig. 264).

A hill is the protagonist scene in the entire garden, with all the architectures being built around this hill. The main gate opens at the northwest corner of the garden in front of clear ripples. A bridge was built in front of the gate so that visitors could have access to the garden. Upon entering the garden, visitors are in front of a

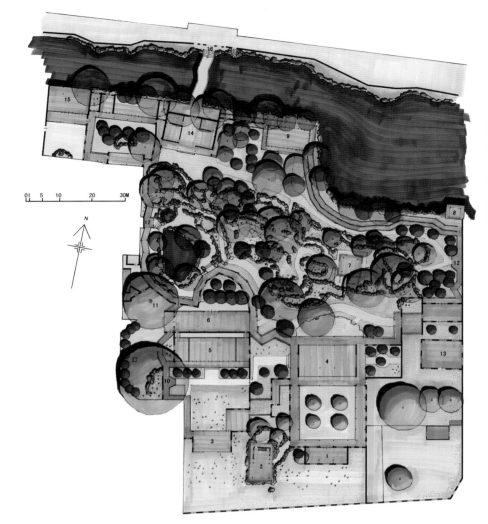

FIG. 264 Ichnography of Great Wave Pavilion
1. Yao Hua Jing Jie Land of Jade Glitters   2. Kan Shan Lou Mountain View Tower   3. Cui Ling Long Exquisite Emerald   4. Ming Dao Tang Hall of Learning Tao   5. Wu Bai Ming Xian Ci Temple of Five Hundred Sages   6. Qing Xiang Guan Lodging of Light Fragrance   7. Cang Lang Ting Great Wave Pavilion   8. Guan Yu Chu Pavilion for Watching Fishes   9. Mian Shui Xuan Waterfront Gallery   10. Yang Zhi Ting Admiration Pavilion   11. Bu Qi Ting Pavilion of Walking along Winding Bank   12. Yu bei Ting Imperial Stele Pavilion   13. Wen Miao Xiang Shi Room for Smelling Appealing Fragrance   14. Da Men Garden Gate   15. Ou Hua Shui Xie Lotus Gazebo   16. Cang Lang Sheng Ji Fang Archway of Wonders in Great Wave Pavilion

lofty and extensive earth hill, which stretches from west to east. Rocks were piled up into revetments at the foot of this hill and stone stair roads along the hill slopes. The east section piled up with yellow stones is an earlier construction, while the relatively depressed west section was patched and repaired with unknown lake rocks. The rock roads wind their way on the hillsides which are sheltered by lush woods, turning and twisting. The roadsides are fully occupied by bamboo rods, presenting a natural landscape. This is a nice

scenic spot among all the classical gardens in Suzhou. The corridor embraces the hill, going up and down according to the geographic features. In the scenic spot of Cui Ling Long (Exquisite Emerald), the small house is located in the bamboo forest, whose surroundings is tranquil and secluded (Fig. 265). Visitors could pace along the corridor here to the small pond located at the southwest corner and then turn north via the pavilion with the imperial stele until they find the garden gate.

The north hillside confronts

FIG. 265 Inside view of the Cui Ling Long Scenic Spot

a pond. A waterside architecture named Mianshui Gallery (Waterfront Gallery) sits on the west bank and a square pavilion named Guanyuchu Pavilion (Pavilion for Watching Fishes) perches on the east bank. The two buildings are connected by a double-pavement corridor and window openings on the wall of the corridor offer visual passages for visitors to enjoy the views inside and outside. Private gardens in Suzhou are mostly fenced with towering walls lest the rockeries and ponds inside the gardens should be exposed to the outside world. Yet, unlike the regular private gardens, this garden borrows part of the scenes outside its walls, and bridges the water surface outside the wall and the hill inside into a holistic one with the help of this double-pavement corridor. This is one of the remarkable examples of borrowing a view. This district between a hill and a lake takes advantage of the geographic superiority and is a good place for sightseeing, where woods flourish luxuriously and a winding corridor curl its way along the pond.

This garden enjoys a prolonged history and manages to maintain its natural taste thanks to the numerous big trees and favorable geographic features. Architectures here are simple and unadorned, presenting a different style from the other gardens. The waterside double-pavement corridor took initiative to communicate the views inside and outside with the window openings, and offer a precedent for the Garden of Pleasure and Lion Grove Garden to follow (Fig. 266). The carved windows (Fig. 267) have very fine and vivid patterns

FIG. 266 The double-pavement corridor and carved windows on the wall

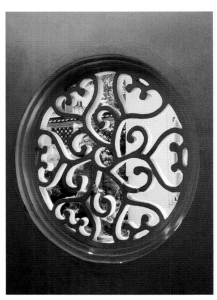

FIG. 267 Carved window

and none of them could find any similar design in the garden. These designs were all creations that artisans made during their construction activities. Both their artistic idea and their practical techniques are worthy of learning.

Great Wave Pavilion

The Great Wave Pavilion, a square building with a gable and hip roof, single eave and round edge, is elegantly designed and a good match for the holistic wild mountainous atmosphere in the garden. This pavilion was built at a high altitude, escorted by several ancient trees of more than 100 years of age, is a more remarkable place to enjoy mountainous scenery compared with other gardens in Suzhou (Fig. 268).

Guanyuchu Pavilion

Guanyuchu Pavilion at the northeast corner of this garden is a waterside square pavilion with four angles and a pyramid roof. The building is embraced by water from three sides, and connected with a double-pavement corridor. Half of this pavilion lands on the riverbank and another half is supported by stone pillars under water. The profile is so rich in diversity and produces distinctive visual layers (Fig. 53). Leaning against the railings inside this pavilion, visitors cold appreciate the fishes in the pond and views outside the garden.

Mianshui Gallery

Mianshui Gallery, a three-room-wide and four-sided hall, sits at the north side of the protagonist scene in this garden, the earth hill. It was connected to the other buildings by the double-pavement corridors in the southeast and northwest corners. When a brook arrives at this site, the water surface suddenly expands extensively, so that both the east and north sides are embraced by water (Fig. 269). The environment here is extraordinarily touching. All four walls have French windows down to the ground, and shell tiles were set in place of window panes. The skirt plate was not engraved with any pattern, simple and unadorned.

Garden Gate

To approach the garden, visitors have to step across a flat bridge first, which is a unique design in all the classical gardens in Suzhou. The garden gate opens to the north, in front of which a flat zigzag bridge bestrides a creek.

Kanshan Tower (Kan Shan Lou, Mountain View Tower)

This tower was constructed in 1873 at the southwest corner of

FIG. 268 Great Wave Pavilion

the garden as a compensation for the visual obstacles, Mingdao Hall (Ming Dao Tang, Hall of Learning Tao) and the Temple of Five Hundred Sages, which block the sceneries in the southwest section. This three-floored tower was built on the base of a rugged rockery. With flying-up eaves and rake angles, this building has very refined structure and a nice profile. Above the tile benches there are plum-flower-patterned window openings on the wall, offering a lofty, remote, elegant, and delighted view (Fig. 270). This is indeed an unusual and ingenious architecture among all of those in Suzhou. The rockery under this tower has a rock cave named Yinxin Stone Room (Stone Room of Printing on Heart).

FIG. 269 Mianshui Gallery

FIG. 270 Kanshan Tower

Yu Garden 豫园
Most Unusually Charming Views among All the Gardens in the Yangtze River Delta

Location: Shanghai
Floor Space: 2.00 hectares
Construction Year: 1559 (in the 38th year during the Jiajing Period of the Ming Dynasty)
Genre of Garden: residence garden

Yu Garden, a classical garden located in the Shanghai urban area, was constructed by Pan Yunduan (1526 – 1601), one of the ministers of the supreme court during the Ming Dynasty. The name "Yu Yuan" refers to pleasing his parents and for them to enjoy peaceful and healthy life. The garden could be divided into the Great Rockery area, the Wanhua Tower area (Wan Hua Lou, Tower in Ten Thousand Flowers), the Dianchun Hall area, the Yulinglong Rock area, and an internal garden inside it (Fig. 271).

The Great Rockery area has several architectures like Sansui Hall (San Sui Tang, Hall with Three Grain Ears), Yangshan Hall (Yang Shan Tang, Hall of Watching Up to Hill), and Juanyu Tower (Juan Yu Lou, Tower of Folding Rains). To the north of Juanyu Tower is a pond. A large-scaled yellow stone rockery piled up on the opposite bank of the pond present grandiose majesty with its rolling ranges, deep valleys, profound gullies, steep cliffs, and rocky caves. When you are inside it, allowing your imagination to extend everywhere, it seems as if you are a part of nature.

Wanhua Tower is the major architecture in the scenic area on the east side of the Great Rockery

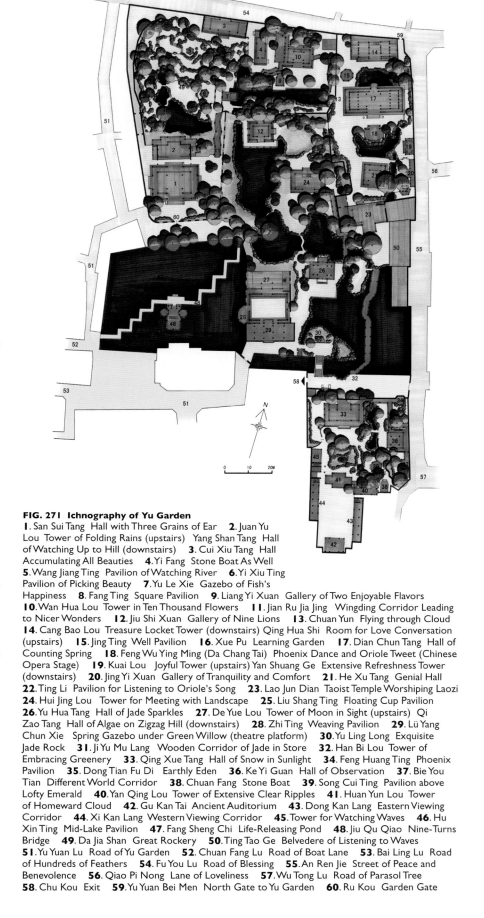

FIG. 271 Ichnography of Yu Garden
1. San Sui Tang Hall with Three Grains of Ear   2. Juan Yu Lou Tower of Folding Rains (upstairs) Yang Shan Tang Hall of Watching Up to Hill (downstairs)   3. Cui Xiu Tang Hall Accumulating All Beauties   4. Yi Fang Stone Boat As Well   5. Wang Jiang Ting Pavilion of Watching River   6. Yi Xiu Ting Pavilion of Picking Beauty   7. Yu Le Xie Gazebo of Fish's Happiness   8. Fang Ting Square Pavilion   9. Liang Yi Xuan Gallery of Two Enjoyable Flavors   10. Wan Hua Lou Tower in Ten Thousand Flowers   11. Jian Ru Jia Jing Winding Corridor Leading to Nicer Wonders   12. Jiu Shi Xuan Gallery of Nine Lions   13. Chuan Yun Flying through Cloud   14. Cang Bao Lou Treasure Locket Tower (downstairs) Qing Hua Shi Room for Love Conversation (upstairs)   15. Jing Ting Well Pavilion   16. Xue Pu Learning Garden   17. Dian Chun Tang Hall of Counting Spring   18. Feng Wu Ying Ming (Da Chang Tai) Phoenix Dance and Oriole Tweet (Chinese Opera Stage)   19. Kuai Lou Joyful Tower (upstairs) Yan Shuang Ge Extensive Refreshness Tower (downstairs)   20. Jing Yi Xuan Gallery of Tranquility and Comfort   21. He Xu Tang Genial Hall   22. Ting Li Pavilion for Listening to Oriole's Song   23. Lao Jun Dian Taoist Temple Worshiping Laozi   24. Hui Jing Lou Tower for Meeting with Landscape   25. Liu Shang Ting Floating Cup Pavilion   26. Yu Hua Tang Hall of Jade Sparkles   27. De Yue Lou Tower of Moon in Sight (upstairs) Qi Zao Tang Hall of Algae on Zigzag Hill (downstairs)   28. Zhi Ting Weaving Pavilion   29. Lü Yang Chun Xie Spring Gazebo under Green Willow (theatre platform)   30. Yu Ling Long Exquisite Jade Rock   31. Ji Yu Mu Lang Wooden Corridor of Jade in Store   32. Han Bi Lou Tower of Embracing Greenery   33. Qing Xue Tang Hall of Snow in Sunlight   34. Feng Huang Ting Phoenix Pavilion   35. Dong Tian Fu Di Earthly Eden   36. Ke Yi Guan Hall of Observation   37. Bie You Tian Different World Corridor   38. Chuan Fang Stone Boat   39. Song Cui Ting Pavilion above Lofty Emerald   40. Yan Qing Lou Tower of Extensive Clear Ripples   41. Huan Yun Lou Tower of Homeward Cloud   42. Gu Kan Tai Ancient Auditorium   43. Dong Kan Lang Eastern Viewing Corridor   44. Xi Kan Lang Western Viewing Corridor   45. Tower for Watching Waves   46. Hu Xin Ting Mid-Lake Pavilion   47. Fang Sheng Chi Life-Releasing Pond   48. Jiu Qu Qiao Nine-Turns Bridge   49. Da Jia Shan Great Rockery   50. Ting Tao Ge Belvedere of Listening to Waves   51. Yu Yuan Lu Road of Yu Garden   52. Chuan Fang Lu Road of Boat Lane   53. Bai Ling Lu Road of Hundreds of Feathers   54. Fu You Lu Road of Blessing   55. An Ren Jie Street of Peace and Benevolence   56. Qiao Pi Nong Lane of Loveliness   57. Wu Tong Lu Road of Parasol Tree   58. Chu Kou Exit   59. Yu Yuan Bei Men North Gate to Yu Garden   60. Ru Kou Garden Gate

FIG. 272 The Chinese Opera Stage

FIG. 273 Roof details on the Chinese Opera Stage

area. This site collects hill beauty, water giggles, moonlight, and floral sweetness in one place. Wanhua Tower, Yule Gazebo (Gazebo of Fish's Happiness), and a square pavilion constitute a courtyard, in which a winding corridor links them together. This area is the best place for watching fishes in the entire garden.

Dianchun Hall is the major construction in the scenic area. Other buildings include Hexu Hall (He Xu Tang, Genial Hall), Cangbao Tower (Cang Bao Lou, Treasure Locket Tower), Kuai Tower (Kuai Lou, Joyful Tower), Tingli Pavilion (Pavilion for Listening to Oriole's Song), and Jingyi Gallery (Gallery of Tranquility and Comfort), which are accompanied by brooks, rockeries, flowering woods, springs, and rocks. Baoyun Rock (Rock Embracing Clouds) sits to the east of Dianchun Hall, leaning against its wall and rising up into the sky. The Chinese Opera Stage built above the water in front of the hall was decorated with exquisite carvings and color paintings (Figs. 272, 273).

The Yulinglong scenic area is composed of Yulinglong Rock, Deyue Tower (De Yue Lou, Tower of Moon in Sight), and Yuhua Hall (Yu Hua Tang, Hall of Jade Sparkles). A lofty rockery perches in the east and a corridor winds its way beside the pond. A moon platform was attached to Yuhua Hall in the front, where visitors could enjoy rockeries and moonlight on the night of Mid-Autumn Day. This scenic area is the essence of the entire Yu Garden because of the distorted rock Yulinglong.

The internal garden was once a part of Yu Garden, yet was

FIG. 274 Entrance to the winding corridor named Jian Ru Jia Jing

FIG. 275 The Taihu Lake rock standing in the Winding Corridor of Jian Ru Jia Jing

sold when the fortunes of the Pan family waned during the late Ming Dynasty. This section of land was then built into a temple garden and named Ling Yuan (Nimbus Palace Garden) and later renamed Dong Garden (Eastern Garden). This internal garden takes up 2 *mu* (0.13 hectares, 0.33 acres) of land, on which Qingxue Hall (Qing Xue Tang, Hall of Snow in Sunlight), Yanqing Tower (Yan Qing Lou, Tower of Extensive Clear Ripples), and Huanyun Tower (Huan Yun Lou, Tower of Homeward Cloud) were built. A rockery and a pond were also arranged inside it. And currently, this garden has been admitted as a part of Yu Garden.

Winding Corridor of Jian Ru Jia Jing (Winding Corridor Leading to Nicer Wonders)

Jian Ru Jia Jing, a winding corridor located east of Yangshan Hall, is also the only access to the Great Rockery. At the entrance crouch a pair of iron lion statues molded in the Yuan Dynasty, which present vivid postures and very delicate molding techniques (Fig. 274). A square pavilion set in the corridor hangs an inscribed board that reads "Jian Ru Jia Jing." Below the board is a piece of Taihu Lake rock named "Beauty's Waist" on account of its posture—as if a charming lady is twisting her tender body to wink at you (Fig. 275). This corridor zigzags, twists and turns, presenting very delicate and exquisite sentiments. Trees and flowers scatter beside this corridor only to add natural liveliness to the layers upon layers of sceneries on the spot.

FIG. 276 Scenery in front of Yuhua Hall

FIG. 277 Indoor scene of Yuhua hall

Yuhua Hall

Yuhua Hall is opposite to Yulinglong Rock, and thus, was named so after the two inscribed Chinese characters "Yu Hua" on the rockery. With two magnolia trees in front, this hall was furnished in accordance with a literati's study, displaying precious furniture like a painting table made from red sandal wood timbers during the Ming Dynasty (Figs. 276, 277).

Yulinglong Rock

Yulinglong Rock is ranked as one out of three most reputable rocks in the Yangtze River Delta, and is the treasure representing Yu Garden. This piece of rock, over 1 *zhang* (3.33 m, 10.94 feet), is very exquisite with holes all over the

FIG. 278 Yulinglong Rock

FIG. 279 Yangshan Hall and Juanyu Tower

body. The criteria for art rocks—thin, crumpled, leaky, and holey—all can be met in this single piece, and accordingly, it could be ranked as a first grade work (Fig. 278).

Yangshan Hall and Juanyu Tower

This is a two-storey tower constructed in 1866, whose ground floor was named Yangshan Hall and whose upper floor was called Juanyu Tower (Fig. 279). Yangshan Hall, a wonderful place to enjoy the Great Rockery, is supported by five front pillars and a winding corridor is attached to it in the back. This winding corridor zigzags along a pond, ready for visitors to stay briefly. Juanyu Tower is a tower with many twists and turns.

When upstairs in a rainy day, visitors would find themselves in an obscure mist through which they could hardly distinguish the charm of a hill. It seems as though they were in a natural hill with a brook and valley on a rainy day. This scenery is the most appealing part of Yu Garden.

Sansui Hall

Sansui Hall was built in 1760 at the front garden gate. The name indicates "a grain bearing three ears means a golden harvest." This spacious and open hall has five rooms, in front of which cypress trees are grouped separately (Fig. 280). Thanks to the big lake to the south, the sightseeing line is pretty extensive and distant.

FIG. 280 The indoor scene of Sansui Hall

FIG. 281 Yi Stone Boat

FIG. 282 Indoor scene of Yi Stone Boat

Yi Stone Boat (Stone Boat As Well)

Yi Stone Boat outside the east wall of Cuixiu Hall (Cui Xiu Tang, Hall Accumulating All Beauties) is known as Boat Hall (Figs. 281, 282). Stone boats at riversides had become a kind of usual construction in the Yangtze River Delta gardens ever since the Ming Dynasty, for people to enjoy the moonlight on the water surface. Yet, such a stone boat directly built on land is pretty rare. This one is an addition to the original garden.

Wanhua Tower

Wanhua Tower is one of the remarkable scenic spots in the west section. The railings of its winding corridor were decorated with carvings of "Eight Celestial Instruments" patterns (namely fish drum, sword, flower basket, bamboo strainer, gourd, fan, yin-yang slab, and a flute, indicating the eight Taoist celestials in Chinese legends), and four carved openings molded into plum flower, orchid, bamboo, and chrysanthemum patterns in the four corners on the ground floor. There are two ancient trees in the front court, one gingko tree 400 years of age and one magnolia 100 years. Several flowers and rock pieces adorn the white-washed wall in the courtyard. The various flowers, grass and seasonal bonsai are placed among the rock pieces to expose the hidden poetic implication here—"in the depth of a thousand flowers" (Fig. 283).

Yule Gazebo

Bestriding above a brook and

FIG. 283 The scene beside Wanhua Tower

leaning against a rockery hill, this gazebo offers a wonderful place for visitors to watch the swimming fishes against the railings. The name "Yu Le" (literally Fish's Happiness) implied that the garden owner expected to enjoy a solitary life, completely free from earthly annoyance (Fig. 284). Furthermore, visitors could experience an imaginary scene created by a lively view-blocking technique: in front of a brook, a white-washed wall decorated with a carved window and a half-circle door opening strides above the water surface, instead of touching it. While the shallow brook flows secretly away under this arch wall, an imagination occurs to visitors all of a sudden— "How can I know where this brook goes?"

Chuanyunlong Wall (Wall of Wavy Dragon Flying through Cloud)

This wall was located on the west side of Dianchun Hall. The head was molded with mud, and the body covered with tiles for scales. The body sticks to a tracery wall, winding its way through the garden like a dragon up to take off above clouds, which is pretty characteristic (Fig. 285).

Great Rockery

This Great Rockery is the largest-scale, the best preserved yellow stone rockery in the Yangtze River Delta. The designer, Zhang Nanyang, a reputable rockery artist in the Yangtze River Delta, composed the general plan in accordance with the artistic conceptions in landscape paintings, took full advantage of the rock materials in line with their specific characteristics, and directed the

FIG. 284 Yule Gazebo

FIG. 285 Chuanyunlong Wall

FIG. 286 Great Rockery

Fig. 287 Brick carving at
Songcui Pavilion

FIG. 288 Jiushi Gallery

construction activity only after he had a mature project in his mind. He piled the rock pieces up in accordance with landscape painting techniques, while taking the local geographic features into consideration. Therefore, he was able to create hundreds and thousands of varieties of mountainous views and remarkable landscapes (Fig. 286).

Songcui Pavilion (Pavilion above Lofty Emerald)

This pavilion stands above the rockery hill to the east of Guantao Tower (Guan Tao Lou, Tower for Watching Waves). This is a small-scale double square pavilion with double roofs, featuring exquisite and unique features and tranquil atmosphere. A stone table and stone stools were placed on the ground floor, responding to the neighboring green woods. It is particularly cool here during the scorching summer. A wavy dragon wall molded with mud in front of the pavilion can connect with Phoenix Pavilion named "Dong Tian Fu Di (Earthly Eden)" to the north and a corridor named "Bie You Tian (Different World)" to the south. Rock steles record the building history of this internal garden—for example, "Record of Reconstruction of Internal Garden" hangs on the wall (Fig. 287).

Jiushi Gallery (Gallery of Nine Lions)

Jiushi Gallery was constructed to the northwest of Huijing Tower (Hui Jing Lou, Tower for Meeting with Landscape). During the rebuilding in 1959, the neighboring private houses were removed to save space for pond excavation and rockery piling. A gallery was built on the north bank of the pond, and named "Nine Lions." A moon platform was attached to the front, where visitors could appreciate the lotus flowers in the pond (Fig. 288).

Guo's Villa 郭庄
Most Supreme Garden among All of West Lake

Location: Hangzhou, Zhejiang province
Floor Space: 0.16 hectare
Construction Year: 1851 – 1861
(during the Xianfeng Period of the
Qing Dynasty)
Genre of Garden: scenic spot garden

Guo's Villa was located on the west bank of the West Lake in Hangzhou, to the south of the Scene of Qu Yuan Feng He (Lotus in Circular Yard in Breeze) and specifically to the east side of Western Mountain Street.

Leaning against a hill and in front of a lake, this garden has rich view-borrowing resources. It borrows the Scene of Su Di Chun Xiao (Spring Morning on Sudi Causeway) to the east, the Scene of Shuang Feng Cha Yun (Two Peaks Penetrating in Clouds) to the west, the Scene of Nan Ping You Zi (Charm of Nanping Mountain in Tranquility) to the south, and the Scene of Bao Chu Qian Ying (Beauty of Baochu Mountain) to the north, possessing extremely attractive spatial landscapes.

Guo's Villa could be divided into two sections: the residential area of Jing Bi Ju (Essential Lodging for Tranquility) and the internal garden of Yi jing Tian Kai (A Heavenly Molded Mirror). In the residential area with a lotus pond as the center, three white swans would alarm their host without stopping whenever a stranger enters. This was where the host resided and received his guests. The indoor furnishings are exquisite and elegant, tinted with antique flavor. The latter section is an

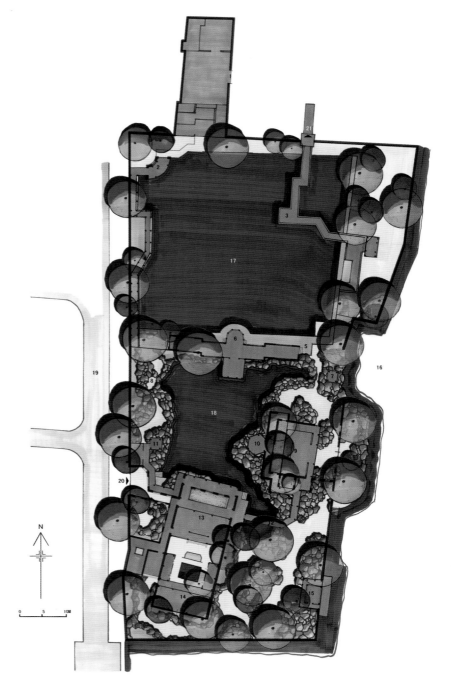

FIG. 289 Ichnography of Guo's Villa
1. Men Qiao Front Gate Bridge 2. Ying Feng Ying Yue Ting Pavilion of Welcoming Wind and Reflecting Moon 3. Wo Bo Qiao Bridge Resting on Ripples 4. Cui Mi Lang Corridor Lost in Greenery 5. Ping Qiao Flat Bridge 6. Liang Yi Xuan Gallery of Two Enjoyable Flavors 7. Zhu Yun Ting (Shang Xin Yue Mu Ting) Pavilion of Upright Cloud (Pavilion Appealing to Eye and Mind) 8. Ting Bu Step Stones; Bi Ting Wall Pavilion 9. Jing Su Ge Belvedere of Revived Scenery 10. Huan Zao Ting Pavilion of Cleaning Algae 11. Ning Xiang Ting Pavilion of Condensed Fragrance 12. Lang Qiao Gallery Corridor 13. Xiang Xue Fen Chun Fragrant Snow Occupying Part of Spring 14. Xi Shan Shuang Qi Refreshing Air in Western Hill 15. Cheng Feng Yao Yue Xuan Gallery of Riding on Wind and Inviting Moon 16. Xi Hu West Lake 17. Jing Chi Mirror Pond 18. Huan Chi Washing Pond 19. Xi Shan Lu Road of Western Hill 20. Ru Kou Entrance 21. Chu Kou Exit

intricate garden with waterscape as the theme. The owner introduced a stream from West Lake into the territory of his garden and made a lake named Suchi Pond, which

looks like a gigantic mirror molded in paradise (Fig. 289).

With zigzag corridors winding their way into the garden, a tiny bridge striding across a

FIG. 290 Cheng Feng Yao Yue Gallery

running brook, rocks being piled up into hills, and flowering woods clustering around the architectures, Guo's Villa is the most characteristic among all of the private gardens built around West Lake, representing the most typical features of the Yangtze River Delta classical gardens.

Cheng Feng Yao Yue Gallery (Gallery of Riding on Wind and Inviting Moon)

This gallery was located in the southeast corner of the garden, closely touching the spacious West Lake. The wooden-structured gallery with a hip roof has a spacious water surface in front of it and a deep and secluded courtyard in the back (Fig. 290). Whenever the partition boards in the door and windows are removed, this gallery will become a shelter-less pavilion, where lotus scent approaches with a cool breeze to

drive away the tedious summer heat. During every winter, the partition boards will be resumed and make this gallery a warm belvedere, where it is comfortable even though snowflakes fall outside the windows.

You can enjoy a pleasant stay here with family and friends, accompanied with cool breezes and a bright moonlight. While trying new tea and enjoying intimate talks, you can appreciate the charming landscapes around West Lake. Extending your sight to the distance, the misty Yangtze River Delta sceneries are profound and thought provoking.

Jingsu Belvedere (Jing Su Ge, Belvedere of Revived Scenery)

Jingsu Belvedere, one of the major architectures in Guo's Villa, was located in the east end of this villa. This two-storey building with a flush gable roof is a brick-wood

structured building used by a lady to make embroidery. The windows and doors are decorated with patters like plum flowers, orchids, bamboos, and chrysanthemums. The front-side eaves stick out to organize a short eaves gallery. Outside the courtyard, a platform was built beside the lake; while inside the courtyard, it makes up an independent world where the windows, door, and passageway are all in a traditional folk house style that is typical of the Yangtze River Delta.

Pushing the eastern windows on the second floor open, you could catch sight of the Sudi Causeway. Watching through the moon gate on the wall, your sight will directly touch the Yadi Bridge (Bridge for Stabilizing Causeway), the third bridge on the Sudi Causeway. Therefore, the bridge, the moon gate, and you are on the same axis, inviting a feeling that nature and

FIG. 291 Jingsu Belvedere

FIG. 292 Shang Xin Yue Mu Pavilion

humans are united in one world. While looking out from the western windows on the second floor, you can see the panoramic view of this entire garden. Then downstairs and pacing out of the small courtyard fenced by white-washed walls, you can stay on the waterside platform where the vague figure of the Sudi Causeway in the distance seemingly appear and disappear from time to time. You will feel relaxed and pleased with wave after wave of a breeze tenderly approaching (Fig. 291).

Shang Xin Yue Mu Pavilion (Pavilion Appealing to Eye and Mind), i.e. Zhuyun Pavilion (Pavilion of Upright Cloud)

Shang Xin Yue Mu Pavilion, a square pavilion with a pyramid roof, is a solitary building in a spacious and vacant space to the east of Guo's Villa (Fig. 292). The charming landscapes around West Lake outside the garden are all in the front, and so the six bridges on the Sudi Causeway in the distance are borrowed spontaneously. While turning back and looking down upon the lake in the garden, you would find the Lake of Yi Jing Tian Kai inside the garden. This picturesque scene with both a remarkable lake and a hill in your sight naturally evokes poetic feelings.

Liangyi Gallery (Gallery of Two Enjoyable Flavors)

Liangyi Gallery is the divisive construction between the residential area of Jing Bi Ju and the internal garden of Yi Jing Tian Kai, the two major scenic areas in the garden. The gallery, the neighboring architectures, and plants are naturally reflected in the Lake of Yi Jing Tian Kai, adding more

FIG. 293 The scenery of the internal garden of Yi Jing Tian Kai from one side of Liangyi Gallery

FIG. 294 The scenery of the residential area of Jing Bi Ju from the other side of Liangyi Gallery

dynamics and charm to the sight and widening the originally limited garden territory (Figs. 293, 294). Visitors could stay inside, drinking a cup of tea and talking in a light mood, with poetic sentiments arising. Or visitors could turn to the outside, where the reflections in the water are so bright and clear,

and fishes play games in the water which provides a zest of life to the view.

Ningxiang Pavilion (Pavilion of Condensed Fragrance)

This pavilion was named for the many fragrant plants planted around it, where a delightful floral scent

FIG. 295 Ningxiang Pavilion

FIG. 296 Cuimi Corridor and Ying Feng Ying Yue Pavilion

rushes to you, and brings a moment of beautiful rejoice (Fig. 295).

Cuimi Corridor (Corridor Lost in Greenery) and Ying Feng Ying Yue Pavilion (Pavilion of Welcoming Wind and Reflecting Moon)

Both Cuimi Corridor and Ying Feng Ying Yue Pavilion lean against the west wall and beside the internal lake. The pavilion is an open building, where you can enjoy the entire lake and mountain views. This is a wonderful place to enjoy the moonlight and the lake (Figs. 296).

Garden of Abundant Shade 余荫山房
One of Four Greatest Gardens to the South of the Five Ridges

Location: Panyu, Guangzhou, Guangdong province
Floor Space: 0.15 hectare
Construction Year: 1866 (the fifth year during the Tongzhi Period of the Qing Dynasty)
Genre of Garden: residence garden

The Garden of Abundant Shade was completed after five years of construction in Nancun village, Panyu. It is one of the four most reputable gardens in Guangdong province.

Occupying a sheer 0.15 hectares of land, this garden has all sorts of architecture, like pavilions platforms, towers, and gazeboes, and decorations like rockeries and flowers. These architectures appear alternatively with corridors, arch bridges, rockeries, flower passageways, and walls. Thus, this garden was constructed into a secluded and zigzag courtyard where the buildings seemingly hide inside. All relieves and furnishings are produce by the hands of renowned and crafty artisans. Furthermore, poetry, calligraphy, and paintings grant the garden with additional pleasurable tranquility and appealing elegance.

The garden could be divided into two halves—the east and west sections. The central view in the west half is a rectangular lotus pond made of rock pieces. On the south bank are simple-structured Linchi Lodging (Lodging Touching Pond), while on the north bank is the major hall—Shenliu Hall (Shen Liu

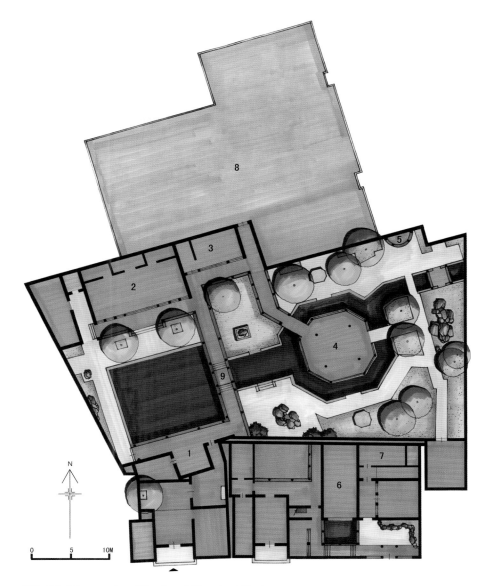

FIG. 297 Ichnography of Garden of Abundant Shade
1. Lin Chi Bie Guan Lodging Touching Pond   **2**. Shen Liu Tang Hall Hidden Deep in Dense Willow
3. Lan He Ting Hall of Holding Cores   **4**. Lin Long Shui Xie Exquisite Waterside Gazebo   **5**. Nan Xun Ting Pavilion of Southern Breeze   **6**. Chuan Ting Boat Hall   **7**. Shu Fang Study   **8**. Ci Tang Ancestral Shrine   **9**. Lang Qiao Gallery Bridge

Tang, Hall Hidden Deep in Dense Willow), in front of which are two vigorous ancient vines on both sides of the courtyard. In the center of the east half is an octagonal pond, with Linglong Waterside Gazebo (Exquisite Waterside Pavilion) in the center fenced with rockeries (Fig. 297).

An intimate neighboring garden, Yu Garden (Garden of Fine Jade), is close by to the south of the Garden of Abundant Shade and is currently a part of it. This is a two-

storey building, where the ground floor is a boat hall, and the second floor offers a view of the Garden of Abundant Shade from above.

Corridor Bridge

A corridor-style arch bridge serves as the boundary between the eastern and western half of the garden views. This is a fantastic combination of bridge, corridor, and pavilion, which fully represents designer's ingenious composition and the artisans' superior

FIG. 298 Corridor bridge

FIG. 299 Linchi Lodging

FIG. 300 Shenliu Hall

construction techniques. This charming scenic spot is known as Hong Qiao Yin Yue (Moon Print on Rainbow Bridge). On nights with a bright moonlight and cool breeze, the moon, the bridge, and people would be reflected together on the surface of the lotus pond, producing a lively view, a touching painting scroll (Fig. 298).

Linchi Lodging

This house was a study where the garden owner played with his brush and ink. It was said that the ancient literati called their ink-slab "pond," and playing with brush and ink as "touching pond," therefore, this house was named "Lin Chi" (literally touching a pond) (Fig. 299).

Shenliu Hall

Shenliu Hall, the major architecture in the entire garden, accumulates the essence of furnishing art and the best antiques in the garden. The two ancient elms in front of the hall are said to have been planted by the garden owner himself and have suffered hard times of a hundred years yet still stand vigorously straight (Fig. 300).

Shenliu Hall has a multitude of precious wooden sculptures in store. The two antique windows in the front walls, two lively wooden partition screen engraved with flower and bird patterns, the peach-wood cabins with 32 painted partition boards in the wing rooms, the several rose-wood folding screens inside the Green-Silk Room are all reputable curiosities (Fig. 301). To the left of Shenliu Hall is a simple cottage named Wopiao Cottage (Cottage of Lying in Dipper), a room for friends to rest.

Linglong Waterside Gazebo

In the center of the eastern half of the garden is an octagonal pond, with an octagonal waterside gazebo named "Ling Long" standing in the center. There are windows on all eight sides, providing eight approaches to sightseeing. A set of rockeries were piled up below the southeast wall, and a straight and charming semi-pavilion named Nanxun Pavilion (Pavilion of Southern Breeze) decorated the northeast corner (Fig. 302). The owners composed poems with wine, extolling cool breezes and bright moonlight (Fig. 303). The eight sides organize eight different scenery

FIG. 301 Wooden carvings in Shenliu Hall

FIG. 302 Nanxun Pavilion

pictures, namely "vermilion osmanthus welcoming sunrise," "poplars and willows tinting the platform green," "winter-sweet in full blossom," "stone woods miniature," "rainbow bridge echoing with moonlight," "appreciating music in Wopiao Cottage," "tranquil orchid

pavement to fruit platform," and "cocktail flaunting tail."

To add more verve to the garden, a great number of precious ancient trees like jackfruit and winter-sweet trees and araucarias were planted around it. This gazebo is the best sightseeing place in the entire garden (Fig. 304).

FIG. 303 Indoor scenery of Linglong Waterside Gazebo

FIG. 304 Linglong Waterside Gazebo

Glossary of Chinese Garden

I. Garden Types

Terms in English	Terms in Chinese and Pinyin	Figures	Introduction
Garden	园 *yuan*		In ancient times, garden or *yuan* referred specifically to a place for planting trees, yet was later expanded to a general term for all natural landscape gardens, including imperial gardens, private gardens, and temple gardens.
Hunting garden	囿 *you*		A hunting garden or *you* was constructed for emperors and noblemen in ancient times to enjoy hunting, touring, and communicating with deities. After a suitable site was chosen, they would define the territory of the hunting garden or build walls around it, and would rear animals, plant vegetations, excavate ponds, and build platforms within the territory.
Palace	宫 *gong*		Prior to the Qin Dynasty, palace or *gong* was a general term for all residential architectures, either built for common citizens or for royal families. After the Qin Dynasty, *gong* became a proper noun applied only to imperial constructions, a collective term for an imperial architectural complex.
Palace garden	苑 *yuan*		Palace garden or *yuan* developed based on hunting garden and palace during the Qin and Han dynasties. Huge palace garden could be as extensive as a hundred miles, including all traditional elements in hunting garden. In contrast, small palace garden was also known as *nei yuan* (internal garden), built inside palaces for residence and entertainment, such as Taiye Pond inside Jianzhang Palace of the Han Dynasty.

Terms in English	Terms in Chinese and Pinyin	Figures	Introduction
Plant garden	圃 *pu*		A plant garden or *pu* was one of the three main sources of Chinese classical gardens. It was basically a place for woods, flowers, and vegetables, serving both as an agricultural base and as a place for sightseeing.
Platform	台 *tai*		A platform or *tai* had been an essential garden type since the Qin and Han dynasties. It functioned initially as a place for people to climb up to worship deities and pray for immortality, and later as a vital construction in gardens for people to enjoy the landscapes in remote places from a lofty position. Platforms vary in form. Those piled up with rock pieces and leveled on the top, those supported with wooden framework and flat without any other architecture on the top, and those built in front of a tower, open and spacious can all be called platforms.
Resort	山庄 *shan zhuang*		A resort or *shan zhuang* is a sort of private garden, usually located in suburban areas with appealing natural landscapes. Such constructions were basically enclosed places with self-sufficient agricultural and sideline productions. The garden owners were mostly officials, officers and noblemen, as well as intellectuals and celebrities. As to their construction scales, they could either be extremely grandiose or small.
Villa	别业 *bie ye*		A villa or *bie ye* is a term for "other estate and residence." House owners usually build another after they possessed one residence. Such secondary residences would be called villas, located in the suburb. The major constructions in such villas are family residential houses.

II. Garden Elements

Terms in English	Terms in Chinese and Pinyin	Figures	Introduction
Belvedere	阁 *ge*		A belvedere or *ge* was a descendent of architectures with railings. Generally, the ground floor would be void, and the entire building with double eaves and windows on all four walls is supported high above. Its ichnography looks almost square. They tend to erect behind halls, either leaning against a hill or perching beside a stream. This picture presents the Wenjin Belvedere (Wen Jin Ge, Belvedere of Literature Taste) in the Mountain Resort at Chengde.
Corridor	廊 *lang*	 	A corridor or *lang*, a sort of covered passageway, is a common type of architecture in Chinese classical gardens. It serves to connect the internal and external spaces of an individual building or link different architectures together. What's more, it helps to introduce visitors to various scenic spots, divide a bigger space into smaller sections, organize scenic spots into architectural complexes and provide travelers with a place to have a rest. Corridors vary a great deal in their shape. Observed from their cross-sections, they could be classified into one-side-view corridor, double-side-view corridor, double-pavement corridor and double-storey corridor. When viewed from their ichnographies, they could be categorized into straight corridor, zigzag corridor and winding corridor, etc. The above picture presents the waterside corridor in the Humble Administrator's Garden. The below one is the circular corridor of Jianxin Studio on Fragrant Hill, Beijing.
Decorative archway	牌楼 *pai lou*		A decorative archway or *pai lou* is also known as *pai fang men*, a magnificent architecture that usually serves as the final touch in a scenic spot. It is often a way-in symbol and so functions as a main gate as well. Decorative archways could be classified into five sorts based on their building materials: wooden, stone, glazed, wood-rock, and wood-brick archways. This picture presents the wooden decorative archway named Jicui (Accumulated Greenery) in Beihai Park.
Gallery	轩 *xuan*		A gallery or *xuan* is a kind of architecture built in lofty and spacious places with a tranquil environment. The picture presents Yiyu Gallery (Leaning against Jade Gallery) in the Humble Administrator's Garden.

Terms in English	Terms in Chinese and Pinyin	Figures	Introduction
Gazebo	榭 *xie*		A gazebo or *xie* are constructed by the side of water for travelers to rest and enjoy the sights. It is typical to set up a platform by the waterside, with half of it landing on the bank and another half extending into the water surface. The second half suspends above water with the help of beams and pillars. Then workers will surround the platform with low railings or swan-neck-shaped armchairs for travelers to rest or stay. This picture presents the waterside gazebo in Outlook Garden.
Hall	殿 *dian*		A hall (*dian*), usually located in the very center in an architectural complex or on the major axis in imperial gardens, was built particularly in royal palaces or for holding etiquettes and religious services. A *dian* could be divided into three sections, namely stairs, main structure and roof. And a *dian* could be rectangular, square, round and H-shaped. This is a picture of Renshou Hall in the Summer Palace.
	堂 *tang*		A hall (*tang*) is the major architecture in a garden. In royal gardens, a *tang* was where emperor and his empress resided and rested; in a private garden, it was the principal building where garden owner dwelt in, relatively large in scale and thus, the center of scenic arrangement in the entire garden. The architecture in the picture is Yuanxiang Hall in the Humble Administrator's Garden.
	厅 *ting*		A hall (*ting*) is a sort of major architecture in a garden, functioning as the principal place for garden owner to host his guests, hold dinner parties and rites. *Ting* could be classified into "lotus hall" which opens at both south and north sides and fenced at both east and west sides, "lovebird hall"—a combination of two halls with one at north side and another at south side, and "four-sided hall" which is open to air at all sides. This picture presents the South Hall in Guyi Garden.

Terms in English	Terms in Chinese and Pinyin	Figures	Introduction
Lodging	馆 *guan*		A lodging or *guan*, a place to have a rest or meet visitors, is usually connected with the major halls in a garden. *Guan*, not grandiose in scale, could enjoy flexibility in its site choice, either connected with the major architectures to construct an architectural complex or standing alone and constituting a small independent courtyard. This picture presents the Linglong Lodging (Lodging of Exquisite Jade) in the Humble Administrator's Garden.
Pavilion	亭 *ting*		A pavilion or *ting* is a type of architecture that was built for travelers to rest and enjoy the scenery. Their environment is open and spacious, and their appearance is relatively compact in scale. This picture is the Gengzhi Tujing Pavilion (Pavilion of View of Cultivating and Weaving) in the Summer Palace.
Room	室 *shi*		Rooms or *shi* are complementary buildings in a garden, smaller in scale and scope. They usually stay in a tiny independent courtyard, constituting a scenic spot in itself. The picture presents Musical Instrument Room in Retreat and Reflection Garden.
Stone boat	舫 *fang*		Stone boats are constructed above a water surface, and are modeled after a real boat. They are used for travelers as a place to host a feast or to enjoy the waterscapes. Three sides of the front section face the water and a level bridge serves to connect its fore with the bank, similar to a gangway. The lower part of a stone boat is usually built with stones, while the upper part with timber. This picture presents the Qingyan Stone Boat in the Summer Palace.
Studio	斋 *zhai*		Studios are usually located in a tranquil and secluded small courtyard in the corners of bigger gardens. This picture presents the Da Studio (Studio of Thorough Understanding) in Zigzag Garden.

Terms in English	Terms in Chinese and Pinyin	Figures	Introduction
Tower	阁 *ge*		A tower (*ge*), is a kind of building with more than one storey and very crucial scenic spot architecture in a garden, usually larger in scale and diversified in shape. This picture is the Foxiang Tower in the Summer Palace.
	楼 *lou*		A tower (*lou*) is a critical scenic spot in a garden, usually with two floors or more and located behind a hall. A *lou* is built for sight-seeing or as a study. Lofty in height, it usually serves as the vertical compositional center in a garden. This picture is the Daoying Tower (Dao Ying Lou, Tower of Reflection) in the Humble Administrator's Garden.
Carved window	漏窗 *lou chuang*		A carved window or *lou chuang*, also known as "ressette," refers to a window with carved patterns. The patterns and compositions of such carved windows are pretty flexible and various, either geometrical or natural shaped. Some of the themes in such windows might represent flowers and animals, while others could orient from fictions, legends and historical accounts. Carved windows serve to divide a big space into smaller sections and connect the internal and external scenes, so that the views at both sides are seemingly divided and meanwhile interlinked, appearing and disappearing from time to time.
Couplet on front pillar	楹联 *ying lian*		*Ying* is a front pillar of a Chinese classical hall. And *ying lian* is the couplet hung on the front pillars, usually carved on wooden boards or bamboo boards. They usually echo with *bian e*, hung vertically either beside the main gates or on the front pillars inside a hall or a pavilion. Couplets on front pillars do not have length restriction, but are quite delicate in the neatly matching of part of speech, rhymed words, tones and artistic charm. They evolved from poetry.

Terms in English	Terms in Chinese and Pinyin	Figures	Introduction
Decorative paving	花街铺地 *hua jie pu di*		A road covered with more than two kinds of cobblestones, or with blue stone, yellow stones, broken jar pieces, porcelain pieces, and other odds and ends. Such roads are very typical features in Chinese classical gardens, especially in gardens in the Yangtze River Delta.
Door opening	洞门 *dong men*		Door openings, *dong men*, are various passable gates with only frames and without any door leaves. They could be an ornament in a garden, and serve to introduce visitors into a scenic spot on their trip, connect different spaces and various sceneries, and frame the views. Door openings have a multitude of shapes like round, gourd-shape, Han-style vase, and *ruyi* shape (s-shape).
Inscription board	匾额 *bian e*		Horizontal inscription boards are called *bian*, while the vertical ones called *e*. They are usually hung above a gate or a door opening, and inscribed with Chinese classical calligraphy, to define or extol the charm of a scenic spot.
Lady stay	美人靠 *mei ren kao*		Lady stay, also known as "swan-neck-shaped armchair," is a kind of railing, providing a place for a comfortable rest. It is more popular in waterside pavilions, galleries, halls, and towers where travelers would spend more time staying.
Stone jetty	石矶 *shi ji*		Stone jetties could be classified into two kinds. The smaller-scaled ones are level rock pieces placed above the water surface. While the larger-scaled ones would be laid out in front of cliffs and stair roads, and piled up into a waterfront platform, constructing a horizontal contrast to the vertical cliffs. Thus, the cliffs spontaneously pass down to the pond.

Terms in English	Terms in Chinese and Pinyin	Figures	Introduction
Stone stair road	蹬道 *deng dao*		A stone stair road or *deng dao* is also known as *pan dao* (circular road), the stone passageway built on the rockeries for travelers to pass through.
Seasonal views	季相 *ji xiang*		Seasonal views refer to the various appeals that plants show us in different seasons. The shape and color of a plant's leaves, flowers, and fruits would definitely change in accordance with the seasons. A plant is of relatively higher value for appreciation when it is in blossom, bearing fruits, or when its leaves change colors.
Flower bed	花台 *hua tai*		A flower bed is usually piled up with lake stones, yellow stones, or a few pieces of bricks with stones. Either regular or irregular in its shape, a flower bed presents natural scenery of flowers, grass, and trees escorted with rock peaks or rock bamboo shoots in it. It is so popular that you can find it in front of a hall, behind a house, by the side of a pavilion, a corridor, a foothill, or a pond.
Famous woods and ancient trees	古树名木 *gu shu ming mu*		Ancient trees are usually those more than a hundred years old, while famous woods have a certain social influence and are renowned in the world. Such trees tend to be older than a century and appear to have experienced all vicissitudes of life, vigorous and primitive.

Overseas Chinese Gardens

Australia

Chinese Garden of Friendship
(谊园, Yi Yuan)

Address: Darling Harbor, Sydney
Completion Year: 1988

The Chinese Garden of Friendship is a scaled-down version of a typical private garden of China's rich and powerful class in ancient times. The Taoist principles of yin and yang and the five opposite elements of earth, fire, water, metal, and wood are the main topic of construction. In the garden, those wild aspects of nature reappeared in artfully designed landscapes that feature waterfalls, mountains, lakes, and forests. To have an exploration in such a Chinese garden is to complete a Chinese cultural journey. Through the serene walkways, the visitors could see private courtyards and traditional pagoda-style pavilions.

Canada

Dr. Sun Yet-san Classical Chinese Garden (逸园, Yi Yuan)

Address: 578 Carrall Street, Vancouver
Completion Year: 1985

Dr. Sun Yet-san Classical Chinese Garden covers an area of 1430 m^2. The whole garden is divided into four sections, each with their own themes and distinct features. Similar to every classical Chinese garden, the design of the garden is based on the harmony of four elements: rock, water, plants, and architecture. In

the year of 1988, it was awarded the special achievement conferred by the International Urban Association.

Dream Lake Park
(梦湖园, Meng Hu Yuan)

Address: 4101 Sherbrooke Street East, Montreal Botanical Garden, Montreal
Completion Year: 1991

Covering an area of 250,000 m^2, the Dream Lake Park is designed after the gardens in the southern Yangtze River region with the architectural style of the Ming Dynasty. Water is a main topic of the scenes in the garden. The Dream Lake, as the main scenic spot, is 60m long and 40m wide. To the south is Qinyi Hall, a center for activities in the garden and also the main scenic attraction. There are ten representative scenic spots. including the Green Shade Pavilion and the Three Stars.

Germany

Fanghua Park
(芳华园, Fang Hua Yuan)

Address: West Park, Munich
Completion Year: 1982

Fanghua Park, covering an area of more than 540 m^2, took part in the 1983 International Horticultural Exhibition. It inherited the traditional Chinese garden features, integrating the beauty of construction and nature together. It not only presents the serenity of those Chinese gardens in southern China, but also the elegance of those

in the south of the Five Ridges of China (Lingnan).

Yingqu Park
(郢趣园, Ying Qu Yuan)

Address: 273 Mülheimer Street, Duisburg Zoo, Duisburg
Completion Year: 1988

Yingqu Park is located in Duisburg Zoo, covering an area of 5400 m^2. In the background of green trees and picturesque natural scenes, one can see many architectural styles, like ornamental gates, halls, waterside pavilions, hexagonal pavilions, and arc-shaped bridges. The design of this garden combines those gardens in southern and northern China, being simple and elegant. Thus, the cultural deposits of Chinese gardens of long history are naturally blended with the beautiful landscapes of Germany.

Chunhua Garden
(春华园, Chun Hua Yuan)

Address: 12 Berger Street, Bethmann Park, Frankfurt
Completion Year: 1989

Chunhua Garden, with an area of 4,000 m^2, follows the construction style of traditional garden in Huizhou, equipped with some architectural elements of the local habitats. Altogether there are 22 landscape views, a marble bridge, pavilions, pond, and waterfall, especially those sculptures in brick, wood, stone, and bamboo. Chunhua Garden, since its unveiling, has won a lot of popularity because of its unique Huizhou style.

Deyue Garden
(得月园, De Yue Yuan)

Address: Gardens of World, Marzahn Recreational Park, Eisenacher Street 99, Berlin
Completion Year: 2001

Deyue Garden literally means "the garden of reclaimed moon," and the moon in Chinese culture always brings good blessings to people. Thus, the plaque, slab, and inscription on the rockery are all related with the moon. In this natural mountain and water garden, apart from greening and water, there are constructions of the classical style of southern China. There is also a statue of Confucius standing at the entrance of the garden. It is truly an ideal place for relaxing and recreational activities.

Japan

Tongle Garden
(同乐园, Tong Le Yuan)

Address: Tsurumiryokuchi Park, Osaka
Completion Year: 1990

Tongle Garden, a Chinese garden taking part in the 1990 International Garden and Greenery Exposition through the invitation of the Japanese government, is in Osaka as a permanent construction. With an area of about 2000 m^2, the design and planning of this garden adapts to the local conditions. On one side, it is separated from the path outside by the wall of lattice windows with brick carvings; on the other side, it has stone boat, zigzag veranda, and a large pond, forming a semi-open and semi-close large space.

Yuhua Park
(渝华园, Yu Hua Yuan)

Address: Central Park, Hiroshima
Completion Year: 1991

Located in the southern-west side of central park of Hiroshima, Yuhua Park covers an area of 1,680 m^2. In the park, there are ponds, corridor, pavilion, hall, and gate, etc. In addition to the traditional construction theory and techniques of Chinese garden, this park makes use of the architectural features of Chonqing's mountain garden in Sichuan province. Different plants make it available for visitors to appreciate the sceneries of all four seasons.

Netherlands

Friendship Garden
(谊园, Yi Yuan)

Address: Hortus Botanical Garden, Kerklaan 34, 9751 NN Haren, Groningen
Completion Year: 1994

Covering an area of 6700 m^2 and divided into 8 sections, the park is an authentic copy of a Chinese mountain and water garden in southern China during the Qing Dynasty. Integrating the rockery, waters, flowers, trees and architectures, people could enjoy the landscapes of the south of the lower reaches of the Yangtze River. This garden also combines the architectural arts of classical Chinese garden with modern life and customs of the Netherlands. Visitors can hold parties, dance, and drink tea in Moaning of Dragon Tea House.

Singapore

Garden of Beauty
(蕴秀园, Yun Xiu Yuan)

Address: 1 Chinese Garden Road, Chinese Garden, Jurong Park
Completion Year: 1992

Covering an area of 5800 m^2, the Garden of Beauty is a penjing park, showcasing a collection of more than 2,000 pieces imported from China and other parts of the world. As the largest penjing garden of Suzhou-style outside China, the garden infuses the essence of eastern horticulture into the arts of Suzhou classical garden. Visitors can not only appreciate those penjing selections, but also roam within the refined, antique but spectacular scenes.

Switzerland

The Chinese Garden
(中国园, Zhong Guo Yuan)

Address: near Lake Zurich, Zurich
Completion Year: 1993

The Chinese Garden is directly located near Lake Zurich, covering an area of 3400 m^2. It is a gift from Zurich's sister city Kunming in China, the capital city of Yunnan province. This garden, on the basic of traditional Chinese garden construction approaches, makes use of the construction techniques peculiar to the Yunnan region in China, the natural and human landscapes being interacting with each other. Though this garden is rather small, people can appreciate the small island, the pavilions, and even a tiny pagoda.

UK

Yanxiu Park
(燕秀园, **Yan Xiu Yuan**)

Address: near Mersey River, Liverpool
Completion Year: 1984

Yanxiu Park is located on the side of Mersey in Liverpool. This park, with the style of Chinese garden in northern China, covers an area of almost 900 m^2. The landscape feature of this garden is the replica of Qinquan Corridor and Zhenluan Pavilion in Jingxing Studio of Beihai Park in Beijing. There are also many plants in the garden, including those mainly seen in Beijing, like pine, weeping willow, bamboo, as well as those specific to China, for example, metasequoia and ginkgo.

USA

The Astor Court
(明轩, **Ming Xuan**)

Address: Metropolitan Museum of Art, 6 East 82nd Street, Manhattan, New York, New York State

Completion Year: 1981

The Astor Court, whose design was based on a famous courtyard of Master of the Nets Garden, was created and assembled by those Chinese expert craftsman through traditional methods, materials, and hand tools. In this 400 m^2 Ming Dynasty style courtyard, most features of Chinese gardens could be available. For example, a circular moon gate, a covered zigzag walkway, elaborated latticed windows, various rockeries, an open pavilion, and a hall.

The China Garden
(中国园, **Zhong Guo Yuan**)

Address: Chinese Cultural Center, Cofco Center, 668 North 44th Street, Phoenix, Arizona
Completion Year: 1997

Covering an area of about 3,000 m^2, the garden is divided into five parts, each representing five Chinese historical and cultural cities, namely Nanjing, Zhenjiang, Suzhou, Wuxi, and Hangzhou. Copies of places of interests in these five cities are gathered together, by plants, paths, and water body, to form a strip park. The scenic spots include the Three Ponds Pools Mirroring the Moon and the Great Wave Pavilion. Visitors can appreciate those scenes and constructions one after another when walking around the garden.

Garden of Flowing Fragrance
(流芳园, **Liu Fang Yuan**)

Address: The Huntington Library, Art

Collections and Botanical Gardens, 1151 Oxford Road, San Marino, California
Completion Year: 2008

The Garden of Flowing Fragrance, the largest Chinese garden in North America was open to the public in 2008. A traditional Chinese garden, based on the blueprint of those in Suzhou, covers an area of 12 acres. Inside visitors could appreciate pavilions, bridges, covered walkways, and windows from the Lake of Reflected Fragrance to the Pavilion for Washing Away Thoughts to the Isle of Alighting Geese. Apart from these attractions, different plants represent the four seasons and endow the garden with various sceneries.

Seattle Chinese Garden
(西华园, **Xi Hua Yuan**)

Address: South Seattle Community College, 6000 16th Avenue SW, Seattle, Washington State
Completion Year: 2010

The Seattle Chinese Garden is the first Sichuan-style garden in the United States. With an area of 4.6 acres, the park shows not only plants, but also stone, constructions, and water elements, customary to Chinese gardens. Those plants specific to Sichuan formed the natural landscape in all four seasons, as if depicting scenes in traditional Chinese painting and poems. The 85-foot Floating Clouds Pavilion soars over the garden, looking at the Space Needle. It is truly a unique and exotic landmark in Seattle.

Bibliography

Chen Congzhou. *Gardens in Yangzhou City*. Shanghai: Tongji University Press, 2007.

Chen Zhihua. *Overseas Art of Garden Construction*. Zhengzhou: Henan Science and Technology Press, 2001.

Harigaya Kanekiti. *Evolution of Western Garden Construction*. Translated by Zou Hongcan. Beijing: China Architecture and Building Press, 1991.

Ji Cheng. *Comments of The Craft of Gardens*. Noted by Chen Zhi. Beijing: China Architecture and Building Press, 1981.

Liu Dunzhen. *Classical Gardens in Suzhou City*. Beijing: China Architecture and Building Press, 2005.

Luo Zhewen. *Chinese Imperial Gardens*. Beijing: Intellectual Property Publishing House, 2002.

Shao Zhong. *Art of Classical Gardens in Suzhou City*. Beijing: China Forestry Publishing House, 2001.

Shen Yuan and Tang Dai. *Forty Scenes of Old Summer Palace and Their Notes*. Beijing: China Architecture and Building Press, 2008.

Wang Yi. *Garden and Chinese Culture*. Shanghai: People's Publishing House, 1990.

Wang Zhideng. Record of Jichang Garden. In *Selected Records of Renowned Chinese Gardens in All Dynasties*, compiled by Chen Zhi, 180 – 86. Hefei: Anhui Science and Technology Press, 1982.

Yu Minzhong. *Imperial Accounts in Capital City*. Beijing: Beijing Ancient Books Publishing House, 1981.

Zhang Cailie. *General Theories of Chinese Garden Construction*. Shanghai: Science and Technology Press, 2004.

Zhang Jiaji. *Chinese Garden Construction Theories*. Taiyuan: Shanxi People's Publishing House, 1991.

Zhou Weiquan. *History of Chinese Classical Garden*. Beijing: Tsinghua University Press, 1999.

Dynasties in Chinese History

Xia Dynasty（夏）..2070 – 1600 BC

Shang Dynasty（商）..1600 – 1046 BC

Zhou Dynasty（周）..1046 – 256 BC

    Western Zhou Dynasty（西周）............................1046 – 771 BC

    Eastern Zhou Dynasty（东周）.............................770 – 256 BC

        Spring and Autumn Period（春秋）.............770 – 476 BC

        Warring States Period（战国）...................475 – 221 BC

Qin Dynasty（秦）..221 – 206 BC

Han Dynasty（汉）...206 BC – 220 AD

    Western Han Dynasty（西汉）..............................206 BC – 25 AD

    Eastern Han Dynasty（东汉）...............................25 – 220

Three Kingdoms（三国）...220 – 280

    Wei（魏）...220 – 265

    Shu Han（蜀）...221 – 263

    Wu（吴）...222 – 280

Jin Dynasty（晋）..265 – 420

    Western Jin Dynasty（西晋）................................265 – 316

    Eastern Jin Dynasty（东晋）................................317 – 420

Northern and Southern Dynasties（南北朝）.......................420 – 589

    Southern Dynasties（南朝）.................................420 – 589

    Northern Dynasties（北朝）................................439 – 581

Sui Dynasty（隋）...581 – 618

Tang Dynasty（唐）...618 – 907

Five Dynasties and Ten Kingdoms（五代十国）...................907 – 960

    Five Dynasties（五代）...907 – 960

    Ten Kingdoms（十国）..902 – 979

Song Dynasty（宋）...960 – 1279

    Northern Song Dynasty（北宋）..........................960 – 1127

    Southern Song Dynasty（南宋）..........................1127 – 1279

Liao Dynasty（辽）..916 – 1125

Jin Dynasty（金）..1115 – 1234

Xixia Dynasty（西夏）...1038 – 1227

Yuan Dynasty（元）...1279 – 1368

Ming Dynasty（明）...1368 – 1644

Qing Dynasty（清）...1644 – 1911

Index